The Eagles
Flying high

LAURA JACKSON

PORTRAIT

Visit the Portrait website!

Portrait publishes a wide range of non-fiction, including biography, history, science, music, popular culture and sport.

Visit our website to:
- read descriptions of our popular titles
- buy our books over the internet
- take advantage of our special offers
- enter our monthly competition
- learn more about your favourite Portrait authors

VISIT OUR WEBSITE AT: www.portraitbooks.com

Copyright © 2005 by Laura Jackson

First published in 2005 by **Portrait**
an imprint of
Piatkus Books Ltd
5 Windmill Street
London W1T 2JA
e-mail: info@piatkus.co.uk

This edition published in 2006

The moral right of the author has been asserted

A catalogue record for this book is available from the British Library

ISBN 0 7499 5113 3

Text design by Paul Saunders
Edited by Jinny Johnson

This book has been printed on paper manufactured with respect for the environment using wood from managed sustainable resources

Typeset by Phoenix Photosetting, Chatham, Kent
Printed and bound in Great Britain by Mackays of Chatham, Chatham, Kent

This book is dedicated to David
– my precious husband

PICTURE CREDITS

CONTENTS

ACKNOWLEDGEMENTS

The following helped with this book: Joe Elliott; Gus Boyd; Clive Whichelow; Elgin Library staff; *Reuters*; *VH1*; *Rolling Stone*; *Uncut*; *Crawdaddy*; *Houston Chronicle*; *Los Angeles Times*; *Interview Magazine*; *Billboard*; *Las Vegas Sun*; *Record*; *Hot Rocks*; *Mojo*; *Toronto Sun*; *Guitar World*; *Detroit Free Press*; *Classic Rock*; *Guitar Player*; *Q*; *Time*; *Sounds*; *Rainbow*; *Melody Maker*; *Zigzag*; *Goldmine*; *Daily Telegraph*; *History of Rock*; *Record Mirror*; *Musician*; *Country Rambler*; *Daily Morning News*; *Q Rock Stars*; *Dallas Morning News*.

Special thanks to: David for his invaluable help and support and to Alice Davis and everyone at Piatkus Books.

Glenn Frey   'the dynamo'

Don Henley   'the cynic'

Don Felder   'the maestro'

Joe Walsh   'the jester'

Timothy B. Schmit   'the hippie'

Bernie Leadon   'the purist'

Randy Meisner   'the homebird'

These are the Eagles ... this is their story ...

CHAPTER 1

Wide-Eyed Wannabes

TAKEN TOGETHER LYRICALLY AND MUSICALLY, the Eagles are arguably rock's most phenomenally gifted band. Certainly, they are one of the most popular of all time. Enjoying colossal success spanning three decades, their every album has gone multi-platinum. They have sold in excess of 125 million albums worldwide. *Eagles: Their Greatest Hits 1971–1975* is RIAA certified as the bestselling album in the history of American popular music. On top of that, recognised as true icons by their induction into the Rock and Roll Hall of Fame in 1998, this legendary supergroup is responsible for influencing generations of artistes in their wake, who seek to blur the borders between country and rock.

Setting their sights on soaring to the top, in 1971 the Eagles embarked on an exhilarating journey that saw them dominate the US music scene in the 1970s, self-destruct in the 1980s, vowing that hell would freeze over before they would re-form, only to reincarnate in the 1990s.

With a new compilation release, *Complete Greatest Hits*, including the new single, 'Hole In The World', in summer 2003, they launched a mammoth two-year-long world tour, during which they reinforced their enduring and deep-rooted appeal. It is hard to remain artistically and commercially relevant, but the Eagles are among the select ranks of those who have managed to do so. It has not been without its pain, and the road to fame and fortune has at times given them a destructively rough ride.

In the 1970s, while at the heady pinnacle of their power, behind the blinding glare of success, the band was spectacularly fractured internally by protracted artistic feuding and fraught personality clashes, not aided by the notorious drug-induced paranoia of some of its members. While the world wallowed in the Eagles' mellow, laid-back southern California sound, at their decadent height the band itself had become immersed in a suffocating sphere at whose axis was a raw and insatiable appetite for cocaine, glamorous groupies, and throwing the wildest parties in rock.

Yet, as hard as they partied, having witnessed the premature demise of other bands in the bruising and ephemeral music business, which was becoming increasingly littered with sad casualties, the Eagles were determined to look out for the pitfalls. But they pushed themselves to the limit from the start.

That start went way back to an America busy recovering in the post-World War II era. 1947 proved to be a vintage year for hatching out future Eagles. Five of the eventual seven band members were born then in states scattered across the US, with music in their veins from an early age. Originally, the Eagles comprised Glenn Frey, Don Henley, Randy Meisner and Bernie Leadon. As singers, songwriters and musicians their individual talents were impressive; collectively they conspired to create a band that had it all.

Frey and Henley formed the creative core of the Eagles, which would be powered by an explosive blend of vibrant personalities. That the four were such diverse characters worked as much for them initially, as it would work against them later. But there was undoubtedly potent value in the counterbalance between Glenn Frey's streetwise city steel and Don Henley's country-bred, deep-thinking sensitivity.

Frey, fuelled with white-hot ambition, had the relentless energy of a speeding bullet; Henley brought an ethereal sense of pain and subtlety. It was little wonder then that, combined, they created commercially strong songs of lyrically intriguing depth and complexity.

The late 1960s/early 1970s were stirring times; an edgy atmosphere prevailed in which anything could happen and everything was up for grabs. America was a political powder keg, with the assassinations in 1968 of Senator Robert F. Kennedy and civil rights leader Martin Luther King, the latter killing leading to race riots in the streets. As community leaders urged restraint and peaceful protest, a year on John Lennon very publicly returned his MBE to Buckingham Palace in disgust at British involvement in the Nigeria-Biafra conflict and UK support of America in Vietnam. Musically, the Californian scene was rapidly changing. Not long after the release of the appropriately titled Mamas and the Papas album, *Farewell To The First Golden Era*, the band so synonymous with the 1960s' west coast sound officially dissolved in 1968. Then the Byrds, the best exponents of electric-folk, began to splinter. The Beach Boys, however, whose *Pet Sounds* album was by then credited with helping to reshape popular music, continued to pack out venues across America.

Like the surf sound before it, flower power was gone. Speed and heroin had rapidly been replacing LSD as the drugs of choice. Whereas music stars like Buddy Holly, Otis Redding and Eddie Cochrane had died tragically in plane and car crashes, things had become dark and decidedly dodgy with the drug-related demise of Janis Joplin and Jimi Hendrix, the sudden exit of Doors frontman Jim Morrison, said to be from a heart attack, and the shockingly subtle murder of Brian Jones, the musical genius and dynamic founder of the Rolling Stones. For the Beatles, too, by spring 1970 it was all over as a four-way working unit. From the ashes of the lately deceased decade, a new musical rebirth was desperately needed.

In Britain, progressive rock from the likes of Wishbone Ash provided true music lovers with a merciful release from the powder puff froth clogging the charts, courtesy of acts such as Sweet and T-Rex. In America, one of the hottest bands to emerge was Crosby, Stills, Nash and Young. Their sound had evolved through various incarnations, mutating from electric-folk into the burgeoning field of country-rock. Snapping at the heels of Crosby, Stills, Nash and Young was the Los Angeles-formed band, the Flying Burrito Brothers, featuring, in 1968, the 22-year-old Florida-born singer-songwriter/guitarist Gram Parsons. Other outfits were attracted to this flame, each one eager to make it big by creating a new LA sound. They were a hungry bunch of desperadoes, haunting the flourishing Los Angeles club scene at popular hangouts like McCabes, the Ash Grove, the Palomino, the Whisky A Go-Go and the Troubadour.

Situated on Santa Monica Boulevard in West Hollywood, the Troubadour was a prestigious club that had once been the preserve of folk singers. In the late 1960s, it changed orientation, and was now where the nucleus of future talent congregated. The place was so drenched in testosterone that a waitress working the front bar once quipped that a girl needed to wear a contraceptive diaphragm just to whisk through the place. To loiter was to risk getting pregnant! Amid this macho melting pot of hopes and dreams, in no one did the flame of ambition blaze brighter in 1968 than one long-haired, 20-year-old musician named Glenn Frey. Born on 6 November 1948 in Detroit, Michigan, Glenn hit the ground running practically from the day he could walk, and was clearly set to break out of the mould. Growing up, the sheer force of his vibrant personality was his trademark, plus an attractive edginess that prompted his mother, Nellie Frey, to tell him affectionately that he reminded her of 'a rattlesnake coiled up in the corner, ready to strike. If you pass by, you better listen for the rattle!'.

The northern state of Michigan was the farthest east that

any original Eagle would hail from; for many, life was tough in Detroit, the industrialised city famous for motor manufacturing. Glenn's father was a machinist making the machines that built car components, and his parents were hard-working, sober-living people, unlike many around them. Glenn recalled: 'I went to school with the sons and daughters of factory worker fathers who beat their wives and kids. The kids would then go to school and beat on me.' Or rather, they would try to. The growing Glenn was not aggressive by nature, but he became streetwise early on, and was too much of a firebrand to be anybody's pushover. He remembers his childhood with deep affection. He never felt that he wanted for anything, and appreciated it that every summer holiday his folks managed to send him to camp for a week.

He didn't set store by material possessions – facing life full on was his preoccupation. The future rock star showed early musical leanings. 'I started taking piano lessons when I was five,' said Glenn. 'I did recitals, the whole thing.' But as he galloped on apace, it was sport that got his juices flowing. Undeterred from playing baseball when he accidentally got hit in the face with a bat, he put his broken nose down to a lesson learned – never catch without wearing a protective mask. At school he excelled at baseball and football. At one stage, wrestling also appealed to him, and his lean build made him something of a natural athlete. It was perhaps inevitable that such a physically high-energy boy would also have a stimulated brain.

Glenn was quick and very inquisitive. Graded among the gifted pupils, he spent years at junior high school thriving in a new, radically streamlined class for students of exceptional ability. Reading and writing, and expanding his mind, became his passions. His teachers positively encouraged his independent streak, and indulged his outspoken challenges to conventional wisdom. As a result, when Glenn moved on to high school, he found himself in advance of many of his peers – even of some of his teachers, who were set in traditional teaching methods – and it was suddenly an unwelcome, stuffy environment. But that hardly mattered, for by the age of 15 Glenn's focus now lay outside school, where he derived his very best pleasures in life from two powerful pursuits.

His luxuriously thick, dark hair crowned a developed athletic body and from his deep-set blue eyes shone the compelling light of his unbridled personality. Undoubtedly a budding looker, Glenn would prove to have quite a voracious appetite for the fair sex. Only a compulsion for music could compete for his attention. He would drive up and down the eight-lane boulevard of Woodward Avenue, glued to the radio, and by now he had progressed to teaching himself to play electric guitar. The combined attraction of music and sex was brought home vividly to Glenn just before his 16th birthday, when he saw the Beatles live in concert in 1964.

Having first landed in America with a bang in February, the Beatles returned for a second countrywide tour, kicking off in August at the Cow Palace in San Francisco. Glenn caught their act when they travelled east in mid September; it was a night he would remember forever. Rock music had been rapidly infiltrating his bloodstream anyway, but the magnetic bedlam from the Beatles' overworked amplifiers, and the ear-busting fan hysteria generated by the four Liverpool lads, were like manna from heaven to Glenn. 'It was awesome,' he recalled of that night. 'Everyone was so caught up in the excitement. I'll never forget how this one girl fell right into my arms in a daze, screaming, "Paul...Paul!" I knew right then, that this was for me!'

So it was no surprise that his burning ambition was now to be in a rock band. The local bands Frey joined in his mid teens included the Subterraneans, the Heavy Metal Kids, a folk-rock outfit called the Four of Us, and the Mushrooms, for which he became lead singer and lead guitarist. Playing dingy Detroit pubs for miniscule fees was as glamorous as it got, but it was exciting, and he felt the Mushrooms just might go places. One of their pet haunts was the Hideout, a teen club where they quickly began to attract a faithful following. The club owned a small record label, Hideout Records, and the Mushrooms cut a single, 'Such a Lovely Child'. Fascinated by this first taste of being inside a recording studio, Glenn was further energised when his band got to perform on the local TV show, *Robin Seymour's Swinging Time*.

At 17, Glenn left high school. His parents had hopes of him attending a good college out of state, but he preferred to stay in Detroit. For now, it was his stomping ground, where his band played. The compromise turned out to be a local community college, but Frey wasn't really prepared to knuckle down to lessons; his other distractions were too powerful. Glenn majored more in the close study of the female form, and the grass was always greener on the other side. He would prowl around the college lunchroom or car park and mourn: 'The chicks are so much better lookin' at Michigan State and, dammit, I couldn't get in!'

In 1967, by the time hippy culture had kicked in across America and was rife on college campuses, Glenn was an out-and-out cool teen king. 'I had a ball in the sixties,' he confessed. He was popular with the lads, and exuded a team spirit. They didn't feel threatened by him. On the contrary, they loved to hang out with him. So did the girls. Glenn was only interested in those on his wavelength. Inasmuch as, he wasn't up for chaste romance. Basically, he was a red-blooded young buck looking to get his leg over any pretty and willing girl he fancied – no strings, nothing heavy. Chaste girls did eye him up in class, but were gently let down.

It has been admiringly claimed of Glenn's spirited mother, Nellie Frey, that she could kill water buffalo at a hundred yards with her laugh. Looking on at her horny son's antics, she was typically blunt with her observations, telling him: 'Glenn, your life revolves around groups of people. You can't relate that well to individuals. If your guitar had tits and an ass, you'd never date!' Glenn understood the unusual appraisal, but naturally he preferred the real thing, and his attitude towards girls was pretty nonchalant. He did not, though, care for the kind of crude locker room talk he overheard when guys would brutally boast about their latest conquests. Said Glenn: 'I'd hear these guys say, "I fucked the shit out of her." And it made me realise that the real test for a man was learning to respect women.'

Having wholeheartedly embraced girls and rock music, there was just one missing ingredient, and while at college in 1967, like almost everyone around him, Glenn began to experiment with drugs. Living out east, he was vicariously soaking up the whole west coast Californian consciousness through television, radio and magazines, and in this spirit he took acid for the first time.

By now, Frey had discovered Buffalo Springfield, the band featuring Stephen Stills and Neil Young, among others. Their single, 'For What It's Worth', about the real-life repressive tactics employed by Los Angeles cops on a defenceless youth, had hit a chord with the prevalent air of rebellion, and would later be hailed as an era-defining social commentary. *Buffalo Springfield* was not a hit album for the inspiring band, but news of it spread by word of mouth among long-haired hippies, and Glenn maintained that as he lay on his bedroom floor listening to this album, it would give him goose-bumps.

Frey's musical taste had firmly zeroed in on west coast groups. The Grateful Dead had performed in January 1967 at the first 'Human Be-In' at Golden Gate Park in San Francisco; with the release of their recent eponymous album, they had begun gigging around America. Glenn cut class to see them at Detroit's Grand Ballroom. It was a wistful time. Not fully sated by catching visiting bands shooting in and out of town, Frey took to watching the sun set every night in the west, dreaming of one day heading out to sunny California, which had come to look like the promised land. Raptly absorbed as he was in tales of a world that seemed like heaven, Los Angeles represented everything he desired, besides making it in music. He said: 'I read about free love and free dope in California and said: "That's the place for me!".'

Not quite yet, it wasn't. Through gigging, Glenn had come into contact with a local celebrity named Bob Seger. Only three years Frey's senior, and from Dearborn, Michigan, the rock singer-songwriter had been recording for a couple of years when his single, 'East Side Story', was released in 1966 on Hideout Records, Detroit. It sold 50,000 copies and made Seger a hit around the Great Lakes area. Seger's song, 'Such a Lovely Child', had earlier been recorded for the same label by the Mushrooms, who had lately begun to share the occasional gig with Bob Seger. He and Glenn became friends, and Glenn also started to hang out at Seger's recording sessions, thrilled whenever he was invited to take part. In 1967, Frey sang backing vocals on Seger's song, 'Heavy Music', which was a big hit in Detroit. Frey also lent his guitar and vocal skills to 'Ramblin' Gamblin' Man', which later became Seger's US chart debut, reaching number 17.

While Glenn delighted in his involvement with Bob Seger and Seger's manager, Eddie 'Punch' Andrews, Frey's mother was less enamoured by what she saw. Ever a woman to take action, Nellie went knocking on the manager's door, and tried to get him to agree not to organise any band bookings for her son until Glenn achieved some academic progress and stopped smoking marijuana. Both of those areas were, of course, outside the man's control, and Glenn soon moved away from any form of guidance. In summer 1968, the lure of the west proved too strong to resist. His concerned parents bluntly warned their headstrong son that if he ditched college and decamped thousands of miles away to California, then they would not give him a red cent. In fact, they did later help him out financially whenever they could afford to, and when the time came for Glenn to go, he left home with their love and best wishes.

Not quite 20 then, Glenn drove west, ultimately to Los Angeles, but with a small detour. In 1975, Frey told *Rolling*

Stone that he had driven first to Mexico to buy himself some drugs, before crossing the border back into North America. Glenn took to Los Angeles straight away. It exuded the kind of nervy, rich energy he thrived on, and with his own perpetual inner edginess, he was ready for anything. One thrill he had not expected was seeing ex-Byrds guitarist David Crosby in the flesh, perched on steps outside a trendy shop on Laurel Canyon. Crosby was swathed in the same dark leather batwing cape that Glenn had seen him wear on TV pop shows, and Frey took this chance sighting of a star he had admired for years as an omen that his own aim to break into music would succeed.

Right then it was tough enough in this sprawling city to find the way to where his girlfriend lived; she had moved from Detroit to LA with her sister. However, it was on arrival at this apartment that Glenn met John David Souther, who would play a major part in his immediate future. Detroit-born Souther had been raised in Amarillo, Texas. Having played in high school bands, he had recently been attracted to the LA music scene. Later he gained acclaim as an accomplished songwriter. That summer, like Glenn, he was struggling. Said Frey: 'JD was going out with my girlfriend's sister, and we really hit it off!'

As the musicians and budding lyricists got their heads together, the girls themselves were in danger of disappearing off their respective boyfriends' attention radar. There was undoubtedly a working chemistry between the two young men, for virtually that very first day they decided to body-swerve rock for now, and form a country-folk duo. They called their acoustic act, Longbranch Pennywhistle; it lasted for over three years. With Souther, Frey had found an affinity and a strong common purpose. Bob Seger had sown the seeds of songwriting in Glenn, though they had yet to flourish. Now JD Souther had something to offer. Said Glenn: 'JD taught me how to sing and play country.' This common purpose proved suffocating for their neglected girlfriends, and before long, as their relationships disintegrated, Glenn and JD were both out on their ear, forced to find themselves their own apartment.

Renting cramped accommodation in one of LA's many impoverished districts, it was hard to make ends meet. JD secured session work. Glenn's parents sent him $10 inside every letter they wrote, urging him to buy himself a proper meal now and again. As Longbranch Pennywhistle, they scrounged up as many paying gigs as they could. They played the Troubadour, but Glenn's initial impressions of the renowned club were caustically negative. Shrewdly, he came to the conclusion that there was a tragic air about some of the characters who haunted the crowded bar, as much among the hopefuls as the has-beens trying to cling on to a sliver of the glory they had once enjoyed. Aspects of the legendary Troubadour thrilled Glenn, of course; but, perceptively, he didn't fail to spot the seamy elements, and he described the club as playing host to some 'spiritual parasites'.

No one could rob him of his artistic energy, however, even though it was sometimes tough to stay buoyant and optimistic. Although he cared about the risk of being lumped among the wasters living on pipe dreams, he hung out there, smoking dope, drinking, scheming his way to success. This involved studying the failures even closer than those who had made it, as well as eyeing up the mini-skirted Californian babes sashaying by his table, and deciding which of them he would make out with next. For all that, it was gigging as Longbranch Pennywhistle at the Troubadour that attracted the attention of Amos Records executives, and led to a recording contract in summer 1969.

Frey and Souther were duly ushered into a recording studio to lay down a collection of harmonised country-rock numbers. Amos Records assigned Jimmy Bowen to produce, and enlisted an impressive wealth of skilled assistance, including the legendary multi-instrumental session musician Larry Knechtel, and Ry Cooder, who played bottleneck guitar, mandolin, dulcimer *et al.* Glenn and JD had come up with an early forerunner of what would be the Eagles' distinctive sound, but when *Longbranch Pennywhistle* was released in September 1969, it just couldn't cut the mustard at such a highly competitive time in music, even though it was an easy listening album. Although dismally disappointed, Glenn was determined to hang in there. It helped that he was recently invigorated by a new acquaintance, a singer-songwriter almost exactly his own age, named Jackson Browne.

Born in 1948 in Heidelberg, West Germany, where his father worked for the US Army, Browne subsequently moved with his family to Orange County, California. From a young age, he displayed precocious musical talent, and quickly became a proficient pianist and guitarist. Heavily influenced by Bob Dylan's fusion of folk-rock, Jackson also began to display an equally impressive lyrical bent. At 17, he enjoyed a brief stint with the Nitty Gritty Dirt Band, then in 1968 became a fixture as a solo act on the LA folk-rock scene at the Paradise club. He signed as a songwriter with a music publisher, and artistes such as the Jackson Five and Tom Paxton were queuing up to record his compositions.

Glenn Frey first met Jackson Browne at a benefit concert in Los Angeles for a free clinic. He later recalled: 'Jackson walked up to me and JD with an acoustic guitar and started singing "Jamaica Say You Will", and we started singing with him.' After that night they kept in close touch, and two months later all three moved into a slum apartment block at 1020 Laguna in Echo Park, Los Angeles. For $60 a month Glenn and JD shared one room that had a bed with a curtain screening it, and a lumpy sofa that had seen better days. They took turns at experiencing the joys of falling off the sofa in the middle of the night in a tumble of pillows and blankets. In a tiny studio apartment directly below, Jackson Browne had moved in with his piano and guitars.

They were spartan surroundings in which to live a hungry, threadbare life, and encouragement was not forthcoming on the recording front. Amos Records would vanish off the scene by the early 1970s, but right then, Glenn had had high hopes of the label – hopes that were not obviously going to be fulfilled. He later confessed that he became so frustrated with the situation that he could barely bring himself to talk about this period. But it was not in his nature to sit with his head in his hands. He declared: 'You can't be short on confidence and expect to do well in the entertainment business. If you're down, you gotta get up.'

When Frey saw that nothing was happening, he took to going to Amos Records' office daily, requesting release from a contract that was benefiting neither side. Every answer was the same – no. So, in disgust or in a flaming temper, he would head for the Troubadour bar. He had no option but to wait for the contract to expire. Longbranch Pennywhistle never did make a second album, and Frey and Souther separated professionally. They remained firm friends, though, and also flatmates in the Echo Park slum where, despite the dire lack of privacy, they coped as best they could.

Irrepressibly, Glenn years later recalled having some great times there, despite the desperate conditions. A night owl, he lived and breathed music out and about the bustling clubs, but what particularly stuck out was hearing Jackson Browne playing the piano and working on songs. Lying flat on his back in bed at midday, with some naked, nubile nymph fast asleep beside him, Frey would stare at the cracked and discoloured plaster ceiling while drawing deeply on a cigarette, and listen intently to the sounds drifting up from the studio flat below. What got Glenn thinking was the sheer painstaking tenacity and repetitiveness of Jackson working at lyrics as they struggled to come together. Songwriting had appealed to him since he first put pen to paper under Bob Seger's encouragement, but till then he had operated on catching a sudden burst of spontaneous thought. What he was listening to with Jackson at work was something altogether different; the enormous discipline required was a dawning revelation to Glenn.

Such fastidious focus was something he had never encountered, but as he lay and listened to a song developing doggedly by trial and error until it knitted together, he realised he was beginning to see what it truly took to become a successful lyricist – how to raise his game. Crummy as the slum at 1020 Laguna was, it was here that Glenn got his first real break when he came into contact with record executive David Geffen. At 21 in 1964, Brooklyn-born Geffen had joined the William Morris Talent Agency as a mail clerk, determined to work his way to the top. He would become one of the most powerful men in rock music. In 1970, along with a fellow former William Morris employee, Elliott Roberts, with $400,000 of his own money he launched Asylum Records, because, as he said later, he couldn't find a record label doing what he envisaged should be done to encourage music forward at that time.

The whizz-kid entrepreneur's initial ambition was to gather a small elite stable of artistes who would be free to be creatively adventurous. He also intended to promote them in a new, more intelligent fashion, and had a marketing philosophy in mind that would dovetail neatly with the newly emerging, laid-back, mellow southern California sound.

Jackson Browne had submitted a demo tape of songs along with a glossy photograph of himself to Asylum Records. David Geffen was daily deluged with such approaches, and Browne's pitch could easily have become buried. But Geffen's secretary fancied the handsome, fresh-faced guy with collar-length dark hair in the photo. At his secretary's hormone-based urgings, Geffen agreed to go see Jackson Browne at his insalubrious Echo Park lodgings. While there, David was also introduced to Glenn Frey and JD Souther. As Glenn later recalled, Geffen was certainly interested in Jackson and JD, but initially only mildly taken with him. Undaunted, Glenn wasn't prepared to let the dynamic record boss forget him, and he started relentlessly rapping on Geffen's door.

David Geffen snapped up Jackson Browne to join artistes such as Joni Mitchell and Neil Young, and Glenn ached to be among that select group set for the big time. Giving in to Frey's unflagging persistence, Geffen eventually heard him play a couple of songs and although he recognised Glenn's intrinsic talents, his advice was not to go solo but rather that Glenn ought to form a group. As at spring 1971, there was no shortage of potential bandmates milling about LA, but Glenn decided to be very choosy. In the meantime he also had to pay the rent, so he sought work as a backing singer and musician – a gun for hire.

One of those who hired Glenn was rising star Linda Ronstadt, an interpretive singer with country-folk rock roots. By this time she had two albums under her belt, and was working on her third when her manager/producer, John Boylan, approached Frey in the Troubadour and asked if he'd like to join Linda's backing road band. Later ribbed about this, Frey retorted that at the time, if there were bucks in it, he would 'Oooh-oooh' for anybody!

To become part of Linda Ronstadt's backing band Glenn was offered $200 a week, which was more money than he had seen in a while, and he gladly accepted. The task of trawling for other talent was Boylan's, but two days before rehearsals were due to start, the backing band still did not have a drummer. In the Troubadour one night, swigging from a beer bottle, Frey noticed another Amos Records signing, standing alone at the bar counter. All Glenn knew about the guy was that he was a drummer who kept himself to himself; he was a shy Texan named Don Henley.

CHAPTER 2

Desperadoes

WHEN GLENN FREY PLANTED a bottle of beer down on the Troubadour bar counter before Don Henley in May 1971, the quiet, shy drummer was stony-broke, disillusioned and dejectedly considering bailing out of the seemingly misnamed City of Angels and heading home. He was just 23 years old, yet it seemed like life had already thrown a lot at him. Although born in Gilmer, East Texas, on 22 July 1947, Don was raised in nearby Linden, a small farming town of some 2000 inhabitants, close to the Louisiana-Arkansas border, in an age when kids could roam freely from dawn to dusk and come to no harm. A deliberate, deep thinker, he was from a tender age a sensitive spirit. Speaking of going fishing as a youngster on Caddo Lake, less than an hour's drive from Linden, the now renowned environmentalist confessed: 'I could never have killed anything, though. It was all about being out in the open.' That, and spending quality time with his father, CJ.

Con Junell Henley owned a shop selling car parts, and his wife, Hughlene, had been an elementary school teacher until their only child came along. From day one, they started making plans for Don's future by rigidly putting money aside at the end of every week. When all the quarters in the piggy bank added up to $100, they bought a bond towards paying for their son's college education. Holding fast to a working class ethos, CJ believed in always paying cash. Years later, as a wealthy rock star, Don was for a long time ultra-conscious whenever he produced his American Express credit card, in case his hometown mates thought he was being flash. Don's love of nature and conservation is again rooted in his childhood. 'My dad taught me that my obligation did not stop in our yard,' he said. And, introduced early to piano lessons by country music-loving parents, home was not where Don's problems began.

With a mass of dark hair, that would later take on an Afro style, and piercing blue eyes, he was a soft-spoken, serious, intelligent boy whose peers were a bunch of rough-and-ready children who didn't share his interest in the classics. The disparity meant that it didn't take Don long to feel he had been beamed down to this East Texas backwater from another planet – a sense of isolation that would grow. More than that, the religion that was rife in the region had a profoundly negative effect on him. In this redneck part of America, the Baptists and Methodists held strong sway, with fervent ministers blasting congregations from pulpits with threats of the hellfire and brimstone that awaited all miserable sinners. Don later vividly expressed the unhealthy power this had over him when he revealed: 'The Southern purgatory they laid on me when I was a kid scared the holy fuck out of me so that I couldn't sleep at night because I thought I would die and go to hell!'

School was an equally arduous ordeal. Don attended Linden-Kildare High School, where he had no difficulty in rising to the top academically, being particularly partial to literature and poetry. But sport – a kind of religion in itself – left Henley cold and out of step. He admitted: 'If you didn't play football, you were nothing.' Longing for the time when he could leave school, he turned to music to get him through each day. Elvis Presley was the first person to give rock and roll a face and figure, and Don quickly identified with the Tupelo-born rebel. Like his future collaborator, Glenn Frey, Henley was also blown away by the Beatles. Meanwhile, in his early teens, he was hooked on the bluegrass music that wafted his way via the New Orleans late night radio shows on WNOE.

Already an adept pianist, Don tried out the trombone. But as he could never resist slapping his palms on the nearest surface while listening to music, it was obvious that he was destined to become a drummer. His natural sense of rhythm led to an invitation to play in a local Dixieland jazz band by the time he was 14. A year later, his parents parted with $600 to buy him his first drum kit, and his horizons began to expand excitingly.

It was music that brought Don his first long-term buddies, among them Richard Bowden; along with the guitarist and a couple of other local lads, at 16 Don joined his first band, called the Four Speeds. In stark contrast to the shy, introverted Don, Richard Bowden was a colourful character with a winning personality and a strong sense of humour. The story goes that, years later, when Richard was in Linda Ronstadt's backing band, he stripped off in a hotel once for a joke, smeared himself all over with shaving foam, then blithely sauntered to reception to ask a startled desk clerk where he could buy a safety razor. Despite this zany streak, the sensitive Bowden understood his friend very well. Reflecting on Don's propensity from a young age to fret, Richard explained: 'When Don solves one problem, he just moves on to something else to worry about.' On the face of it, Don's nature did not make him an obvious front man. Yet he became the Four Speeds' lead vocalist as well as its drummer – mainly because his name was drawn out of a hat for the job everyone else ran scared of. But he took to it with a will, and spent a lot of time at the Bowden family home. 'Richard's house was a haven for musicians,' recalled Don. 'His parents would hang out with us and let us practice in their living room.'

The Four Speeds changed their name to the Speeds, then later to Felicity when they gigged at Linden venues such as the American Legion Hall and the Lions Club. Playing cover versions of James Brown and Otis Redding songs, Don developed a distinctive rasp in his singing voice.

It was curious that a teenager who had felt distinctly out of step with and oppressed by his surroundings should draw extra attention to himself, but he did just that, simply by growing his hair down onto his shoulders. In 1964, long hair in teenage boys was reviled by people in middle-American towns such as Linden, Texas and, like his bandmates, Don was given a hard time because of it. Looking as the 17-year-old Henley did, you fell into one of three categories – a filthy communist, a criminal or a gay pervert. Since you were also a sissy if you played in a rock band, a long-haired sissy became a target of particular persecution, but Don made a pugnacious stand, to the bewilderment of his conservative parents. Like teenagers the world over, Don, by now a mystery to his mother, began to come into conflict with his father. Fearful that Don was becoming unruly, CJ would try to clamp down on him; Don would automatically rebel. They were a very close, loving family, and it was no more than adolescent growing pains, but it was difficult at the time.

Don sometimes used his car to let off steam. He had learned to drive in his back yard at 14, when he'd had to sit on a cushion to be able to see over the steering wheel. By now he owned his first car, a 1948 Dodge sedan that he dubbed 'The Blue Goose'. Don recalled: 'It had "suicide doors" and wide flat front fenders that were perfect for sitting on, clutching a beer in one hand and the chrome hood ornament in the other. You could remain on this perch even at high speeds, around sharp corners.' At 16, Henley had won a trophy for stock car racing at a drag strip in Hallsville, Texas, but he kept it hidden from his parents for years, knowing that they would only have worried about him taking part in such a dangerous sport.

The Blue Goose had a broad back seat, handy for a growing adolescent who made this precious car his home-from-home. He said he and his friends slept, ate, drank and threw up in it – hardly an appealing passion wagon, then! 'We occasionally got girls to enter our mohair-upholstered domain, but I don't recall that anything major ever happened!' confessed Don. In such a tiny town it hadn't taken very much for Don to appear the way-out hippy. Things did not improve at first when he went to college. In 1965, Don enrolled at the Stephen F. Austin State College in Nacogdoches, where he majored in English. It was hard to flourish in this environment. Henley later reflected: 'Kids today don't realise how difficult and dangerous it was for musicians with long hair back in those days. We were threatened all the time. We had to be very careful about where we went.'

When it came to sex, in keeping with his deep thinking character, the teenage Don was no rampant skirt chaser. He was more prone to intense devotion. Throughout his adult life, Henley would attract the most beautiful young ladies around him, and at 18 he was involved with the prettiest girl in town. Henley would never be happy revealing details of his love life, but his oldest friend, Richard Bowden, believed that Don had become deeply attached to this local beauty. According to Richard, Don bought his sweetheart an engagement ring, but later the couple reached a crossroads where they were each looking for different things from life. Years later, Bowden expressed his belief that Don was given an ultimatum by his fiancée – to marry and lead a conventional life, or to pursue music. If true, the fallout from that option could, by the mid-1960s, have easily been predicted. It's also Richard's personal opinion that he detected elements of that fractured relationship in some of Henley's later lyrics as an Eagle.

Music certainly dominated Don's life in 1965. To his list of favourite artistes, he had now added a liking for the Byrds, but best of all was the lesser-known bluegrass band, the Dillards.

One day in Shreveport he caught a performance that sent him off excitedly in search of Dillards' records. Despite being immersed in music, at this point Don still envisaged himself becoming a teacher, but could no longer tolerate the atmosphere at Stephen F. Austin. In autumn 1967 then, he switched to continue his education at North Texas State University in Denton, where he was delighted to discover a bohemian culture and a climate in which he felt safe. By now he had developed a deeper aversion for small town mentality, and broke out even more. Turned onto psychedelia by the Beatles' *Sgt. Pepper's Lonely Hearts Club Band*, Don dropped acid for the first time.

His band had been gaining experience playing the demanding fraternity circuit, attracting the battle scars that came with the territory. Changing their band name yet again – this time from Felicity to Shiloh – bookings in country clubs, nightclubs and for debutante parties steadily flowed their way, and life was full of invigorating promise. He actively enjoyed class now, particularly English study, where his tutor was something of a renegade. He turned up to teach in hippy clothes, and lectured while perched cross-legged on his desktop. His students thrived on his unorthodox style, and Henley took to heart some particular advice he got from this tutor. Taking a keen interest in their son's future, Don's parents regularly approached the tutor, eager to learn which direction he was headed in. What this bohemian told Don was: 'Frankly, if it takes you your whole fucking life to find out what you want to do, you should take it. It's the journey that counts, not the end of it. That's when it's all over.'

What was all over for Don, come spring 1969, was college. After almost four years, despite being a bright student, he did not graduate. He suddenly quit North Texas State University and went home to Linden to spend time with his father, who had just been diagnosed with arterial disease. It seems commonplace for sons to see their fathers as somehow invincible, and the skids go from under them when they discover their error. Don took his father's ill health hard, describing himself later as having been 'very disturbed' by it.

Back home, Don often took off into the countryside, with which he had always had an affinity, sometimes walking, other times riding dirt bikes, but always seeking to find some solace in the hills from his increasing worries. Because he rejected conventional religion, Don was never likely to lean on the church at this troubled time. Instead, he looked elsewhere for answers to some of the big life questions he suddenly found himself forced to face. Among those was the eternally burning one to eat up a teenager with a sick parent: Why do good people die before their time? Don started to connect spiritually with nature. As a former English major, he began reading works by Henry David Thoreau and Ralph Waldo Emerson. 'I found transcendentalism,' said Don. 'I could see God in nature rather than sitting in church listening to someone yell at me about damnation.'

The 22-year-old's other lifeline was music. Along with Don in Shiloh was Richard Bowden, bassist Michael Bowden, Al Perkins on pedal steel, and keyboard player Jim Ed Norman. Collectively, all five had developed a more structured approach, and were regularly rehearsing in an old abandoned church. They'd come to realise that cover bands got nowhere, so they had been writing their own original material. With anxiety a constant companion, Don was ripe for writing poignant lyrics; when he wasn't communing with nature, he pored agonisingly over his thoughts. He also kept up with the latest sounds and not necessarily only those from the major hit-makers dominating the airwaves.

Around now the record wearing thin on his mono turntable was *The Fantastic Expedition of Dillard and Clark*. Doug Dillard and former Byrd, Gene Clark, were among the first exponents of country-rock, and this 1968 album featured the skilled musicianship of a future Eagle who had joined Dillard and Clark's expanding line-up. 'That's how I first found out who Bernie Leadon was,' said

Henley. 'I knew it was the scene I'd like to be involved with.' Don and his bandmates had by now financed some demo records, but nothing was happening for them. Then a chance encounter promised to change that.

In August 1969, Houston-born Kenny Rogers sprang to international prominence with the hit single, 'Ruby, Don't Take Your Love To Town'. Months before that, not long after Don had left university, Shiloh bumped into Kenny Rogers while browsing in a Dallas boutique. Rogers was always on the lookout to produce other bands, and after talking with Henley and his bandmates, the country singer took in a Shiloh performance and thought he spotted potential. Don recalled: 'Being fellow Texans didn't hurt. We had a regional and cultural connection.' Kenny had been around the block enough times to know how desperately hard it was for mid-American bands to make it, and he promised Shiloh he would try to help. It wasn't cheap talk, though nothing happened in the immediate future.

They kept in touch by telephone for about a year. Then one day in February 1970, Rogers invited Shiloh to Los Angeles to record a single for Amos Records. Not surprisingly, the budget was small, and Don didn't feel that he, or any of the other songwriters in the band, had really developed their craft. It couldn't, therefore, be their finest showcase, even though they gave it their best shot. With unvarnished honesty, Henley later confessed that it proved to be most valuable as a learning experience, though he was grateful for having been given this early opportunity. The single, 'Jennifer', bombed, and Shiloh went home, but not for long. In June 1970, the band drove back to LA in an assortment of trucks. This time, they recorded an album with the same label, but nothing came of that either. Like countless wannabe rock stars, on his first visit to Los Angeles, Don Henley had made a beeline for the legendary Troubadour when it made its customary impact. He had walked in and promptly spotted Graham Nash, Neil Young and Linda Ronstadt. Said Henley: 'She was standing there in a little Daisy Mae dress, barefoot and scratchin' her ass. I thought: I've made it! I'm in heaven!'

Viewed from Linden, East Texas, California had seemed like paradise. Don had often wondered if it was true what they said: that the women there were bronzed, leggy, gorgeous, and outnumbered the men two to one! The darker side to the sun-kissed state and its high-profile inhabitants, however, was brought home to Don at the beginning of October 1970, when he was shocked to see up close in the Troubadour the reality of what Texan star Janis Joplin had by then become. Henley had regarded the raucous wild woman of rock as someone who'd been determined to show folk back home in Port Arthur just how successful she had become. What Don saw led him to describe Joplin sympathetically as resembling 'a wounded animal'. He wasn't that wide of the mark. Three days later, on 4 October 1970, Janis Joplin was found dead at the Landmark Hotel in Hollywood with fresh needle marks in her arm. Joplin's squalid death, coming just two weeks after Jimi Hendrix's shock demise in London from inhaling his own vomit due to barbiturate intoxication, had sunk the music world into a dark gloom.

Closer to home, it was hard for Henley to keep his spirits up. Shiloh's album had flopped. The band scratched up as many gigs as it could, but money was near non-existent and his accommodation bleak. Although no doubt disappointed at their son not graduating, his parents could see where his heart lay, and as best they could they helped him out financially as he struggled to get by, even while coping with their own strains. Don's flit to LA did not mean that his thoughts stopped revolving around his ailing father's battle with heart disease.

Come spring 1971, then, Don was in a fairly lonely and desperate state when Glenn Frey bought him that bottle of beer. Frey's face wasn't totally unknown to Henley, but his first impressions of the Detroit city kid were none too complimentary. Don later declared: 'I thought Glenn was another fucked up punk.' He quickly revised his opinion once they got talking at a tucked away table. Henley was all too aware that he was at a crossroads. His band was patently going nowhere; he was drinking a lot, and with only loose change to his name he was seriously on the cusp of quitting Los Angeles. Glenn Frey then threw him a lifeline when, almost the second he parked himself at the table, he put a proposition to him. Said Don: 'Glenn asked if I'd like to go on the road for $200 a week with Linda Ronstadt's band. I said, "You bet I do!"'

As the night progressed, Henley was blown away by Frey. A man with a plan, Glenn had the eye of the tiger. Don recalled: 'Glenn kept telling me about this David Geffen. I didn't even know who Geffen was, but I decided I would stick my neck out and team up with Glenn.' Frey's mission that night was to fill the gap in Linda Ronstadt's backing band with a fine drummer, but he had a grander plan. Geffen's advice to form a band was burning him up. He wanted a band with no dead-weights. He had chalked up the groups who would carry a relative or flatmate out of friendship. That wasn't for him. In Don Henley, he felt he had found his first prospective partner.

On the face of it, Glenn Frey and Don Henley were not the most obvious pairing. Although in a band, Henley was by nature a loner. In LA he had always hung out at the Troubadour on his own, making no attempt to mingle or network. Frey was intrinsically a team guy, and not easy to overlook. With brutal candour, Don described his new friend as having been really cocky, but professionally, they were a yin-yang combination. Don declared: 'Each of us embodied both things and we would rotate roles.'

Henley had never been on the road before, and the prospect exhilarated him for the first time in a long while. But it also forced him to split from the hometown band he had fronted, and that upset him. These guys were his friends, and he took separating from them badly enough to liken it to getting divorced. It was as well then that time to mope was rationed the moment he joined Frey at rehearsals.

Out on the tour circuit, backing Linda Ronstadt, the first stop was playing the Cellar Door in Washington, D.C., and it took Glenn and Don just that one gig to be sure that they ought to start forming a band together. They were on the road for six weeks, and in that time a strong bond of friendship developed between them. Away from the stage, they schemed endlessly about their prospective band. 'We were sure we could learn from the mistakes of others and put together a group that could avoid some of the roadblocks to success,' maintained Don.

For Frey, teaming up with Henley was a godsend. Lately, he had been hugely frustrated. He was sitting with a collection of original songs, but was unable to make a record since he'd set his mind on forming a band at a time when he was forced to job as a backing musician to keep the wolf from the door. Now things were looking up, and he began to fire on all cylinders.

Frey hardly lacked ambition; his plan for the band was breathtakingly precise. Glenn wanted a four-man unit, in which everyone had to be able to write excellent songs, sing really well, play even better and look cool while they were at it. According to Don, Glenn thought that if all four were also blue-eyed, long-haired and skinny, so much the better. Frey had a definite concept in mind, and he envisaged amalgamating the best of all features. His need for this band to be musically dynamic and lyrically strong was for it to be capable of engendering three things: delirious crowd reaction, peer respect and commercial success. He was hell-bent on avoiding the risk of losing vital momentum.

Drawn to the nascent country-rock music genre, Glenn not only sought bandmates who could individually take turns singing lead, he also wanted voices that would blend into a tight harmony. He had a natural knack for musical and vocal arrangement. Not for nothing would he earn the nickname in the Eagles – 'The Lone Arranger'.

The pool of potential musicians in LA in spring 1971 was as headspinningly wide as it was deep. But to make up the optimum foursome, Frey had set his sights on two very specific targets, and he began to talk to Henley about Randy Meisner, a prodigiously talented bass player with one of the highest harmony singing voices in the business, and Bernie Leadon, an extraordinarily gifted multi-instrumentalist, whose name Don was already familiar with.

Randy Meisner was born on a farm on 8 March 1946 in Scottsbluff, Nebraska, a breadbasket US central state sandwiched between South Dakota to the north and Kansas to the south. A fresh-faced, dark-haired boy with trusting eyes, he had an inner energy that set him apart from the start. That his path would lie in music became apparent by the impact Elvis Presley had on him on 9 September 1956 when, just 10 years old, along with a third of America's population, Randy tuned in to see Presley's first appearance on *The Ed Sullivan Show*. Presley had blazed onto TV screens the length and breadth of the country with his brand of audaciously sexual charisma, grinding out the rocker, 'Hound Dog', and the as yet unreleased ballad, 'Love Me Tender'.

Record shops were suddenly inundated with advance orders for 'Love Me Tender'. 'Don't Be Cruel' topped the US singles chart, and young Randy Meisner, whose family won blue ribbon awards for sheep rearing, began to dream avidly of becoming a rock star. This unrelenting ambition propelled him into his early teens, by which time he had discovered his distinctive high register singing voice and a precocious talent for bass guitar.

At 15 he was a founder member of the Dynamics, a high school rock 'n' roll band for which he was bassist and lead singer. Having changed their name to the Drivin' Dynamics, in 1962, the band paid to record a self-produced album on which Randy sang lead on a cover version of Sam Cooke's 1957 chart-topper, 'You Send Me'. The album was chalked up to experience, and most of Meisner's energies were ploughed into harvesting regional support for his band as they gigged around several states, as far south as Texas.

While most teenage boys were avidly chasing girls, Randy was steadier – before he was 20 he married a local girl. He would fiercely guard his privacy, and his wife, Jennifer, would prefer to make a private life for herself (and their children, when they came along) in Mitchell, Nebraska, while Randy pursued his professional ambitions. Later, as an Eagle, he would head home from Los Angeles every chance he got.

For now, Meisner moved to Denver, Colorado where he joined a midwestern outfit called The Soul Survivors (not the Philadelphia band, Soul Survivors, which had a Top five hit in 1967 with 'Expressway to Your Heart'). Other members of The Soul Survivors included guitarist Allen Kemp and drummer Pat Shanahan, and around 1965 they had a stab at cutting a couple of singles. Nothing was happening, however, and the band relocated to Los Angeles, where they played the bars and small clubs. Soon, though, it was all change again, and Meisner, Kemp and Shanahan sacrificed The Soul Survivors, to team up with guitarist/vocalist Randy Naylor to form a new band they called the Poor.

Financially skint, they certainly were. Randy recalled: 'There was one guy and his wife and four others living in a one-bedroom apartment in east LA. We slept on the floor.' Over two years from mid-1966, the Poor recorded a few singles. In the prevalent style of the times, these were folk-rock numbers, heavy on harmonies. The problem was, a hundred other wannabe bands were turning out the same sort of songs. Life was pretty downbeat for Randy Meisner around this time. He had a dingy room in the insalubrious Tropicana Hotel, and worked during the day as a newspaper seller on Sunset Boulevard; he did what he had to, to make ends meet and to buy himself some marijuana. He has admitted that he was sometimes so desperately cash-strapped that he exchanged some of his grass for cash to be able to pay the rent.

Come spring 1968, the winds of change had begun to blow

again, and the Poor folded, becoming another in a lengthening line of bands not destined for stardom. With folk-rock being left behind for a more country-oriented sound in California, Randy heard it wherever he went, and found it seeping under his skin. He was only 22, but had already garnered useful experience, which he was determined not to waste. Meisner hung out at the usual haunts, and had played several times with the Poor at the Whisky A Go-Go, which was where he first met Buffalo Springfield. In April, Randy was asked to audition for a bassist vacancy in that band. His try-out took place at guitarist Richie Furay's house, but it wasn't to be. In May 1968, Buffalo Springfield broke up, each band member going his own way. Most notably, Stephen Stills formed Crosby, Stills & Nash, while Neil Young found success both solo and when he annexed with CS&N.

Meanwhile, Richie Furay and fellow guitarist/vocalist Jim Messina asked Randy Meisner to form a new band called Poco, whose other members were drummer George Grantham and pedal steel player Rusty Young. It felt right to Randy from the start, and he said yes. Poco, which became one of the longest lasting country-rock groups, studiously rehearsed throughout summer 1968 in Topanga Canyon, and gave its debut live performance in November at the Troubadour. Poco then played to a far more daunting audience just weeks later when, on 26 December, they joined the Steve Miller Band and Sly and the Family Stone to perform at the Fillmore West in San Francisco.

In January 1969, Poco were signed to Epic Records, and subsequently sent into the recording studio. For Randy Meisner, it should have been the start of what he had spent years dreaming of, but this period turned completely sour. Randy recalled: 'I was dissatisfied with the way our sound was coming out on record.' It has otherwise been claimed that a personality clash set in. Whatever the reason, the upshot was that Meisner quit Poco. Strangely, the musician offered his place in Poco was future Eagle, California-born Timothy

B. Schmit. Disgruntled and disillusioned, Randy Meisner left California and headed home to his wife in Nebraska, where he found work as a parts man in a tractor factory. He didn't desert music, though. Forming a band called Gold Rush, he played local bars on weekends, but it wasn't enough. He soon up-sticked again and returned hotfoot to LA, where in late spring he was invited to join a new backing band for the former 1950s teen idol, Rick Nelson.

In the Stone Canyon Band, Randy found himself in the familiar company of Allen Kemp and Pat Shanahan, plus steel player Tom Brumley. The band debuted at the Troubadour, where they recorded *Rick Nelson In Concert*, released in January 1970. The Stone Canyon Band's live sets came especially alive when performing a cover version of the Rolling Stones' latest number one hit, 'Honky Tonk Women'. Randy also played on the band's next album, *Rudy The Fifth*, released in 1971, but he began to wonder if he would ever feel fulfilled.

John Boylan produced Rick Nelson as well as Linda Ronstadt, and some work backing Ronstadt was on the horizon, but Meisner was frankly bored, and acutely aware that he would never get anywhere eternally playing back-up. He had no idea that his Troubadour performances with Poco and the Stone Canyon Band had attracted Glenn Frey's attention, or that being roped into supporting Linda Ronstadt would prove to be significant.

Like traffic at a busy inner city intersection, future bandmates were crossing each other's paths unnoticed all the time. In early summer 1971, Randy Meisner didn't know that Bernie Leadon, another musician who occasionally joined the Ronstadt pool of backing talent, would come to feature so heavily in his life.

Born on 19 July 1947 in Minneapolis in the northern state of Minnesota, Bernie Leadon moved to San Diego with his family when he was 10. A bright-eyed, lean boy with curly hair, he mainly passed up on traditional childhood pursuits by becoming deeply immersed in his patently remarkable talent for playing virtually any stringed instrument he could lay his hands on. This talent telegraphed early on where he was headed. Bernie had eclectic musical taste, was naturally drawn to rock 'n' roll, and developed a penchant for country music. But bluegrass, a form of folk music originating in Kentucky, which requires a virtuosic talent for guitar and banjo, quickly got into his veins, and he became an astonishingly proficient bluegrass player before entering his teens.

Such outstanding ability inevitably brought him into contact with other passionate bluegrass prodigies, such as Chris Hillman, a Los Angeles-born musician four years his senior, who later became a member of the Byrds. When Leadon was 15, he teamed up with Hillman in the local bluegrass band, the Scottsville Squirrel Barkers. Bernie Leadon was a revelation to anyone who encountered him, and was eyed covetously by every other band around. A future singer-songwriter too, right then he excelled on acoustic and electric guitar, banjo, mandolin and dobro, a type of acoustic guitar with steel resonating discs inside the body under the bridge, named after its Czech-American inventors.

In 1962, the Leadon family left San Diego for Gainesville, Florida, where for the next four years Bernie continued to let normal schoolboy life pass him by in favour of furthering his deep passion for performing. Here, too, there was no shortage of local bands keen to butterfly net him off the street. Bernie could not know it, but when he met and teamed up with one particular guy in Gainesville named Don Felder, he was befriending a fellow future Eagle. Already a highly accomplished lead guitarist, Felder had earlier played in a band called the Continentals, who had performed on the back of a pick-up truck. Felder recalled: 'Bernie moved to Gainesville for his junior and senior years in high school. We put together two bands, which we finally merged. One was a fraternity/high school prom dance band, and we also had a bluegrass band. Bernie was already a master – a killer five-string banjo player.'

In his late teens, then, Leadon found himself in a fertile hotbed of fledgling talent. The Allman Brothers Band were as yet the Allman Joys, playing teen dances at the YMCA, and young Gainesville-born Tom Petty, in his pre-Heartbreakers days, in a few years time would lead a band called Mudcrutch, which included Bernie Leadon's brother Tommy on lead guitar. Playing a mix of country and rock in Daytona clubs, Bernie honed his considerable skills, unknowingly laying the groundwork for the future Eagles sound.

After high school, as Don Felder headed north to New York, Bernie moved back west, this time to Los Angeles. Leadon didn't forget Felder, and by phone he kept urging him to come to California too. In 1967, soon after arriving in LA, Leadon infiltrated the folk circuit, joining the group Hearts and Flowers. The band did not have a long lifespan, but still Bernie played on their second Capitol Records album, called *Of Horses, Kids and Forgotten Women*, released in 1968. By that summer Leadon had moved on to join the band Don Henley so admired – Dillard and Clark. Bernie was thrilled to get to know Doug Dillard, who had always been one of his idols. Said Bernie: 'We played music all day and all night for six months.'

As well as playing on Dillard and Clark's debut album, *The Fantastic Expedition of Dillard and Clark*, several months later Leadon also contributed to its follow-up, *Through the Morning, Through the Night*. Guesting on this latter album were steel guitarist 'Sneaky' Pete Kleinow and Bernie's old friend from the Scottsville Squirrel Barkers, Chris Hillman, both of whom were right then members of the Flying Burrito Brothers.

In May 1969, Bernie restlessly broke away from backing Dillard and Clark to fill a post in the Corvettes, who became a backing band for Linda Ronstadt's summer tour. On the move again, in September, Leadon was lured into joining the

Flying Burrito Brothers. Bass player Chris Ethridge had left, and Chris Hillman, hitherto on guitar and mandolin duty, switched to bass, leaving room for Bernie Leadon to take over on guitar and dobro. Though bursting with talent, the Flying Burrito Brothers' main lightning rod between late 1968 and summer 1969 was singer-songwriter/guitarist Gram Parsons, who has since attained near mythical status in music. Around the time Bernie Leadon joined these respected exponents of country-rock, Parsons started to drift away from the group, spending a lot of time with the Rolling Stones, who had taken up residence in LA. Leadon remained with the Flying Burrito Brothers long enough to play on the albums, *Burrito Deluxe* and *Flying Burrito Brothers*, then quit in July 1971.

At 24, Bernie Leadon already had valuable recording experience. He was a stunning lead player on banjo, dobro and electric guitar, as well as a poundingly strong rhythm guitarist. He had also become a good harmony singer. In short, he was too talented to fade into the background.

In summer 1971 the same, of course, could be said of Glenn Frey and Don Henley. With Randy Meisner and Bernie Leadon at the forefront of his mind for weeks, Glenn, along with Don, continued to play support across the US to Linda Ronstadt. Then, when they pitched up at Florida in July, fate took a hand as Ronstadt's manager John Boylan drew together for one night the chance combination of Frey, Henley, Meisner and Leadon. It took place one evening midway through Linda's short residency at a Disneyland club, but it made its mark. John Boylan stated: 'The first time they played, it was clear there was something worthwhile there.' For Frey, the fact that even then the four of them had naturally knitted only reinforced his faith in his own judgement. When Ronstadt's tour was over, therefore, he set out to rope Randy Meisner and Bernie Leadon in with himself and Don Henley. Glenn was at his most persuasive and so brimming with confidence that neither recruit put up much of a struggle.

John Boylan had fleetingly fantasised about Frey, Henley,

Meisner and Leadon constituting a strong supergroup to support Linda Ronstadt, but the as yet unnamed Eagles were nobody's backing band. Frey counted Boylan a friend and was candid with the producer/manager when the idea was mooted, telling John upfront that that was not what they wanted. Though disappointed, Boylan understood and generously wished them well. They promptly set about rehearsing, and all four were ambitious to make it. Glenn Frey had added to his criteria for success, the obvious wish to make a pile of money. Don Henley concurred, considering the amassing of great wealth a much saner goal than the pursuit of fame. 'They'll both drive you crazy,' he later declared. 'But if I'm gonna blow my brains out for years, I want something to show for it!'

CHAPTER 3

Where Eagles Dare

WITHOUT SO MUCH AS a demo tape in hand, in September 1971, Glenn Frey, Don Henley, Bernie Leadon and Randy Meisner showed up at David Geffen's office on Sunset Strip, Los Angeles, with the brass-necked attitude: Here we are! Do you want us? 'It was a great moment,' Henley recalled. 'Geffen kinda said: "Well...yeah."'

Running on adrenalin, all four had hyped themselves up to having the balls to make one of the most audacious approaches ever to an influential record label chief. But Geffen, one of the shrewdest entrepreneurs in the music industry, was not bounced into signing them on impulse. He grilled the young, high-energy musicians, almost attracting a tan from the glow given off by the limitless ambition they radiated, and both sides were completely in sync. The band believed passionately that their potent combination of tight harmony vocals, lyrically complex songs and blindingly impressive musical ability would create an exciting new and commercially very strong rock sound. Geffen agreed. He also absorbed their deep devotion to a disciplined, hard-working professionalism. Like fine marksmen, they were aiming direct for the bullseye.

Geffen even approved of the name the band chose for

themselves – the Eagles. With the majestic bald eagle as America's proud national symbol, it had a sturdy patriotic connotation. Alternative versions exist as to how the band arrived at their name. It has been said that the Eagles appealed to Glenn because it sounded like the name of a street gang. Then again, Bernie and Don, in particular, had developed an interest in Native American folklore, specifically in the Hopi Indians, whose mythology venerated the eagle as sacred. For them the eagle, which flies closer to the sun than any other bird, was spiritually the richest of them all.

According to Leadon, he and his bandmates were intrigued at the time by the writings of Carlos Castaneda, and so had decided to select a name with a mythological ring to it. Bernie somewhat earthed this profundity when he also baldly conveyed their collective attitude as being: 'We're the fuckin' Eagles! Kiss my ass!' Signing the Eagles to Asylum Records then, David Geffen became their manager, advanced the band $125,000 and set up rehearsals in LA for a couple of weeks.

The powerhouse energy and white-hot ambition with which the Eagles had overwhelmed David Geffen was no facade. All four had the fire in the belly. Talking of his passion to make it, Don described himself as 'a man possessed', and the difference in the individual personalities was a stimulating plus. 'We didn't all agree on things from the beginning, but we were so enamoured of one another, that was okay,' recalled Henley. The binding element for four talented guys with disparate personalities was Glenn Frey. He was the band's de facto leader, but not in an autocratic sense. Glenn saw the Eagles as a sports team in which everyone should be encouraged to play to their individual strengths. To Frey, this was their best shot, and not to be squandered by foolish one-upmanship. 'We'd all wandered around with different bands,' he said, 'but as the Eagles, we'd found our power spot.'

To refine their act, David Geffen sent the Eagles to Aspen, Colorado, to play at the Gallery, a small club that could cram in a few hundred people, wall to wall. It was to be a month-long residency, during which they played four sets a night, six nights a week. Part of the thinking behind this was that the band should gain first-hand experience of playing live to a feisty audience but that was hardly necessary. The Eagles were not sheltered boys. Every one had paid his dues already in chalking up hair-raising experiences. As Don Henley revealed: 'From 1963 to 1970, I'd played in absolute dives in Texas where guns were whipped out and there were knifings.' An après-ski crowd would scarcely faze them. They did, however, need to iron out the wrinkles when it came to performing together, and these exhaustive gigs would tighten the Eagles musically.

Squashed into one van piled high with equipment and instruments, in late October 1971, the four drove from Los Angeles east to Arizona and into New Mexico, before heading north to Colorado on a journey that would leave an indelible imprint on their young minds. In New Mexico, they stopped off to spend a night in a hippy commune, and ended up playing a concert in an underground cavern. The hippies somehow managed to run an electricity cable for over a mile to tap into the nearest source of energy, to get power for the band's amplifiers. As gigs go, it was the weirdest yet. They performed standing on a dirt floor in a claustrophobic, subterranean space, before a blazing log fire around which the hippies danced wildly, freaking out to the music, throwing shapes and casting oversized dark silhouettes on the cavern's rough walls, made more madly menacing by the flickering orange firelight.

How the band and the hippies were not choked to death by smoke from the raging open fire is anyone's guess. But the Eagles' audience feverishly lapping them up, looked like remnants of a long-lost Inca civilisation doing a frenzied war dance around the campfire and all sense of time and place vanished. That dislocation from reality was helped on its way by the hippies' hospitality, which included, for anyone who wanted it, a supply of peyote, an hallucinogenic drug prepared from a small spineless cactus native to south America, containing mescaline. After leaving their hosts in a happily mumbling, exhausted heap on the madly trampled dirt floor, the band staggered up to the surface for much-needed oxygen – at least two of them by now drugged out of their minds.

In the cold night, in the wide-open, date-defying desert, the vastness of the universe seemed awe-inspiring. Overhead, magnificent eagles were soaring and dipping with the wind under their wings and gazing skywards, the band took it as a good omen. It wouldn't have been so good if their spaced-out drummer, who was stumbling about alternately giggling and throwing up, had wandered off and got lost! No search parties were required, however, and next day the band moved on, making it intact to Aspen, where they knuckled down to playing at the Gallery.

It was Glenn who set the band's repertoire, which consisted of numbers that appealed to all four of them. Their sets were packed with cover versions of songs by the Beatles, Chuck Berry, Bob Seger, Neil Young and Sonny Boy Williamson. When they hammered into country and bluegrass numbers, Bernie Leadon's blistering banjo work would set the club alight. There were odd nights when the Eagles equalled the audience in numbers, and two of those were bartenders, but mainly, the Gallery was bursting at the seams with a crowd often on the wild side. If the Eagles had thought tribal-style dancing was the preserve of the hippies in the New Mexico commune, Aspen opened their eyes. Some in the audience were regularly high as kites on LSD and tripping into a zone of their own, they would enthusiastically jig to the music until they literally fell down. Others drank and danced until they dropped senseless. 'It was fantastic,' recalled Randy Meisner. 'Everyone had a great time.'

Young and optimistic, each Eagle had near unlimited reserves of stamina. Their whole lives lay before them, and with a recording contract newly signed and sealed, they shared a tremendous sense of the possibilities out there to be explored. There was something special right then about being in the Rockies, with the snow falling and an abundance of free beer and pretty girls on tap. And all the while they were cutting their creative teeth. Spliced between the staple diet of the cover versions they played over the course of almost a hundred sets in that month, they road-tested some original songs which would be worked up for their first album. Randy felt that 'it tightened up the group pretty well. Then we went to play a club in Boulder, Colorado'.

When they returned to Los Angeles in November, enriched from their trip, courtesy of David Geffen's advance, each Eagle was able to leave behind slums like 1020 Laguna in Echo Park and the Tropicana Hotel. Frey, Henley, Leadon and Meisner got their first taste of moving up in the world. Bernie opted for a place in Topanga Canyon. Randy wasn't far away, while Don took a house on the corner of Camrose and Tower in the Hollywood hills, close to the famous Hollywood Bowl. Glenn's new abode was a house in Laurel Canyon on Kirkwood Drive. Mouldy, mildewed mornings were a thing of the past. The pressing business now was pulling songs together for their all-important debut album. This period pre-dated the dominant songwriting partnership of Glenn Frey and Don Henley, and so lyrically it was one of the Eagles' most democratic albums. Don later made it clear: 'From the beginning, we tried to keep this band on an equality basis. Everybody writes, everybody sings. The important thing to realise was that the whole is bigger than the sum of its parts.'

Randy Meisner came up with solo compositions: 'Tryin'', a high-energy rocker, and a contrasting atmospheric number, 'Take The Devil'. He also teamed up with Bernie Leadon to co-compose 'Early Bird'. Leadon's song, 'Train Leaves Here This Morning', had been co-written with Gene Clark back in Bernie's Dillard and Clark days, and was now given the Eagles' treatment, with Leadon providing understated vocals. The upbeat 'Nightingale', penned by Jackson Browne, was one of only two songs on the ten-track album to be provided by a non-Eagle. Glenn sang lead on this track, which was highlighted by Randy's high register vocals in its close harmony passages.

Frey assumed the lion's share of lead vocal work on the album, and also provided two diverse solo compositions: 'Chug All Night' and 'Most Of Us Are Sad'. The former song, a hard, gritty rocker, celebrated the hedonistic drinking and womanising lifestyle with which he was so familiar. To match Glenn's sensitive and intuitive flip side, the latter song was a meaningful ballad. The standout songs, however, were the three that, released as singles, gave the Eagles a hat-trick of hits.

'Peaceful Easy Feeling', the work of songwriter Jack Tempchin, was sung by Glenn, whose melodic lead vocal perfectly suited the song's laid-back style. Frey admired songs by the Byrds, the Beach Boys and Poco, whose vocals were always cut-glass sharp, and he wanted to be that pristinely precise. He was also particularly attuned to the bittersweet irony sewn into the lyrics of the otherwise contented country-rock of 'Peaceful Easy Feeling', and could throw himself wholeheartedly into this number. Likewise, Glenn would become synonymous with the very essence of the emerging Eagles by taking lead on the rousing belter, 'Take It Easy'. Though Frey is credited as co-lyricist with his friend Jackson Browne, he has revealed that he had very little to do with writing this now classic rock number.

Glenn had a good memory for songs he heard, even in passing. His introduction to 'Take It Easy' had been listening to it struggling to form, while he was living in the slum apartment above Jackson Browne's studio flat in Echo Park, and he had collared Jackson about the song before the Eagles went to Colorado. Browne confessed that he'd never been able to complete the song, which celebrated the louche lifestyle of cruising in an open-topped convertible, happily on the pull for frisky young women. When Jackson played it for Glenn, it was obvious that it wasn't short of much. Glenn instantly turned the situation round so that it was the girl doing the cruising, boldly eyeing the song's protagonist in return – and that was the missing link.

Thrilled at finally nailing the song, Browne magnanimously insisted on sharing the songwriting credit with Frey, and few would argue against 'Take It Easy' as the best way to kick off the Eagles' debut album. The chiming, opening chords, played on 12-string guitars, sounded like a proclamation that this new band had arrived on the scene. 'Take It Easy' became the band's lead-off single, but the most unusual number was unquestionably 'Witchy Woman'; this song marked Don Henley's only contribution to the album as lead vocalist and as co-composer, along with Bernie Leadon.

Don had been at his Hollywood hills house when Leadon showed up one evening, on fire about a tune that was haunting him. When Bernie began to play this compelling riff in a dramatic minor key, it immediately conjured up images of those cowboy and Indian movies churned out in the pre-politically correct days when it was okay to portray rampaging redskins fearsomely scalping any white man foolish enough to trespass on their land. The sound immediately captured Don's imagination; installed behind his drum kit, he and Bernie recorded a rough version on audio cassette tape. Soon afterwards, Don came down with the flu but he stubbornly wouldn't let that get in the way of this song. He was running such a high temperature, at times he became semi-delirious, and it was during this fever that he penned most of the lyrics, drawing on an amalgamation of the dangerously alluring women he had encountered after dark. 'Witchy Woman' showcased Don's distinctively rasping voice and marked the start of his professional songwriting career.

The startling contrast between the flowing, guitar-led harmonies of 'Take It Easy' and the tribal heavy rock of 'Witchy Woman' signalled the Eagles' wide musical range. They had the recipe for mass appeal, and with this hive of productivity yielding such honey, David Geffen was keen to shepherd the Eagles into the recording studio. Although he was surrounded by excellent facilities and experienced producer/engineers in Los Angeles, in the new year Geffen despatched the fledgling band to Britain, to Olympic Studios in Barnes, London. Geffen had also managed to enlist the services of Glyn Johns, one of the most sought-after record producers in the business, though it had not been easy. David Geffen had earlier persuaded Johns, on a chance visit to America, to go see the Eagles perform in Aspen, an experience that had left the Epsom-born producer flatly unimpressed.

Glyn Johns later declared: 'They were playing Chuck Berry, badly. You had Bernie Leadon on one side, a great country player, and Glenn Frey on the other, a good rock 'n' roll guitarist, and they were pulling the rhythm section in two.' To Johns' ears, there was a lack of proper cohesion. All he could hear initially was a complete cacophony. The next time Geffen got Johns to attend a performance, he turned up early, and caught the Eagles in rehearsal. Suddenly he sat up and took notice. He recalled: 'Bernie and Frey picked up acoustic guitars and played a song Randy had written – just two acoustics and the four of them singing. And that was it!'

At Geffen's instigation the Eagles flew into London in February 1972 for two weeks' recording at Olympic Studios. Don recalled: 'They packed us off to England and stuck us in this little apartment, picked us up, took us to the studio, and then we'd go back to this little place and drink ourselves to sleep. Next day, we'd get up and do it all over again.'

Glyn Johns had established himself in the 1960s as a first-rate engineer, then producer. Most recently, he had helmed the 1971 album, *A Nod's as Good as a Wink...to a Blind Horse*, for the Faces, fronted by Rod Stewart, which had hit number six in the US charts in December. Professionally, Johns was a proven asset to a band, but he did not always enjoy harmonious relations with the musicians with whom he worked. In 1963, the first unknown but promising group

Glyn Johns had brought in to record at IBC Recording Studios in west London was the Rolling Stones. Glyn went on to develop a successful working relationship with the Stones, but due to a clash of personalities, Johns and the Stones' creative genius and founder, Brian Jones were in constant conflict. Johns admired Jones' incredible professional abilities, but personally thought Brian an asshole. The feeling was entirely mutual, though it didn't prevent them from working together.

The relationship between Glyn Johns and the Eagles, just flexing their wings, was sometimes fraught. Don Henley found the 30-year-old British producer unnecessarily intimidating. He described how he felt Glyn would compellingly confront him. 'You couldn't help but get emotional,' Don confessed, adding: 'We even cried a couple of times.' The producer could not know it, but Don's inner fears for his father's deteriorating health were crowding in on him. Thousands of miles from home, he was especially vulnerable at that time, and he certainly did not need to feel harassment in the work place. Glenn Frey was also forthcoming about Glyn Johns' propensity to highlight flaws in the band members. Said Glenn: 'He pointed out a lot of bad habits in everybody. It's hard to be friends with someone who does that to you. It's a basic premise for friendship that you accept the threat that everybody else poses to you.'

In fairness, it must be said that there was some provocation at work. Glyn Johns had a strict 'no drugs in the studio' rule, which Frey and Meisner all too frequently chose to break. Frey knew full well that he was irritating the hell out of the producer when, during breaks in recording, he would sneak off to the toilets to smoke some weed, and come back stoned. Johns had perfectly legitimate concerns. Grass was making Glenn so malleable that he would temporarily lose his edge. He always got it back, but by then time had been lost. When Glyn confronted Glenn about what he saw as juvenile behaviour, Frey pleaded guilty, but went his own way, possibly to assert some independence in the face of such a strict atmosphere created by someone he and Henley saw as an authoritarian producer.

Friction also arose from the fact that Glenn and Don envisaged more of a rock direction to the album. Frey was fearful of ending up with a collection of smooth as glass country-rock numbers, and didn't want what he termed 'a limp-wristed record'. They wanted a tougher sound. It appears that the producer felt – and did not hesitate to baldly tell the band – that there were scores of British groups able to rock a lot harder than the Eagles. So they should know when to leave well alone. At the time, young, green and not wishing to capsize an already rocking boat, Frey and Henley backed off and settled for fuming on the quiet. Not far down the track, however, raucous numbers such as 'Heartache Tonight', 'Life In The Fast Lane' and the very Free-sounding rocker, 'Victim Of Love', would effectively prove that not every respected producer is right all the time.

On the positive front, working with Glyn Johns did produce a debut album that would put the Eagles on the map by spawning three hit singles. And valuable lessons were learned from the experience, for the Eagles had been keen to discover how their American music and attitude would sound when filtered through the ears of an experienced English producer. Glenn Frey's and Bernie Leadon's syncopated ringing guitar work, Don Henley's and Randy Meisner's hypnotically tight rhythmic bedrock beat, Glenn's smooth lead vocal and the pitch-perfect exquisite three-part harmonies of Glenn, Don and Randy, when combined with inspired arrangement and mind-boggling musicianship, conspired to create a sound that would give the band its wings and would become inextricably synonymous with southern Californian rock.

Having been bundled over to Britain to concentrate solely on making the album, the band were severed from all the usual distractions, like women and hanging out at the Troubadour. There had been no struggle to enforce a closed recording sessions policy to exclude an army of friends from disrupting proceedings, because the band knew no one in London. A divorce from their usual milieu had been necessary, but once the album was in the bag, the band was very glad to be heading home. Back on US soil, the Eagles discovered that David Geffen next wanted them to gain some live experience by touring as the support act to a few different bands, one of which in April would be Procol Harum, then on a 13-city American tour. But career considerations took a nosedive in summer for Don, when his father's condition worsened.

In the three years since being diagnosed with arterial disease, CJ had had several heart attacks, and on each occasion Don had faced the ordeal of rushing to his father's bedside in the intensive care unit of the local hospital, enduring the heartbreak of seeing his parent so helplessly weak, frightened and bravely fighting for life. 'You don't know what's real until then,' said Don. 'Everything else gets real trite.'

After yet another cardiac arrest, Mr Henley died on 7 July 1972. Don was almost ripped apart. Two weeks shy of his 25th birthday, he was a vibrant young man with his whole future before him, and inwardly he raged that the path of life had meant that his father had worked and worried himself into an early grave. To Don, CJ died way before his time, and Don blamed his father's suffering on God. All the philosophy study at university suddenly became meaningless to him. He'd studied, he'd thought out and queried these teachings, and he had believed ultimately that there *was* a power up there that made things come right. This was very wrong. And for the next two years, as Don put it, he went around 'cussing God'.

CJ had so wanted his son to do well in life, and when Don's direction had deviated from his plans, he had still supported him. The Eagles had recently released their first single, 'Take It Easy', and Don had hoped that a successful music career would repay the belief CJ had invested in him. Mr Henley had heard 'Take It Easy' and 'Witchy Woman', Don's own composition, but he died just as the first single became a hit, never living to see his son succeed. It is sad that two such significant events had to happen for Don, one almost on top of the other. Don's anger at the unfairness of life, and his resulting cynicism at the world, coloured his attitude and emerged in a variety of ways in his future songwriting.

In July 1972, a mere ten months after forming, the Eagles made their impressive recording debut by chalking up a number 12 hit with 'Take It Easy'. Suddenly the music press noticed this raw new talent. Bernie Leadon told *Rolling Stone*, already knocking on their door: 'We're a synthesis of all the sixties' music that has evolved from folk, country and rock & roll. The LA music scene is a progression through the same family.' Robert Christgau for *Newsday* weighed in with: 'The Eagles are the tightest and most accomplished rock band to emerge since Neil Young's Crazy Horse.' He further declared that the Eagles espoused a new hedonistic brand of American individualism, and were 'the ultimate in California dreaming'. Bernie and Randy happily lapped up the praise. It is doubtful if Don, in mourning, remotely paid it any attention. Glenn was cagey about it – one swallow did not make a summer. As a man who still studied where other artistes had gone wrong, Frey cautioned against getting carried away, telling journalists: 'People haven't decided to like us yet.'

That reluctance to accept premature talk of success was reinforced when the band went back out on the support tour circuit. The Eagles opened for the British group, Jethro Tull, and Glenn recalled: "'Take It Easy' would be the seventh song in our nine-song set, and no one would pay any attention to the first six. Then we'd do 'Take It Easy', and people would say, "Oh yeah! *That's* who you are!"' Undertaking various support engagements meant gaining valuable exposure, and the Eagles had the company on the road of their friend

Jackson Browne, who would collaborate on future Eagles' numbers.

When not on tour, between August 1972 and the end of the year, the Eagles concentrated on writing songs for their next album. Meantime, their debut album, *The Eagles*, made its presence felt when it climbed to its peak of number 22 in October. As new kids on the block they were there to be shot at, but some attacks came from surprising sources. The Flying Burrito Brothers' debut album, *The Gilded Palace of Sin*, had peaked at 164. In 1971, the third album from these hallowed exponents of country-rock, *The Flying Burrito Brothers*, fared even worse, dropping anchor at 176. Yet Gram Parsons, who died in 1973 from heart failure following a drug overdose, felt entitled in 1972 to lead the charge on the Eagles, declaring: 'The Eagles' music is bubblegum. It's got too much sugar in it. Life is tougher than they make it out to be.'

Parsons had missed the point. The Eagles had not set out to expose the unfair imbalances and infidelities in life. In the very near future their lyrics would become far more complex. But for now they had openly served up songs about the free rolling life with willing women, tales of lost love and of restlessly youthful spirit. Glenn called it a commentary on their collective background experiences, and stressed that the Eagles had been conceived as a song-oriented band. It mattered not a jot, he maintained, how musically good they were if the material itself was inferior.

Rolling Stone did not class it as inferior, and hailed *The Eagles* as one of the finest debut albums of the year. From his first fired-up conversation with Don Henley over a beer in the Troubadour, Frey had fiercely wanted the band to establish a vocal signature, to create a sound that people would instantly identify as the Eagles as soon as it came wafting over the airwaves. US radio adored the Eagles' sound, and this debut album was destined for platinum status.

An entire concept surrounded the Eagles. In addition to what would become their trademark sound, the band itself became a symbol for a relaxed, rich, don't-give-a-shit lifestyle. In time, they came to represent to the world the image of southern California. The band had chosen a concept cover, too, for their album. They were four individually-styled, striking young men, but instead of their intent faces being emblazoned on the front sleeve, they had opted for an atmospheric shot of the Joshua Tree desert at dawn, mainly in dark blues and shadowy, with cactus silhouetted and an eagle flying high at the top centre. The band's name was spread across its regal wingspan. The band were pictured in an inside cover shot taken in the evening in the desert as they huddled around a blazing campfire. As far as Don Henley can recollect, all of them had been smashed out of their heads on peyote when the photo was taken.

As well as drink, girls and gambling, drugs occupied a fair chunk of life for Frey and Henley during the last quarter of 1972, the start of a riotous party lifestyle that would spice up the rest of the decade. Bernie Leadon preferred to stay detached from this mad social whirl, and Randy Meisner would take himself off home to his family in Nebraska when he was not needed professionally. The nerve centre of the sybaritic decadence was Glenn's house in Laurel Canyon. Don lived just two blocks away and could easily hotfoot it over. Frey's sense of humour led him to dub this colourful community of theirs as the Kirkwood Casino and Health Club.

There was nothing wholesome about it. For spells, days on end followed a pattern of sleeping until mid-afternoon, then rising to begin drinking, sampling drugs and settling down to long drawn-out games of poker. All sense of time became blurred. The only aim in life was to sate their appetite for every excess they fancied, at any given time, quitting the gaming tables only long enough to eat or to have sex with the perfumed predators only too happy to flock to Frey's plush home, and to wait around in various bedrooms until their tender attentions were required. 'We were young and having a good time,' said Don. 'What more could you want?' At intervals, the rollicking house party would move *en masse* to the Troubadour or to a nearby restaurant, normally attracting more members of LA's music community by the time they staggered back to flake out in Frey's house.

Life wasn't all about partying, however, and the business of imprinting themselves on the music map kicked back in, taking the Eagles off on tour, again in support slots, backing a variety of established acts. But their own star was inexorably rising, as was proved when their second single, 'Witchy Woman', hit number nine in the US charts in November 1972. Bernie Leadon opined: 'We had every confidence that eight of the ten album tracks could have been singles. So we put out the ones we felt were most representative of the overall trip.'

On 24 November, the Eagles took part in a star-billed KROQ radio station sponsored 'Woodstock Of The West' festival, before hitting the road again on a trip that would take them into the new year and out of the country once more. In February 1973, their latest single, 'Tryin'', failed to chart on its American release, a disappointment that was counterbalanced when the Eagles were nominated in the Best New Artiste category for the Grammy Awards. When 'Peaceful Easy Feeling' reached number 22 in March, the Eagles could relax in the knowledge that, from the proceeds of their first three hit singles alone, they had already repaid David Geffen's substantial advance.

Keen to capitalise on this cleared slate, the band had by then returned to London to start recording their second album – this time at Island Studios, and again, despite the previous tensions, with producer Glyn Johns. Transplanted to London, this time around the band knew the score better and feeling less claustrophobically marooned, they were able to unwind more. They took in the clubs and scouted out the British opposition, studying the charts and how music was watermarked on this side of the pond. The band avidly scoured the British music trade papers, as well as those from back home, to keep abreast of everything that was happening across the board in the industry, ever eager to identify pitfalls that had trapped other bands.

With a debut album almost cracking the Top 20, and three hit singles, the Eagles' press could only make for positive reading. And since they were four very distinctive individuals with diverse musical backgrounds, journalists were quick to publicly peg their personalities or place in the band. Bernie Leadon was seen as the purist, a maestro musician bent on creating meaningful music. Randy Meisner, credited with providing the throbbing heartbeat of the band's sound, was the home-loving quiet one. Don Henley was pinpointed as the very intense, intellectual Eagle, and Glenn Frey was affectionately branded the rowdy playboy, even though behind the mischievously glinting eyes and risqué smile there lurked the soul of a literate artiste.

The Eagles had very quickly become a tight collaborative unit, within which Frey and Henley would become a prominently potent songwriting force. This was richly apparent in the band's next work, which they hoped would elevate the Eagles to higher realms.

CHAPTER 4

Egos and Excess

THE CREATIVE CORE of Glenn Frey and Don Henley began to evolve when the time came to write songs for the Eagles' follow-up album. Although 'Witchy Woman' had been Henley's sole lyrical contribution to the band's eponymous debut offering, he was clearly capable of much more. Don had now acquired a taste for songwriting, but he needed encouragement to blossom. He got that from Frey. To Glenn, this was a crucial time. He was as convinced that his friend had an untapped reservoir of talent, as he was certain that writing superior songs was the key to building upon the band's promising beginning. Despite having three hit singles to their credit, he did not feel flushed with confidence. On the contrary, carefully analysing their situation, Glenn concluded that for their survival the Eagles needed to set themselves apart.

Asylum Records was a new label. David Geffen and Elliott Roberts, as GR Management, handled them. But they also managed such lyrical talents as Neil Young and Joni Mitchell, and it was Glenn's growing belief that the Eagles had a limited period within which to make their mark or risk being cut loose. It was a dog-eat-dog business in which, talented or not, it was easy to slip between the slats.

It is typical of Frey that he did not try single-handedly to seize the songwriting initiative – always assuming that the others would have let him. Instead, with his indefatigable enthusiasm, he swamped Don with his desire that they collaborate. Used to the guitarist's relentless energy, Henley was happy to see if it would work. Don already considered Glenn an excellent lyricist and arranger, but once the pair actively put their heads together, he discovered that Glenn had another natural knack. 'When I would pull out all my book learning, he would help me put it into the vernacular. He had a wonderful sense of street language,' said Don.

The rapid professional symbiosis of Frey and Henley was an extension of the complementary yin-yang personalities that made their friendship work. In time, the two would emerge as co-leaders of the band when, as Don once put it, he was able to provide 'stability and country common sense to Glenn's vital impetuousness'. He explained: 'I tempered him in a way, and supplied logic, calm and a certain rootedness.' Ingenuity was never in short supply, as each band member bent his mind to the question of the direction the next album should take. It was common for artistes to take the vicissitudes of life and the pursuit of success as the general basis of their sophomore work, but the Eagles created a bold concept album. Why it should assume a cowboy theme is easily nailed down.

Ever a renegade spirit, Glenn later opined: 'When a kid sees a guitar in a shop window, he sees it the same way the outlaw in the Old West saw the gun. It's the mark of a new kind of man, a way he can make a fortune and a name for himself while thumbing his nose at the things society wants him to be.' The Wild West had never been far away from any young boy's consciousness in the 1950s/early 1960s. The staple diet on the small or silver screen was the western, projecting a romanticised image of the tough, enigmatic loner living on the edge, always a whisker away from death by bullet, knife or the hangman's noose. Growing up, Frey, Henley, Leadon and Meisner had all soaked it in, imagining themselves as quick-draw outlaws. It was almost un-American – not to say, unmanly – not to have done so.

As adults, Glenn and Don still had reminders around them of those desperately lawless days. Frey had a gunfighters' photo album knocking about the house, and Jackson Browne had a book he had been given years earlier for his 21st birthday, all about various outlaws, including the Doolin-Dalton gang. The Eagles did not see themselves as outlaws, but as far as Glenn and Don were concerned, they both led a radical life – transposing night for day, chasing women and smoking dope. And the deeper they sank into talking of the dusty trailblazers of old, the easier it became to see a thread between the restless, rootless, rascally outlaws, and the itinerant life of modern day reckless rock stars, shocking society and succumbing to a sense of wanderlust, while indulging in every excess to sustain a sometimes soulless existence.

Originally, they anticipated an album of songs about several different rebels, and not necessarily time-capsuled. One evening, however, Glenn and Don sat down together to work on a song specifically about the Doolin-Dalton gang. For Frey, it had begun life earlier when he had bounced ideas around with drinking buddies Jackson Browne and JD Souther at the Troubadour. But, in tune with Henley, the same song seemed to acquire an extra evocative dimension. Although the Eagles were newly into the system, Henley has maintained that the whole cowboy/rock star analogy that developed for their second album stemmed from an inner urge to rebel against the corporate aspect of the music business – his cynicism beginning to kick in. Certainly cynicism tinged the moodily pessimistic 'Doolin-Dalton', in which contemporary references are laced into the fabric of a song otherwise set in the past. And what became a recurring theme of faithless women began to show itself.

Fairly quickly then, Glenn and Don came up with three

dual compositions, one of which was the title track, 'Desperado'. Again, Henley has maintained that this was a reaction to the band's initial success. Interestingly, the perennially deep thinker debated with his collaborator for hours about the propensity for people in the early 1970s to seek escape, Don's own belief being that there is a danger in escaping too thoroughly from life's realities. 'Desperado' was not released as a single, yet went on to become one of the Eagles' most distinctive and best loved numbers. The song about an anguished, unfulfilled soul who has deliberately built barriers around himself, grew from the seed of an idea Henley had been nursing for years. At the tail end of the 1960s, he had no more than promising but disjointed song fragments, which were set to take on a Southern gothic complexion. But post his father's untimely death, Don was a very different young man, who now came at songwriting in a new way.

He had the title, some lyrics and parts of the melody. His canyon house, not far from Glenn's, was built on stilts; on windy days it would tend to rock disconcertingly from side-to-side. It had an unsettling effect on Don, and one particularly gusty day, while struggling with 'Desperado', he welcomed the company when Glenn turned up to get down to work. Having ditched its original form, Henley was convinced that his patchwork song had the potential to be turned into a western style number suited to their new thinking. When he showed it to Glenn, Frey immediately got excited and set about fleshing it out at the piano with his own inspired lyrics, rapidly bringing structure to the song. 'Glenn was great at that,' said Don. 'That was the start of us becoming a team.' Frey summed up his professional partnership with Henley as: 'I brought him ideas and a lot of opinions. He brought me poetry.'

Within days of completing 'Desperado', Glenn and Don created 'Tequila Sunrise', a smooth sounding ode to a young man's footloose way of life. Glenn came up with the title, only to fret that it was too obvious. The tequila sunrise cocktail was very popular at that time, and though Frey loved the song, he feared it was too clichéd a title. It suited his energetic nature that it came together quickly and apparently seamlessly. Don afforded his cohort the credit, too, for coming up with the clever changes in the song's bridge, and felt that the reference to needing some Dutch courage would hit the spot with shy young men countrywide. Henley revealed that he often needed a swig or two of the potent Mexican liquor to give him the nerve to approach the ladies. Having co-composed what would become two classic songs in relatively short order, Don's self-confidence was slowly beginning to build. 'From then on,' he said, 'I felt I knew what I was doing.'

A heavier number, called 'Out of Control', about a gambling drifter arriving in town, looking to get lucky and laid, was another Frey/Henley composition, this time with a contribution from songwriter Tom Nixon. Bob Dylan-influenced lyricist David Blue provided 'Outlaw Man', the only non-Eagle composition for the upcoming album. Glenn and Don collaborated with Randy Meisner on 'Certain Kind of Fool', and the melancholic, regret-laden ballad, 'Saturday Night', was a four-way band collaboration.

It was an inspiring time for the Eagles, when a willingness to be mutually supportive reigned supreme. Encouragement and enthusiasm abounded, and there was no shortage of stimulus between four opinionated guys, none of whom would pull any punches with the other. Proposed songs could be just as brutally denounced as shit, as others glowingly hailed superb, as they whittled their way ruthlessly down to the final selections. Before they were half way through this ego-bruising process, they could see that the outlaw/rock star analogy would hold together; it made them determined to execute every aspect of this concept album to the best of their developing abilities. Two more songs made the final playlist, both solo Bernie Leadon compositions. These were 'Twenty-

One', an impressive bluegrass number, and a touching ballad called 'Bitter Creek'. 'Doolin-Dalton', it was decided, would surface twice more – mid-way as an instrumental, and again as a reprise at the end, which would make it an 11-track album.

From early on, the Eagles gained a reputation for poring over every word and every melody of every song deemed to be recordable, and then transferring that meticulous attention to detail to the studio. From this point on, too, band tensions began insidiously to seep in. The germ of the dissent that later debilitated the band came with the emergence of Frey and Henley as close songwriting collaborators. This is invariably a tricky development in a band, since it tends to project a shift in the power base. All four members were indisputably vital to the success of the Eagles, but Glenn and Don were beginning to appear more prominent. Don declared: 'The only two people in this group who tend to think alike are Glenn and me.'

Whether Bernie and Randy considered that as sufficient justification, outsiders were noticing. Producer Glyn Johns, with whom Glenn and Don had a fraught working relationship, commented: 'Frey and Henley had the common leadership approach. The other two were treated very much as country cousins in the songwriting department.' Bernie Leadon felt that this was not what he had signed up for. The way he saw it, the original premise had been that the band would consist of equal partners, all writing songs and all given equal time in the spotlight. Every Eagle *did* write material, and some were more at home than others with being centre stage, but Bernie stated: 'There was supposed to be no leader, no second-string members! It was meant to be a total democracy.'

In February 1973, these simmering grievances were in an early enough stage to be put behind them when they flew out of Los Angeles for London, eager to record their clutch of new songs at Island Studios, once again with producer Glyn Johns.

This time, they had just over a month in which to lay down their concept album. For the duration of this visit the band rented an apartment in the King's Road, and took a firmer stand about pleasing themselves when off duty. Not the tidiest young men in the world, they quickly turned the bachelor pad into a tip. The wreckage of late-night gambling sessions saw strewn playing cards and dice discarded willy-nilly, and an abundance of empty beer and spirits bottles lying, like themselves, keeled over. With the stamina and resilience of men in their twenties, however, they never failed to show up at the recording studio on time and sober.

Working relations with Glyn Johns were watermarked pretty much as they had been the first time around. But naturally, the Eagles had acquired more self-confidence since the previous collaboration. Frey was just as incorrigible as he had been 12 months ago, but Don was not so vulnerable. Having penned such obvious gems as 'Desperado' and 'Tequila Sunrise', the pair saw no reason not to assert themselves a bit more from the get-go. Glyn Johns had always admired Bernie Leadon's incredible musicianship; in turn, the multi-instrumentalist rubbed along well with the redoubtable producer. For as uneasy as Leadon was starting to feel about the dynamics within the Eagles, publicly he was upbeat. He told journalists willing to flock to the Americans in London: 'The new album will be a lot looser and more relaxed than the first. We've been writing a lot collaboratively. This time around it's more thematic.'

When they'd recorded their first album, the Eagles had deliberately remained within the realms of what they could reproduce on stage. It was important to them to be the kind of group which replicates live, what their fans were getting from an album. But this time they adopted a more layered approach in the studio with, for example, Bernie overdubbing three instruments on a single song. In a concert situation, that would obviously not be possible with just the four of them.

While the Eagles were recording in London, they played live concerts at the Oxford Polytechnic and, on 16 March, at London's Royal Festival Hall, during which they performed numbers from the forthcoming album. There was no such thing as second-rate placings on stage. Don Henley, as drummer, took up the traditional elevated post behind the rest of the band, but from the audience's view, from left-to-right Randy Meisner, Glenn Frey and Bernie Leadon, each with vocal and instrument mikes, stood in a three-way pole position. All four sported the moustaches that were in, in 1973. To go with his Afro, Don had also grown a full beard, while Glenn's hair waved well down onto his shoulders. Bernie took to the stage wearing a pudding basin style hat perched on his springy curls, and Randy looked mellow, with an easy smile and collar-length locks. Taking lead vocal on most songs, Glenn had a distinctly roguish gleam in his eyes, occasionally flashing a matching disreputable grin, but the band wasn't big on talking overmuch to their audiences. Cliché or not, they preferred to let their music speak for them.

The early 1970s was a period in music, on both sides of the Atlantic, which accommodated a variety of genres before radio and TV popularised particular trends. Guitar-led, progressive or country-rock bands were avidly supported by music lovers, who were able to appreciate the skill that went into these non-showy performances. It was also still a time when exponents in the same field did not feel so threatened by each other. Bernie maintained: 'None of us feels it's a competition.' No one knew which genres would stay the distance or which bands would survive in play – questions which burned into Glenn's consciousness quite a lot as he tried to see into the future. 'You realise that longevity and keeping your band together is the ultimate goal,' said the 24-year-old, with some perspicacity, adding that 'it takes ten years to write that overnight sensation.'

The Eagles and Asylum Records also wanted to push this

emerging concept album to the nth degree, and so it was decided to go for the Old West look on the album sleeve. Booked into shooting scenes at Shepperton Studios, near London, with photographer Henry Diltz, the band took over the studio backlot of a western. All four dressed up as the epitome of the mean, lawless desperadoes of their songs – and they came out the other end with one of the most famous album covers in rock music. Frey, Henley, Leadon and Meisner were authentically transformed back in time. They suited the dusty trail look, complete with spurs and buckskin, and armed to the teeth. Wearing a wide-brimmed, battered hat pulled low on his brow, Don projected the aura of the enigmatic loner-drifter. Bernie and Randy were believably menacing lean guns for hire. Glenn, having seriously trimmed back his moustache and grown a close stubbly beard, easily assumed the casually charismatic gunslinger role.

As this Younger Brothers-style gang, the four had a whale of a time pretending to rob the local bank, or lounging about as feral up-to-no-good types, aching to make mischief with the sheriff and his men. To liven up the inevitable spells of hanging around on set between shots, the band knocked back a few beers and set up quick-draw challenges between themselves. In each case, the boy was still inside the man. They were toting real six-shooters, mercifully loaded with harmless blanks. Once back in business, extras were brought in for shots of the band-cum-bandits grimly depicted as lying dead in the dust, roped together after capture by the gloating town sheriff. For the album's back cover, the sepia tinted photograph displaying this mock death scene was remarkably effective. And included in the line up of 'bodies' was Jackson Browne, who had come over to Britain and had happily got involved. The front sleeve shot was guaranteed to stand out, with the four Eagles, like true yesteryear renegades, staring morosely into the camera.

It certainly caught the eye of leading film director, Sam

Peckinpah. He had already made his name by directing blood-spurting, violent westerns such as *The Wild Bunch*, and he had lately been at the helm of *Pat Garrett and Billy The Kid*, starring Bob Dylan, among others. Peckinpah was so impressed by the Eagles' concept album that he took an option on *Desperado*, with the aim of turning the tales unravelled in the album into a follow-up film to *Pat Garrett and Billy The Kid*. The movie never materialised, and likewise the concept album, *Desperado*, considered by many to be the Eagles' masterpiece, initially failed to live up to the band's commercial expectations when it was released in June 1973. In time it would go double platinum, and be credited with launching what became 1970s cowboy-chic. But in terms of chart performance, it dropped anchor at a disappointing number 41 in America, and took two years to appear at number 39 in the British album chart. Similarly, in the US in summer 1973, the future classic, 'Tequila Sunrise', stalled at a lowly number 64.

The reason for these surprisingly poor chart placings lay in the two worlds the album spanned. The Eagles were moving towards being more of a rock band than exponents of country-rock, which was itself distinct from pure country music. *Desperado* was viewed as too rock sounding for the countless traditional country music radio shows. At the same time, DJs at America's plethora of rock music stations took one look at the band dressed as cowboys, and promptly passed the album by for being clearly country. Falling between two stools, the album was starved of prominent and sustained nationwide radio airplay. The album's chart performance disappointed more than the band. Producer Glyn Johns stated years later: 'Although *Desperado* has since gone platinum, it should have taken the world by storm. It has become a milestone, and I'm very proud of it. But it's very strange that it wasn't a hit at the time.'

Desperado intrigued some critics. David Koepp for *Super Rock* hailed the concept work as the Eagles' most important effort, declaring that it was 'less a rock opera than a rock movie, a drama of defeat by a sympathetic, cautionary but carefully detached observer'. It did not take the band long to realise that they had been saddled very firmly by the music press with an outlaw image, a tag that was alright for a while, but which became tedious after a time, and not a little foolish on the part of those sections of the media which persistently took it too far, since it had simply been an album idea. Every so often over the years, Don Henley would kick out frustratedly at this practice: 'We never pretended to be cowboys [in real life],' he would stress. 'I wear boots, sure, but I've worn boots all my life. I don't like that whole schlock outlaw trip. It's a myth that everybody around here rides around with cactus up their butt!'

A decade on, Don was still batting back the cowboy/outlaw rockers image, which by 1987 he ended up describing as having been a bit bogus anyway. But it is true that, for a moment, the Eagles did capture their time and their culture. And in real life, circa 1973, theirs *was* a modern-day lawlessness – not living the regulation 9 am–5 pm life in the steady job, and settled in conventional relationships. Some of them called it living outside the laws of normality. Frey and Henley had an unrelenting itch for any action, any hedonistic thrill which, when transferred to song, played well live with their rapidly expanding fan base.

There was no hiding, though, from the disappointment of failing to better their debut album's success, and some in the band were forthright about their desire to make money. Glenn and Don also continued to be eager to learn about the music world's business end – something too many of their contemporaries did not bother to do, to their ultimate cost, and something for which, rightly, the pair made no apologies. Henley was blunt: 'You can't be sensitive artistes all the time. You have to be able to fend for yourself. I don't want to be like the 1950s stars, walking around now completely broke and trying to make a comeback.' In summer 1973, the Eagles were not exactly flush in the pocket, and in the quest of familiarising more people with their new material the band went out on tour across America. It was a trip that would become most memorable for two events.

One was for putting the east coast rock critics' collective back up by slagging off the New York Dolls from the stage of Madison Square Garden, New York. As a commercial force, the New York Dolls had a short lifespan. Staten Island-born singer David Johansen was considered, by some, to be a dead ringer in looks and voice for Mick Jagger. Another band member, Johnny Thunders, seemed similar to Jagger's sidekick, Keith Richards. The Dolls, however, were synonymous with their garish transvestite stage wear. They released their eponymous debut album in summer 1973, but within two years were slipping off music's radar.

Such cross-dressing was certainly not to the taste of the Eagles, whose stage wear of jeans and shirts was decidedly dressed down. But it was not on a sartorial level that the Eagles were said to have had a go at these new kids on the block. It appears that they denounced the New York Dolls for not being a proper group, claiming that they couldn't play their instruments. It could reasonably be argued that such a musically gifted band as the Eagles were well qualified to voice such a professional opinion. But their stark candour made a cross for their backs with the riffled up new wave of reviewers. On the bright side, the other significant event was coming into contact with rock manager Irving Azoff, an experience guaranteed to leave its mark.

Born in 1948, and from Danville, Illinois, Irving Azoff became the *enfant terrible* of the music business scene. As *Rolling Stone* admiringly put it: 'He is the American Dream taken by the balls!' Referred to by the Eagles as 'Big Shorty' (he is around 5'3"), Azoff had been impossible to overlook from the day he could make himself understood. In Chicago in the late 1960s, while in his early twenties, he was handling the affairs of dozens of artistes, including Reo Speedwagon, and shaking up club owners with his full-on style of doing business. Promoting his growing roster of acts over five states, he was gaining experience at a rate of knots, and leaving an indelible impression wherever he went. People marked him down as someone obviously going places. Yet Azoff himself would read about David Geffen, whizz-kid entrepreneur, and consider Geffen godlike.

By the time the Irving Azoff whirlwind moved to Los Angeles, his client list included Dan Fogelberg, Steely Dan, JD Souther and Joe Walsh. Initially, Azoff could not afford to open his own management office, so he went to work with GR Management, bringing his clients with him. Irving Azoff's memory of first making contact with any of the Eagles was by telephone. He recalled: 'I was in the office one day and the secretary tells me I have to take a call from this raving madman, Glenn Frey.'

The band had been badly rattled by a series of hiccups. Then the promised transport had not shown up to take them to the airport in time to catch their flight. So Azoff, himself an explosive personality, came up against a fuming Eagle in the shape of Glenn in a towering temper. Azoff later claimed that Frey ear-bashed him for a full 15 minutes over the transport blunder. The first face-to-face encounter between Azoff and the Eagles came when Irving arrived in Kansas City to steer the band through the mid-section of their tour. Far from meeting with flaming arrogance, he found a band suffering from low morale. The Eagles were disheartened at zigzagging across America, only to perform to half empty theatres; there seemed to be a lack of focus behind them, which had made the band worry that GR Management was perhaps not concentrating on them as much as they had expected. When a mole within the company seemed to confirm these suspicions, it led to the four, rightly or wrongly, feeling neglected. Financially, too, they were deeply disappointed. In the days when they had been on the other side looking enviously over the wall at signed recording artistes, bands with two gold albums under their belt seemed to have hit it big. Reality, they had discovered, was something very different. Said Glenn: 'When we first met Irving, we had two gold records and $2,500 in the bank.'

Irving Azoff was like an adrenalin jab in the arm. His reputation for employing unorthodox business techniques had preceded him, and the Eagles had heard how, to extract top dollar contracts for his clients, Azoff had been known to erupt verbally at record label executives, to physically tear up an unsatisfactory proffered contract, even occasionally to dash inanimate objects to the ground to emphasise a point. Startling as this behaviour was from a manager – and Azoff would become renowned for it – it had the desired effect for the artistes he handled. Don Henley described Irving Azoff as 'Napoleon with a heart. But I'm always awed, because he's screaming at some guy twice his size and never gets his face crushed for it!' Glenn Frey jokingly maintained that Azoff was strikingly like a real-life version of the cartoon character, Dennis the Menace.

That apart, the first night on the road that the band actually sat down with the dynamic manager, sparks flew in a good sense. There was something so right about the chemistry. Both Glenn and Don felt able to air their particular concerns, opening up about problems they had experienced in working with a producer whose determination to give a glassy polish to their records did not tally with their own vision. In turn, despite his brash, over-the-top reputation, Azoff revealed that he had come into the management set-up on the west coast with clients and experience, but that he himself was in a growing process which was not as certain as he made it appear on the surface. In effect, Azoff was in the throes of working hard to catch his rising star, just as the Eagles were.

It was several months before Irving Azoff took over the job of managing the Eagles and giving them a much-needed boost. For now, matters stayed discouraging. Their latest single release, 'Outlaw Man', barely bettered 'Tequila Sunrise' by reaching a humble 59 in the US chart in October. Disappointment made the perfect bedfellow for the creeping dissent that was now starting to develop artistically. The beef centred around songwriting, and began to come to a head in summer 1973, while they worked on new material for their third album. It came down to one half of the band disagreeing with the other. Frey saw no problem in sometimes altering lyrics written by Meisner or Leadon. Although, when Glenn brought the subject up with musician friends outside the Eagles, some of them were openly shocked that he would dare do this.

Henley agreed with Frey. He deemed that making such adjustments was a way of helping Meisner and Leadon to express themselves even better in song. It was not, Don maintained, that he and Glenn did not recognise that their bandmates had a need to write lyrics, or that they had something valuable to say, but putting together the very best song possible surely benefited everyone. Henley pointed out that critics were not interested in distinguishing who had written what, and therefore any weak song on an album would reflect badly on the Eagles as a whole – an argument for taking collective responsibility, therefore requiring collective involvement.

But often this did not cut any ice with Randy and Bernie, who were becoming increasingly conscious of the conjoined force of Glenn and Don. Henley owned up candidly to the fact that he and Frey had assumed the role of major songwriters within the Eagles, because they genuinely believed that that was where their particular forte lay. Equally, they deemed Meisner and Leadon to be *well* ahead of them as musicians. It came back to the basic belief Glenn had started with, that for the band to attain optimum success, each member ought to play to his individual strength. This sturdy belief did not stop Glenn and Don from being sensitive to outside criticism that they just couldn't help themselves, and itched to rewrite any lyrics that hadn't flowed from their own pens. For Randy and

Bernie, it certainly didn't sufficiently alleviate the feeling of gradually being marginalised within the Eagles.

These strained relations in the band were hardly the best basis for a return visit to London in October, to record their next album with Glyn Johns. Henley made no bones about the fact that he and Glenn assumed what he termed 'a bulldozer attitude' before setting foot inside the studio this time. There was still an intrinsic clash of ideas between a producer who continued to want to corral them in a country sound, and a band determined to bust loose and prove their credentials as a rock group. Like oil on water, they were never going to blend, and it could only be fraught. Stress in the recording studio, in fact, sometimes became so explosive that it seriously hampered progress. In this septic atmosphere, simmering resentments within the band itself over songwriting issues also surfaced, making everyone tetchy. A depressing cloud dampened what was supposed to have been an all out push to pull themselves out of the slump their recent US chart placings had left them in.

There was one ray of sunshine during their stay in Britain, when the Eagles deserted the recording studio for a week in early November 1973 to play support to Toronto-born 28-year-old Neil Young, then on a short UK tour that commenced at Manchester's Palace Theatre and ended at London's Royal Festival Hall. In spring 1972, his fourth solo work, *Harvest* had garnered him the number one slot in both America and Britain. This Tonight's The Night tour was an exhilarating trip from the start, and the Eagles relished the chance to escape the studio and join Young on the live circuit. Backstage excess in the 1970s was par for the course, but it would still go down as a tiny piece of folklore, that at the end of a poker game on the tour bus journey from Birmingham to London, Don Henley won $7,000 from one of Neil Young's producers.

Frey and Henley both thrived on the thrill of high-stakes gambling. But sobering sensations once more swamped the

Eagles when they returned to work on their new album. After a six-week slog to make it take shape, only two tracks had been recorded: 'You Never Cry Like A Lover' and 'Best of My Love'. Frustration on both sides was sky-high, and the sessions were a rolling disaster. That much was obvious, but neither band nor producer would agree that they were to blame for the difficulties. Don admitted that 'there was a lot of fighting'. Glyn Johns later maintained that at that point in late 1973, the Eagles had a lot of hang-ups in the recording studio, both individually and with one another. Johns believed that the recording sessions for the Eagles' third album going awry was in no way his fault. He stated: 'The whole thing was that Glenn Frey wanted the Eagles to be a rock band and, of course, that's what they became when I stopped producing them.'

With these London sessions in tatters, the Eagles left Britain for Los Angeles at the end of 1973, washed out, thoroughly demoralised and anxious about their future. Irving Azoff was assigned the task of booking the Eagles into an LA studio and bringing in a producer to replace Glyn Johns. In the meantime, the band were despatched out on to the road in early 1974 to play some live US gigs. Opening for the Eagles was singer/lead guitarist Joe Walsh, whose business affairs Azoff also looked after. In a couple of years' time, Joe Walsh was destined to become a fully-fledged Eagle, but right then he was a solo act, having recently earned his first solo gold disc for the album, *The Smoker You Drink, the Player You Get*, which had hit number six in America the previous summer.

That album had been produced by Walsh and Bill Szymczyk. It was the latter whom Azoff enlisted to help shunt the Eagles back on the recording track when they picked up the cudgels again, this time at Record Plant Studios in Los Angeles. Bill Szymczyk had also worked with blues and heavy rock artistes such as B B King, which particularly pleased Glenn Frey. Proof that this was the right match came when the rest of the album pulled together in little over three weeks. Producer and band found a mutual rhythm straight away, largely because Szymczyk did not peg the Eagles as country-rock artistes. He had not saddled them, either, with *Desperado*'s cowboy image; he was all for the closet rockers in them breaking out.

The Eagles, of course, still wanted to develop their own recognisable musical identity. Bill Szymczyk understood this, and was fired up with ideas of how best to achieve both goals. The challenge was stimulating and along the way it led to the introduction of the man who would become the fifth Eagle – lead guitarist, songwriter and Bernie Leadon's long-time friend, Don Felder.

Born on 21 September 1947 in Gainesville, Florida, Don Felder had found music fascinating from an early age. Like countless youngsters across America, it was seeing Elvis Presley on *The Ed Sullivan Show* that inspired him, aged 11, to acquire his first cheap guitar. 'I traded a handful of cherry bombs to a kid across the street for a horrible acoustic that was full of holes,' Don Felder recalled. He promptly tried to enlist anyone he could find to show him how to play it. But he largely relied upon teaching himself, by listening to records and to the radio, then endlessly copying the sounds he was hearing. It was a painstaking process but, bitten by the bug from day one, he never lacked dedication or application. He upgraded as soon as he could to electric guitar, and within two years was amazingly proficient. Being content with impressing friends and relations with blindingly fast, intricate party pieces was not his style. His heart was too set on perfecting his craft, even though he was operating at this time with very makeshift equipment. His Silvertone guitar was adapted with a de Armond pickup, and was amplified through a tape recorder. 'Anything you could plug it into,' said Felder.

His musical inspirations included Chet Atkins and Elvis Presley's guitarist, James Burton, and he continually sought to extract the best sounds out of ever-improving instruments. He moved up to a Fender Musicmaster guitar, on his way to owning a Stratocaster. The actual process of recording also absorbed him, and when his father brought home one of the first stereo tape decks with a sound on sound function, Don began experimenting with primitive overdubbing. Playing live soon naturally became a must, and at 15 Felder joined the Continentals, who at one point included Stephen Stills. The band played junior high schools and teen dances. 'We were pretty successful, considering that we were all teenagers lying about our ages,' recalled Don.

It was around now, in 1962, that Felder met Bernie Leadon, newly arrived in Gainesville from San Diego. Don was blown away by Leadon's bluegrass banjo licks, just as Bernie enviously eyed Felder's electric lead guitar wizardry. According to Felder, he and Bernie 'traded lessons'. Folk, country and bluegrass music was popular in Florida at this time, and soon Don and Bernie branched out together and formed a bar band they called the Maundy Quintet, with local musicians 'Boomer' Hough, Barry Scurran and Tom Laughon, again bluffing it out, claiming to be 18 when they were not.

The local college fraternity circuit also helped keep them busy. They took it very seriously and, image-conscious, scraped together the money to buy matching red Gibson guitars. Felder said: 'We were the hottest thing in Florida at the time, except for the Allman Joys [later the Allman Brothers Band].' Felder and Leadon also formed a bluegrass band, tailored to fulfil specific bookings. By 1965, as a 17-year-old gigging musician, Don Felder was making a reasonable enough living, which he augmented by giving guitar lessons at a local music shop for $2 an hour. As his reputation spread, wannabe rock stars in the region wound their way to Felder; one of the young, up-and-coming stars he taught guitar to was Tom Petty, then knocking about with a band called Mudcrutch.

In 1967, after high school, the Maundy Quintet broke up.

Bernie Leadon headed back west, and Don Felder felt his musical future lay in New York. He decided that to improve his prospects he would be wise to develop a lot of styles, and so be versatile enough to play country, jazz, rock and pop. For a while, therefore, he concentrated his energies on learning to play classical guitar and pedal steel. It was also in New York in 1968 that Felder began to plough his hopes into his latest band, called Flow, a four-piece jazz-rock outfit that had been formed in Florida, featuring alongside himself on guitar, Mike Barnett playing drums, John Winter on piano and saxophone, and bassist/vocalist Chuck Newcomb. Flow stayed together for three years and cut one album.

Felder fitted in well with these guys, whose personalities were like his own – placid and reflective. The four moved into a sprawling farmhouse in upstate New York, worked endlessly at the art of performing smoothly, and lived on their collective dream of making it, while writing a wealth of original material. Flow picked up gigs at universities and colleges within a workable radius of their base, and began to attract the eye of local reporters, earning themselves little write-ups here and there that invariably praised Flow's unique style. Like rough diamonds, they and their material were not perfect but showed stimulating promise.

Most plaudits stemmed from an appreciation of their strong musicianship, and while Felder deserved to be singled out as an inspiring lead guitarist, what was perhaps most interesting was that he had the strength of character to blend, not to showboat. His subtlety and concentration on making the music mesh into the best achievable ensemble sound, marked out his approach as different to most of his ilk. With fair hair and compelling, almond-shaped eyes, Don was a looker too – a vibrant spirit, enjoying what were very stimulating times. The shift in popular music was already pronounced when the era-defining three-day Woodstock Music and Art Fair took place at Yasgur's Farm, close to the village of Woodstock in Bethel, New York state, in August 1969. Torrential rain had turned the place into a mud bath. The Grateful Dead were among those who took part, as was Jimi Hendrix, whose fee of $125,000 was the highest of any performer there. Bob Dylan snubbed the momentous event. Joni Mitchell pulled out, but did pen 'Woodstock'. And as the classic song said, the crowd which flocked to this hitherto unremarked upon location was half a million strong – or thereabouts.

Felder, like the rest of Flow, looked on enviously in one sense, yet with a raw awareness that as one exciting decade was dying, a new dawn might see different bands with longevity emerge. Determined to be part of any such new musical movement, the band were energised, and set their sights higher. As Woodstock already began to wallow in a mythical glow, Flow moved up a gear. They managed to wangle an appearance on one of the Tuesday Nites At The Fillmore East shows, and straightaway caught the ear of experienced record producer, Creed Taylor, who had recently started his own label, CTI. Taylor invited Flow to be one of the inaugural groups to record on CTI, but the experience did not live up to expectation for Don Felder. 'It was a dreadful album,' he revealed. 'The whole thing was done in three days. Creed Taylor was used to people who came in with, say, a trio, turned on the machine and let it rip for four hours and that was it – they had the record. That was a total failure.' Released in 1970, *Flow* sank without trace. Felder remained in New York for another 18 months playing the clubs, but Flow was feeling suspiciously like a spent force.

Felder had kept in touch with Bernie Leadon, and had heard all about the band he'd joined. So whenever the Eagles came east, Felder would team up with Bernie and meet his mates, who were happy to hang out with him. Felder recalled: 'I'd go jam with them when they came through town, and built up a relationship with them.' Felder particularly remembered when the Eagles gigged over the eastern seaboard during their first tour. One night in New York, he jammed backstage with Bernie. 'I played slide guitar,' said Don, 'and Glenn Frey freaked out!' While Frey never forgot Felder's musical expertise, Don looked to his future and headed north to live in Boston, Massachusetts, where he delved into the production side of the record industry, working in a recording studio for two years, sometimes sweeping floors, but mainly learning how record engineers operated.

Bernie Leadon was frequently on the telephone, encouraging him to come to Los Angeles, where there was plenty of work. But Felder went his own path, stimulated by learning studio and musical techniques. He focused more on songwriting, and thrived on performing. It was a tiring life, and didn't pay so well, but he kept at it. After his day job at the recording studio was over, he would be out gigging in edgy clubs, playing R&B for five hours a night until 2.00 am. Eventually, Boston and the east coast lost its lustre, and in 1972 Felder went west after all, where with his abilities he quickly landed session work in Los Angeles. Much in demand, Don played guitar on a David Blue album being helmed by Graham Nash as producer. When David Blue went on tour, opening for Crosby & Nash, Felder went too as part of his backing band.

Over the course of the next two years, Felder made ends meet as best he could. In addition to his session work, he played the bars and the fraternity clubs. 'Any gig that would round up a dollar,' he recalled. Then, at the start of 1974, Don's days of living hand-to-mouth ended. Graham Nash had newly asked him to play guitar on his upcoming solo tour and Felder was on the brink of accepting, when the Eagles tapped on his shoulder. Don Felder explained: 'Glenn called and asked me to come play a slide solo on a track called "Good Day in Hell".' Felder was thrilled. He hared round to Bernie Leadon's home, borrowed a 1957 Deluxe tweed amplifier and, armed with a Les Paul guitar he pitched up at Record Plant Studios, where the Eagles were laying down their third album, now to be titled *On the Border*.

Launching himself into the task, Felder had a ball, and the

Eagles were thrilled. Don had brought exactly the harder, darker edge they were looking for. The next day, Frey rang Felder and asked him to join the band. 'I didn't even ask how much I was gonna get paid,' said Don, 'I just said, "Sure!"' Felder later recalled being blown away to be invited into the Eagles, then shocked at what he found once he entered the studio with them on a permanent basis. Hostility raged behind these closed doors, with the majority of the quarrels centring on this determined drive towards the Eagles becoming more rock than country. The path hotly favoured by Frey and Henley was not nearly so attractive to Leadon and Meisner, who were becoming ever more openly resentful of being swept along on this strong current. To Leadon and Meisner, the introduction into the band of a 'hot rod' guitarist like Don Felder was further proof of the inevitable.

The Eagles had always been highly combustible characters, but few knew it, and Don Felder could only gape in disbelief at the reality behind the highly skilled band's serene facade. Looking back, Felder revealed: 'Bernie was bouncing off the walls. Randy was threatening to quit. Everyone was yelling at each other and fighting. I thought: What have I done?' As Felder has frequently stated over the years, he thought he had just joined a band that was in the throes of a spectacular break-up. 'Everybody was really pissed off,' he said. In time, Felder also found out that this cauldron of discord was not a one-off bad phase. Speaking of the fiercely fluctuating dynamics within the Eagles, Don graphically revealed: 'The band was always like a keg of dynamite with the fuse lit. You just never knew how long the fuse would burn before the next explosion took place. There was always a struggle, always chaos, arguments and fighting over lyrics. It was difficult because everybody thought he was right.'

Yet for all the squabbling over direction, the Eagles could see that their new album was finally getting beyond the sticky start it had had under Glyn Johns' aegis. Glenn Frey, for one, was heartened to see the immediate difference that adding Don Felder to the team had made. 'Bernie and Felder are proud guitar players,' he enthused; 'to me they're carrying on the work of Clarence White and Duane Allman.'

Don Felder quickly discovered that one of his roles was to beef up the Eagles' sound in a live context. He said: 'They'd been having trouble with concerts because the music was too quiet.' He appreciated the fact that as the band was becoming more complex with their arrangements in the studio, it meant that to reproduce these same songs properly on stage, they needed another hand on deck. In early 1974, the Eagles' playlist was heavy on bluegrass material, and Bernie, although a master of multi-tracking on vinyl, could obviously not simultaneously cover all the various instruments featured in one song in front of an audience. With Don Felder on board, therefore, while Leadon finger-picked banjo, Don took over on mandolin. When Bernie concentrated on pedal steel, Don would play flat-top acoustic. The rock-oriented material was also double and triple track. Felder explained: 'Bernie would play a B-string bender and Glenn played harmony lead parts on top of that.'

As a five-piece band from January 1974, the Eagles were an even more enthralling live musical experience. On 6 April, they performed before a 200,000-strong audience at the 'California Jam' rock festival, but that spring their entire focus was on their new album's worth of songs, a collection of which they had high hopes. When the Eagles resumed work on this third album in Record Plant studios with producer Bill Szymczyk, the first song they laid down was 'Already Gone', a high-energy rocker which was one of three non-Eagle compositions on the 10-track album. Written by Jack Tempchin and Robb Strandlund, 'Already Gone' epitomised the free-spirited, male 'don't try to pin me down girl' attitude and it had come the Eagles' way via Glenn Frey's mailbox.

Jack Tempchin, who had already given the band a hit with 'Peaceful Easy Feeling', had sent a tape of 'Already Gone' direct to Frey. Bill Szymczyk called it 'Drums, bass and two guitars turned up to ten.' Glenn delighted in its pumped-up adrenalin-driving thrust. It was the perfect opener for the new album. In the studio, it gave Glenn the spontaneous feeling he hoped they would capture in the improved environment of Record Plant, a far cry from working with Glyn Johns. It was perhaps to be expected that with Johns and Frey both having very strong personalities, there would be problems. Glenn's own view was that his relationship with the producer had been particularly strained. So unsurprisingly, Glenn thrived on being in LA with Szymczyk with such a positive vibe abounding. Glenn said of 'Already Gone': 'That's me being happier...freer!'

The mate to 'Already Gone' on the album was 'James Dean', a raucous tribute to the late 1950s screen actor, which had been penned by Jackson Browne, Glenn Frey, Don Henley and JD Souther. Curiously, in 1977, Glenn called James Dean, star of *Rebel Without a Cause* and *Giant*, the first rock and roll casualty. Frey maintained that Dean, who was killed in a road accident, had trademarked a certain style for young bucks – blue jeans, white shirts and light jackets. Said Glenn: 'Jimmy Dean was my first hero – that first angry young man. I had a lot of heroes. But Dean? Man, he's it!' The song is said to have been written round a table in the front bar of the Troubadour. Don Henley had been interested to hear the reverential way the dead actor was being spoken of, for he personally had never bought into the whole iconic status given to the late young film star. That did not hinder Henley, however, from tuning into the feel of the belter in the making. Although, he says, the prime lyricist on the song was actually Jackson Browne.

Perhaps proving their intention to be even-handed, Bernie Leadon's solo composition, 'My Man', was a gentle ode to the late Gram Parsons. Similarly tender was 'Is It True', Randy Meisner's solo song about lost love. The other two non-Eagle entities were 'Midnight Flyer', a bluegrass number by Paul Craft, and a Tom Waits' number, 'Ol' 55'. Henley particularly welcomed the inclusion of 'Midnight Flyer', because with Bernie's blistering banjo playing, it stamped the Eagles' versatility. Even in the new millennium, the Eagles remain labelled by some as a country-rock band, when their range far outstrips the confines of that category. As a bluegrass fan, the drummer enjoyed recording and performing this number.

'Ol' 55', in turn, appealed strongly to Frey from the moment that David Geffen had played him a tape of it in his Sunset Strip office. Glenn had taken it to the others for possible inclusion on the album. When he played the tape to Don Henley, Glenn suggested that they split the vocals. Frey was already ahead of himself, thinking out neat vocal arrangements that would interplay between them, to make the best use of their diverse singing styles. Hailing from America's motor city, the Detroit-born singer loved 'Ol' 55' because it was 'that car thing'. Doubtless, the references to Lady Luck also appealed to the gambler in Glenn.

The Glenn Frey/Don Henley composition, 'Good Day In Hell', the rock number that had brought Don Felder into the fold, was another of those dual compositions that cast women in a devilish, manipulative light. The Eagles' lyrics throughout the mid-to-late 1970s would frequently intrigue fans and critics alike, exciting speculation as to which of the two principal songwriters, Frey or Henley, had the cynical attitude towards the nature of the female sex. The devil connotation was meant in terms of women being alluringly dangerous to men, but other references to a deep distrust of women would appear more prominent.

Don Henley had already refused, two years earlier, to say whether any specific lady inspired him in 'Witchy Woman', and in 1974 he maintained this stance, preferring to say that the women he wrote about were composites of some he had known. Still, when Henley teamed up with JD Souther to come up with 'You Never Cry Like A Lover', Don was quizzed again as to whom he had meant. Some thought it one of the angriest songs they had heard, that there was bitterness to it – even that it spoke of frigidity. But Henley proved elusive when asked if it held a sense of personal vengeance. He was unable to say if JD Souther had had anyone in mind when putting pen to paper, but he did admit that his own contribution had sometimes been specific. Said Don: 'It's about repressed emotions. I thought it was sympathetic at the end.' Challenged on the imputation of frigidity in the song, he replied: 'She just didn't want to do it with the lights on.' Teasingly, Don declined to say who 'she' was. As to whether 'she' knew the song referred to her, Henley quipped: 'Don't know. I never asked her.'

The other number to have been produced by Glyn Johns was 'Best of My Love' – a three-way collaboration between Don Henley, Glenn Frey and JD Souther. The music for this ballad came about by accident. Glenn had been sitting with his acoustic guitar one day at home in Laurel Canyon, busily working out something Joni Mitchell had recently shown him. But the more he tried to concentrate, the more his fingers strayed off into realms of their own, which ultimately became the sound for 'Best of My Love'. According to Don Henley, most of the song was written in Dan Tana's, an Italian restaurant the Eagles frequented in Los Angeles. 'Best of My Love' came to them as young men on the make, eyeing the stream of beauties who in those days, before the band's huge success, Don felt wouldn't give him or Glenn the time of day. For Henley, the number conjured up that period when he could still be frustratingly insecure with women. Emotions like jealousy combining powerfully with lust made for a vividly memorable phase. Looking back, Don considered it a flaw in their characters that he and Glenn tended to lust after the 'unattainable' women who looked askance at them, while overlooking the girls eager for their attentions.

In a complete change of tack, the title track, 'On The Border', written by Frey, Henley and Leadon, addressed issues such as personal privacy rights and political persuasion. Richard Nixon was at the time hip-deep in the Watergate scandal, which brought down his presidency and although the song had not started out that way, it ended up taking a swipe at the practices of the beleaguered US government.

Clearly, *On the Border* more closely resembled the Eagles' debut album, in that there was no concept theme, and each track was potentially a hit. Released in spring 1974, it claimed the number 17 slot in the US chart, becoming the Eagles' fastest selling album yet, and giving the band their best album chart position to date. It also went double platinum, and was the album that broke the Eagles to an international audience when in late April it lodged at number 28 in the British chart. The quest for a harder edge had caused ructions within the ranks, but *On the Border* proved to be the Eagles' breakthrough to the big time, although the first two spin-off singles did not exactly shine. In June, 'Already Gone' stalled at number 32 in America, and five months down the track, the best 'James Dean' could manage domestically was a creaking number 77. Neither single impinged on the British music market, but this could not change the fact that *On the Border* had stepped the Eagles up a gear. For a while, this success papered over the cracks in the band.

To fuel the momentum, the Eagles had to get out on the road with their expanded line-up and increase their visibility. The rigours of touring did not suit everyone, and years later Don Henley revealed: 'There was always some guy who didn't like to go on the road. It was basically just immaturity coupled with neurosis and [in some cases] drugs.' Henley enjoyed roadwork, as did Frey, whose pronounced penchant for generating a team spirit continued to show itself on and off stage. He often wore sports jerseys for gigs, and when the Eagles were backstage, primed to return to the spotlight for an encore, Glenn had a habit of having the five form a huddle, like American footballers do, each throwing his arms around his neighbour, heads bent together to discuss a game plan. Like a team coach, Glenn would suggest which numbers to hit 'em with next, before breaking and bounding on stage to soak in the ever louder cheers, whistles and applause.

As is vital for the longevity of any rock-pop band, a good proportion of the Eagles' building fan base was male, and it became obvious that *On the Border*'s success had revived interest in *Desperado*, when teenage boys wearing battered cowboy hats began turning up to fill front rows of theatres across America. The reward for some of these wildly enthusiastic fans was being given access later backstage – these were the days before watertight security became essential. Frequently these devotees formed unofficial travelling support units which drove hundreds of miles across several states to catch the Eagles in flight time and again. Glenn Frey would happily grin alongside the exuberant fans for endless photographs, and would sign autographs, as did some of the other band members. Randy Meisner's excruciating shyness meant that he preferred to back away from flashing cameras, and was uncomfortable when it came to press interviews on their travels.

As the band crisscrossed the country, in private minus their adoring public, the five often got stuck into lively debates about the government, what was right and wrong with their country, and analysing the music business. Regardless of the differences within the band, they did have a lot in common – shared beliefs that gave them reassuring common ground. When not on stage, though, they seldom hung out together. Randy was family oriented, and telephoned his Nebraska home at least once a day to speak with his wife and children. Bernie Leadon was a dedicated loner. Whenever the band hit a new town, during off duty hours he liked to trawl through the music shops, rarely returning empty-handed. By the mid-1970s he had an impressive collection of musical instruments, valued in the tens of thousands of dollars.

The differences in each Eagle's lifestyle on tour mirrored their home set-ups in Los Angeles, with three of them living a very different life from the other two. Meisner hiked off home at every opportunity, while Leadon and Felder were virtual recluses. Out on the road, Felder clowned around and verbally bantered with Frey and Henley, just as he liked to jam with Randy and his long time friend Bernie. He had had no teething trouble settling into the band, but he was married, and he and his wife Susan had recently had a baby son. So, disliking the LA scene when back at base, Felder would shoot off home, choosing to live quietly with his family in a beautifully rustic house nestling off the beaten track, miles down a dirt road along one of California's coastal canyons.

Frey and Henley were birds of an altogether different feather, accustomed to leading a nocturnal life, which they still thoroughly enjoyed. Glenn particularly liked the home he had moved to in Coldwater Canyon, an opulent bungalow that had once belonged to James Cagney's brother, Ed. It appealed to him that the actor, famed for his gangster movies, had latterly used the house as a refuge, where he found solace in playing the piano. The house had also witnessed some legendary parties, and did so again now with Frey in residence.

The second half of 1974 saw the Eagles shift rapidly through the gears as their pace of life accelerated. With them more than ever on this next leg of the roller coaster journey was Irving Azoff. Changes were afoot, in that David Geffen moved away from the management scene when Asylum Records merged with Elektra Records. Azoff explained: 'It ended up just me and Elliott [Roberts] running the office. I was a nervous wreck. We had everybody – Crosby & Nash, Joni Mitchell, Neil Young, America and the Eagles. David had signed Bob Dylan, so we were working on a Band tour too. Elliott and I were going fucking crazy!'

Frey and Henley often mulled over just what was and wasn't happening for them, in terms of management. And while these situations always have two sides, it was the opinion of these particular Eagles that the band was still not being paid the attention they felt it deserved and needed. It was their understandable wish that the Eagles be considered top priority, and they did not believe that was happening. So when Irving Azoff started up his own firm, Front Line Management, and asked the Eagles to come onto his roster, the band did not hesitate. GR Management was letting artistes go, and the Eagles were free to make that choice. Henley has said: 'Finding the right manager is kinda like finding the right girl when you finally get the perfect one.' In 1975, Glenn Frey nut-shelled their good fortune in hitching their wagon to Azoff's when he declared: 'Getting Irving then was like catching Geffen on the upswing six years ago.'

Irving Azoff's sales pitch to the Eagles that he would play hardball and get them deals that would make them rich was scarcely original, but he made good on his pledge. Azoff's reputation for unorthodox, hard-nosed business tactics had, if anything, steadily strengthened. With a distinctive hairstyle and thick rimmed glasses, the diminutive human dynamo had 'terrorised' the powers that be for long enough now to make him stand out in a neurotic city renowned for its business barracudas. Frey certainly approved of Azoff's tendency to pound on record executives' desks when hammering out his terms on behalf of the Eagles. Over the years, too, Glenn got a kick out of lounging in a chair on the opposite side of the office from Irving, listening fondly to the manager 'kill' on the phone. What mattered, though, was that Azoff got results, and quickly made an appreciable difference to the band both financially and in terms of thrusting them to the fore.

Azoff has openly admitted that when preparing terms for his artistes, he would work out a fair figure, then boldly add a third on top, and that was what he would go into meetings insisting on obtaining from record companies. And he would get it. He negotiated better concert contracts and secured far bigger radio airplay for Eagles records, thus enhancing their profile. A year later, Frey was transparently delighted, revealing to the press that each Eagle was coining in half a million dollars a year.

Increased financial success and elevated status dovetailed with an explosion in the adventurous pursuit of pleasure by the two footloose, fancy free Eagles, and as the band hit the road in summer 1974, it was an off-duty carnival of reckless excess and outrageous antics. Sex, drugs and rock 'n' roll were synonymous with the likes of the Rolling Stones, The Who and Led Zeppelin, but when this pair of Eagles let rip, they were no pale imitators. Not so long before, Don Henley had recalled a time when he felt that the foxiest ladies had looked upon himself and Frey as scruffy sorts with 'no calling card'. Those days had gone. With sage cynicism, Glenn quipped: 'The difference between being seen as boring and laid-back is a million bucks.'

Neither Frey nor Henley was looking yet for that special woman. Far from it, they were happy to sample the many delights on offer, which, it is reputed, during this tour included a two-for-one special in the shape of a comely young lady and her youthful looking mother. Glenn confessed that it was their habit when they arrived in town to amass 'as many beautiful girls as we'd meet between the airport and the hotel'. Obviously, the swamp of groupies moved in after each show, and the licentiousness that ensued became known as the Third Encore. In the hedonistic 1970s, before words like HIV and Aids came to blight the landscape, there was stiff competition when it came to deciding which rock band took the crown for memorable backstage debauchery. With no qualms, though, Frey has declared: 'I think we had the greatest travelling party of the decade.' Speaking of one particular celebration, Glenn revealed: 'Don had a birthday party in Cincinnati and they flew in cases of Chateau Lafite Rothschild. The wine was the best, the drugs were good and the women were beautiful.'

Their manager, being their own age, was hardly fazed by the on the road antics of the high-spirited ones among his charges. The Eagles' public image was smooth, soothing even, while well able to rock. But behind the scenes, some band members could be every bit as wayward as the acknowledged bad boys of rock. For certain stretches of the 1970s, it was not unheard of for the Eagles, on their travels, to be held accountable for trashed hotel rooms when high jinks spun out of control. They always paid for any damage done before moving on. But one unusual jape occurred during this particular trip when a record company accountant found himself temporarily imprisoned inside his hotel room when the door was nailed up from the outside! Quite who specifically was responsible for this outrage is not clear. When hotel security had no option but to take a fireman's axe to the door to smash their way in and release the seriously irritated but unharmed accountant, as splintered wood went flying in all directions, Irving Azoff stood nearby peeling off $100 bills one after the other into the outstretched palm of the unimpressed, stony-faced hotel manager.

To Frey, going on the road meant playing music, then the rest of the time going crazy, getting drunk and high and making money, which didn't only come from the band's gigs. Gambling still fascinated Glenn, and Henley enjoyed this other source of entertainment too. Between them they came up with their own high-stakes game they called Eagle Poker. Glenn recalled: 'We were into a big gambling thing – cards all the time.' In the middle of their 1974 tour, the band had a couple of days off and were not particularly enamoured of kicking around New York. Armed with $5,000 stake money, therefore, a foursome decided to go to the Bahamas in search of the gaming tables. Flying south by private jet for a two-day spree were Don Henley with a lady friend, Glenn Frey and Irving Azoff.

The plan was that no one would be carrying drugs, and they all agreed – innocent cherubic faces all round. Only it did not work out that way. Glenn Frey later told *Rolling Stone*: 'On the plane over, Irving took 20 Valium tablets and put them in a sugar package and stuffed them in his shoe. I put half an ounce of marijuana in my boot. We figured there was no way we were gonna get caught for that little bit.' Neither Henley nor his lady friend had drugs in their possession, but on arrival at customs, when Don's girlfriend's bags were routinely searched, cigarette papers were found. Suddenly a senior customs officer swooped and next minute the arrivals were shepherded away to be searched.

Two young customs officers were to physically search the three men, and for Frey and Azoff it was an anxious time. Describing the scene, Glenn recalled: 'Irving and I looked at each other, knowing we couldn't reach into our boots.' Glenn would later progress to doing cocaine, and half an ounce of marijuana hardly seemed so criminal, but he fully expected to be busted and didn't relish it. Irving Azoff went into the ante-room first; assuming the balloon would immediately go up, Glenn resigned himself to being arrested. However, no charges were laid. Years later, Frey set out publicly what happened that day. He maintained that once alone in the ante-room with the two customs officers, Irving produced his 20 Valium tablets right away, explaining what the pills were, and that he did not have the prescription bottle with him.

Irving then apparently went into his most persuasive mode, explaining that the long-haired guy wearing a blue shirt [Glenn] had a tiny amount of grass on him, but that he was a rock star with gold records to his name and on the rise. Appealing to the young guys, Azoff is said to have explained that if Glenn were to be busted it would affect his ability to take the band's music abroad, and could even kill his career. Thinking quickly on his feet, and with his grasp of human nature, Irving cleverly talked himself and Glenn out of trouble. Minutes later Azoff re-emerged, surreptitiously winked at Glenn, then walked out. Don, who had nothing to worry about, was searched, and Glenn was completely overlooked. All three were free to go. 'I didn't know what the fuck was going on,' said Frey, but he credits the band's resourceful manager for having saved them from winding up with a criminal record.

Putting this narrow escape behind them, the two Eagles rejoined the others after that Bahamas break to carry on with the US tour, which was taking its toll on Bernie Leadon. Long journeys between endless pit-stops in unfamiliar places, being constantly surrounded by strangers and bolting junk food on the hoof had never appealed much to the serious musician, who only really liked the performing part. On the morning after the Eagles had played their last date of the three-month trek, the band stopped off en route home at a Holiday Inn café. Something, no one would later pinpoint what, triggered an exhausted and low-spirited Leadon to erupt. To bewildered onlookers it seemed like Bernie was raving as, losing his rag, he suddenly started screaming. Then, just as abruptly, he slumped forward in his seat, and his face and arms slapped jarringly onto the cold Formica-topped table. Alongside the cafe's patrons were the rest of the band and Glenn's parents, who had driven up from Detroit to be with him. It is a measure of how tired the Eagles were that, as Bernie mumbled incoherently into the Formica, his bandmates just carried on with their breakfast.

Bernie was certainly not in the habit of behaving like this, and it was an extremely worrying episode for him. The Eagles had been promoting *On the Border* exhaustively, but they had ventured close to the edge. Stress and tension were building, and perhaps the writing was on the wall that Bernie Leadon would begin to think of leaving the Eagles. In the meantime, he pulled himself together as the cavalcade finally made it back to Los Angeles. Soon afterwards, he met a woman who would feature in his life; something that, in turn, would pile more pressure on him. She was pretty, young, free-spirited Patti Reagan, daughter of Ronald Reagan, then Governor of California. The one-time actor had turned to politics, joining the Republican party in 1962 and, an extreme right winger, with his second wife Nancy at his side, he twice stood unsuccessfully for the presidential nomination before winning through on his third attempt and going on to topple Democrat President Jimmy Carter in 1980 to become the 40th President of the United States.

In 1974 the Eagles were beginning to fly, and Patti Reagan played *On the Border* virtually non-stop. She also often studied the photos on the album cover's insert, and one day Bernie's image drew her so strongly that it felt fateful. Days later, Patti drove to the Westwood Music shop to browse. It was a store often haunted by the cream of the LA-based music stars, and as she was about to cut her car engine 'My Man', Bernie's lyrical tribute to the late Gram Parsons, came on the radio. It already seemed portentous when Patti went into the shop. Minutes later, Leadon walked in and came to stand nearby.

In today's more guarded society it seems unthinkable, but three decades ago it was not uncommon to strike up instantaneous connections, and for a girl to be happy to just take off with a good looking stranger. Bernie Leadon was one of the Eagles, certainly, but Patti could have had no idea of his character or anything else. Yet after striking up a conversation, in no time at all she agreed to his suggestion to go to the beach. For her part, Patti had given Bernie only her Christian name; she kept quiet about being the Governor's daughter for now. That day, the pair spent a few hours on a private stretch of golden beach belonging to some friends of Bernie's. They waded out into the crystal clear ocean where, bobbing up and down in the glinting water, they ended up in each other's arms. Patti felt surprisingly at home with Bernie, as if they had known one another for ages.

Later, Leadon took his new acquaintance to his house perched on a hill in Topanga Canyon. Looking at the breathtaking views, the couple got even closer by the time the sun sank in the sky. Years later, Patti romantically recounted how that evening she and Bernie 'made love outside with an acacia tree spilling yellow blossom around us'. That night

Leadon promised to get in touch with Patti once he had had a chance to recharge his batteries, following the gruelling experience of the recent tour. And he did. It was soon after he began dating Patti, who lived in her own apartment, that Bernie was startled to discover that her father was the Governor of California; although he had quickly deduced that his new girlfriend's parents were high-powered in some capacity.

Six years after failing to secure the Republican party presidential nomination, Ronald Reagan was beginning to think of making his pitch to stand again in a couple of years' time; bearing in mind the media scrutiny that that involved, Patti's parents were having to look closely at all angles of their private life. They were concerned, then, when a couple of months after Patti started seeing Bernie Leadon, they learned that she intended to accompany him when the Eagles went to play some tour dates in Europe, and would be sharing hotel rooms with her boyfriend. Patti knew that those with aspirations of holding high political office laid their entire family wide open to press scrutiny, but she believed herself to be in love with Bernie, and they planned to live together. Whether or not Patti's parents were happy about it, Leadon retained his house in Topanga Canyon and bought another property on Old Topping Canyon Road.

When Patti accompanied Bernie to the Los Angeles International airport on the day the band left for Europe, photographers were out in force to snap the couple, and within days, *People* magazine ran an item that Governor Ronald Reagan's daughter Patti was travelling on tour with Bernie Leadon of the Eagles. Patti's recollections of this period would be of a time crammed with all the glamour, drama and excitement of being suddenly in the midst of the maniacal music scene – bedlam gigs, flash photography, rampant fans and fast getaways from gingered up venues in speeding limousines.

Behind the pizzazz, though, Bernie's problems with being in

the Eagles were beginning to surface. Already feeling frustrated and unfulfilled songwriting-wise, he had become deeply concerned that the lyric nucleus of Glenn Frey and Don Henley was strengthening even more. The unease within the band over the developing grip these two had did not pass the newest member's notice, but Don Felder took a more pragmatic view. He pointed out: 'When you put out an album that had ten songs on it, which songs were the hits? It was always the songs that Glenn or Don wrote or sang. So, after three or four albums, you go: "You guys have got the stuff. I bow to you humbly. Show me the way!"'

Even though the subservient aspect of that was meant tongue-in-cheek, the point is that not every Eagle was able to be quite so sanguine about it. Stellar success was just around the corner for the band, but ructions were set to make it a very bumpy ride indeed.

CHAPTER 5

The Eagles Have Landed

IN MARCH 1975, the Eagles hit the coveted number one slot in America for the first time with 'Best Of My Love', the last cut from *On the Border*. The acoustic guitar-based ballad became the band's first million selling single, and broke the Eagles to a much wider public. Don Henley's smoky lead vocal was tinged with a country boy drawl. But unlike songs from *Desperado*, which fell between two stools, this single successfully crossed over and received generous airplay on pop and country radio stations. 'Best Of My Love', indeed, went on to earn Grammy nominations in both pop and country categories.

Notching up the success of this country-flavoured ballad gave its producer, Glyn Johns, an undisguised satisfaction. Johns didn't rate the Eagles as a rock band and was forthright enough to say so publicly. When Glenn Frey read remarks he didn't care for in the music press, which were attributed to the British producer, he retorted with his own characteristic bluntness that everything had got better for the Eagles once they had teamed up with a producer who was prepared to give them the rope to explore. While they were inexorably heading in a more rock-oriented direction, Frey readily acknowledged that 'Best Of My Love' was 'the song that did it'.

The success of *On the Border* had raised the bar for the Eagles, and they were up for the challenge to better their performance. Said Henley: "Best of My Love' kicked off the whole big thing for us, moving us from being in the top 90% of bands in America to the top 10%.' At the very least they wanted to maintain that, and to this end, with their new album in mind, the two principal songwriters decided it was time to move in together. It was the start of what became a pattern. Don explained: 'Glenn and I would go through a series of moving in together and then moving out. We'd have girlfriends and live with them for a while. Then we'd get ready to do an album and we'd move back in together.' It was to make collaboration easier, but by the start of 1975, Frey and Henley were also virtually inseparable as buddies.

They rented a plush mansion up on Briarcrest Lane in Trousdale, once the home of Hollywood film star Dorothy Lamour. Frey and Henley christened their new temporary abode, 'The House With The Million Dollar View', and indeed, for two young stars who had never lost sight of their working class roots, seeing the twinkling night lights of Los Angeles sprawling below them was truly breathtaking. They also nicknamed the mansion, 'The Eagles' Nest', and as footloose free agents, they were determined to have a ball. Dudes on the rampage was how Henley summed themselves up then, as a steady stream of curvaceous beauties helped warm the nest after many a night on the tiles.

As Glenn and Don compulsively chased women during their off-duty hours, their friends looked on at the bedlam life the two live wires were leading, and affectionately shook their heads. Jackson Browne revealed: 'We called them the odd couple in those days. Glenn always went around messing things up and Don always followed him around cleaning things up.' It's a set-up that Henley has confirmed. 'I was sort of the housekeeper, the tidy one. Glenn was the lovable slob,' he said. 'All around the house he'd leave these little cigarette butts standing on end, like miniature cities!' Soon, the furniture and floor coverings were pockmarked with cigarette burns, and the pair were in danger of disappearing under a rising tide of discarded coffee cups and other unwashed crockery.

They took bedrooms at opposite ends of the house for the privacy to indulge their individual sex lives. But Sunday afternoons would be strictly a female-free zone, as they surfaced only to slouch on the lounge sofas, beer cans in hand, to watch football on the TV and yell abuse and encouragement at the screen. For all that, Frey and Henley got down to serious songwriting, and their close friendship fuelled their drive to reach new heights. Creatively, they were coming to the boil. As Glenn put it, the very best of their material was penned during this mid-1970s period. 'Don came out of his shell,' said Frey. 'The times we were living together, we were on such a roll.' At an oak table in the lounge, armed with writing pads and pens, they would start sparking off one another. Stimulatingly, most times bursts of songs would flow almost too fast to write down. Other times, it was like wading through treacle. But they kept their noses to the grindstone, and with the mansion's music room converted into a temporary recording studio, they could capture what was crystallising from their intensive efforts.

Inspiration came from several sources, including the prevailing political and social climate. The recent turmoil in Washington had cast a gloom over politically aware Americans and engendered an edgy atmosphere of unrest on the streets again. Musically, the mosaic was diversifying. Disco in its full blown form was a way off yet, but Henley favoured their new material placing more prominence on a throbbing beat. At the same time, it was essential that the Eagles' guitar-heavy hallmark sound should not be sacrificed. Although it has become fashionable to blame the 1960s for everything amoral, the 1970s was a debauched, morally bankrupt and decadent decade, sliding on sleaze and corruption, and in southern California it reached a new dimension in bacchanalian hedonism. Highly susceptible to the social mores around them, Frey and Henley were well acquainted with decadence, and when they added their own personal cynicism into the mix, they had a potent brew into which to dip.

Glenn and Don co-composed more than half of the nine tracks ultimately laid down for the fourth album, and producer Bill Szymczyk saw an immediate difference in the material. 'The songs had a darker, edgier tone to them,' he later recalled, adding that the Eagles seemed to have assumed what he called 'an us against the world attitude'. Certainly, a harshness was traceable in their lyrics. Don Henley stated: 'Rock music is, by its nature, angry and rebellious. We were rebelling against what we saw as the Establishment. Also we had dry, cynical senses of humour. I think we were misunderstood at times, but we *were* arrogant. You have to be, if you're going to be in a rock band.'

Henley queried the ceaseless quest to fulfil the next dream, when landing the previous one had failed to satisfy – an eternally emotive ache which he and Frey wove into a number called 'After The Thrill Is Gone'. Don wrote the bridge for it, and collaborated with Glenn on the verses. Imbued with much inner reflection, innuendo and irony, both Frey and Henley fully related to the work, and Glenn considered certain poignant passages to be pure Henley. For Don, this song mirrored the meshing of their personal and professional lives. When it came to recording 'After The Thrill Is Gone', its lyricists shared lead vocals.

One fear they shared was becoming so insular within their own created universe that they lost touch with the wider music world. To avoid this danger, they consciously laid themselves open to different influences. Rhythm and blues began to get under their skin, and they became avid fans of Al Green, the 29-year-old Arizona-born R&B singer-songwriter with a distinctive high-pitched vocal style. This leaning towards rhythm and blues tinged the album's eventual title track, 'One Of These Nights'. With references to inner demons, and revisiting an earlier devil-woman connotation, it was a distinctive song with a moodily dramatic sound. It had come to Glenn almost from the ether. Frey once compared the process of nailing a song to pushing a big boulder arduously up a steep hill. Not so, here. He had sat down with an acoustic guitar and almost instantly come up with the rhythm sections.

'One Of These Nights' would showcase the Eagles' strength in high harmony singing, and ingenious instrumental work in the studio led them to experiment with harmony guitar passages that were made to resemble horn riffs. For Frey, it was Henley's lead vocal which gave the song its haunting quality, and he had the intense satisfaction of knowing that, as lyricists, he and Don had taken a significant step up with 'One Of These Nights'. Invigoratingly, they could see the album taking shape from early on. Said Don: 'The theme of all our albums has been basically the same – looking for it, whatever it is – whether it be a woman, or peace of mind, or satisfaction, success, riches or happiness. Looking for it and trying to deal with it.'

As he and Glenn indulged the high rolling life up in the Hollywood hills, the easy availability of women became a double-edged sword. Uncomplicated sex was what the guys wanted with women who knew the score – there were no innocent lambs unsuspectingly lured to the den. Yet the open promiscuity in the willing women they encountered, fed an already noticeable cynicism towards the fair sex. Untrustworthy women featured in Eagles' songs to a significant degree during these years, and this time around Frey and Henley came right out and named a song that became one of their most recognisable hits, 'Lyin' Eyes'. Blatantly about a scheming girl who had cynically married a sugar daddy, only to cheat on him, the song does yet contain a strain of sympathy for the central character, caught up in a life of deceit that clearly makes her rue having made wrong choices. Still, 'Lyin' Eyes' would re-ignite accusations that, in their songs, the Eagles were often sexist and harsh towards women.

'Lyin' Eyes' had been Glenn's baby. Drinking one night in the Troubadour, he had spotted an old man with a buxom young blonde hanging on his arm. Cynically concluding that the guy must be loaded, Glenn was quick to catch it when, sure enough, the beauty's eyes strayed the second the man's back was turned. With a rumble of knowing laughter Glenn remarked to friends: 'Just look at those lyin' eyes!' Not so much a spontaneous sexist remark, as baldly stating a fact.

Frey had already batted back attacks over the devil imagery in their songs by explaining that the witchy-bewitched stuff was meant in seductive terms. But now a growing number of female journalists were choosing to take issue with this perceived sexism, although they couldn't figure out which songwriter was to 'blame'. To the charge of being anti-women in song, Don Henley would later say: 'Glenn's attitude toward women was a little different to mine sometimes.' He also pointed out: 'Rock and roll *is* sexist and always has been. To single out the Eagles for that is absurd. We weren't any more sexist than anybody else.' Never a man to hold back, and with glorious disregard for how it sounded, in 1979 Glenn Frey declared: 'Women *are* objects for men, whether or not sex objects. They are a goal. That's the way we're brought up.' Frey did not mean that he thought that was right, and since he was a renowned ladies' man, he could scarcely be accused of hating women. So no one was any the wiser. *Rolling Stone* would say of this period in the Eagles' career that their lyrics 'did a brutal job of depicting the walking wounded from the great sexual wars of the seventies'.

'Lyin' Eyes', on which Glenn assumed lead vocal, ran for six minutes, 21 seconds. Yet Glenn's juices had run so freely when writing this number that he had in fact penned verses that were not finally included in it. It had been one of the easiest songs to emerge, and he and Don brought it swiftly to fruition.

In the lounge of their mansion with the million dollar view, Frey and Henley successfully came up with 'After the Thrill Is Gone', 'One Of These Nights' and 'Lyin' Eyes' and that roll Frey spoke of continued with 'Take It To The Limit', a soaring number for which they brought in Randy Meisner as co-lyricist. The lead vocal on this song was tailored exactly to Meisner's unique capabilities. Frey and Henley had actively striven to write the right song for the bass player to shine centre stage, and were thrilled with this end product. When it was released as a single, 'Take It To The Limit' went gold.

'Hollywood Waltz' was the fifth number to feature the songwriting team of Frey and Henley, this time in conjunction with Bernie Leadon and his brother Tom. Lyrically, it seemed to operate on two levels. Either the song's protagonist is a good-time woman past her sell-by date, who engenders a sort of pitiful affection, or 'she' is Hollywood itself, a fading system losing its lustre. The Eagles were beginning to encapsulate in song the seamy underbelly of the outwardly glamorous Los Angeles with a perfection that would reach a pinnacle in their next album.

For now, writing this new album occupied much of the first quarter of 1975, and at times Henley felt bogged down. Sunk in creating with the right touch, a certain mood in order to pull out a super-sensitive song, he would suddenly rock back in his chair, wrench off his headphones and curse aloud just who the fuck gave a shit about a song's content. He began to wonder deeply if they weren't perhaps taking themselves just a tad *too* seriously. To alleviate this creative strain, Frey and Henley partied with a passion. Their friend and future bandmate, Joe Walsh, called it burning the candle at both ends, to get twice the light in half the time. And on this hectic schedule, productivity galloped on as they developed these five songs, while welcoming contributions from the rest of the band. Randy Meisner and Don Felder came up with an atmospheric, rhythmic rocker, 'Too Many Hands', which would also feature Meisner's lead vocal. Felder teamed up with Henley to write 'Visions', a wistful song about ultimately settling for less in life, on which lead vocal fell democratically to Felder.

This left two numbers to complete the nine; both came from Bernie Leadon. One was an indulgently long instrumental called 'Journey of the Sorcerer', and the other, a ballad, 'I Wish You Peace'. Its inclusion on the album caused anything but tranquillity. It was co-composed by Leadon and his girlfriend, Patti Reagan. And Don Henley had very specific views on the song, and the way he thought Leadon's new amour was impinging on the band. Bernie sang lead vocal and played lead guitar on 'I Wish You Peace', in addition to having co-written it. It was diametrically different, though, to the other compositions, and thus was viewed by some as something of a cuckoo in the nest.

Patti later maintained: 'I didn't know when I sat on my bed one night, writing a song, that it would increase the tensions that already existed.' When she had played 'I Wish You Peace' to Bernie, he had helped her to complete it, and was determined to submit it as his other cut for inclusion on the new album. It was a dogged desire that led to trouble. Patti believed the Eagles had made a new rule that henceforth they would not involve outside lyricists on their albums, but in this instance, the plain fact was that the band simply did not care for the song. More than a decade later, Don Henley bluntly stated: 'I sort of resented Patti being around at the time, because I thought she was butting in. She co-wrote this song, and Bernie *insisted* it go on the album. We didn't want it on there. We didn't feel it was up to the band's standard. But we put it on anyway as a gesture to keep the group together.'

According to Patti, Bernie's stance over this song's inclusion actively hurt his already fractured relationship with his fellow Eagles. 'I felt guilty about it,' she admitted, 'but I was also ecstatic that I was going to have a song on an Eagles' album.' Don Henley did not share her joy when – and he has conceded that she may have been misquoted – he read press reports in which Patti expressed delight that she 'wrote songs for the Eagles!'. Today, it is water under the bridge, but at the time the tension increased once recording commenced.

In spring 1975, with their clutch of new numbers ready, they headed east to start work at Criteria Studios in Miami, Florida. The Eagles didn't allow girlfriends into the studio, so when Bernie wanted Patti to be present while laying down his tracks, resentment swelled. She wasn't omnipresent like Yoko Ono had been in the latter days of the Beatles. But from taking stock of the strains that had affected groups like the Rolling Stones, the Beatles and Crosby, Stills, Nash & Young, the Eagles had hoped to avoid personal conflicts, clashing egos and/or women disturbing the unity of the band. In this instance, Bernie's harmony with the Eagles was already under threat, and Patti's presence on the scene was an added source of edginess. Randy Meisner, whose wife had always remained well in the background, nevertheless could sympathise. He felt: 'When you love someone and the guys in the band don't like her, or she can't stand them, it's hard on you. It's painful.'

Work at Criteria Studios had to be spliced with undertaking live tour dates spread over several months which added to the strain, and took a toll which the band would only be able to recognise in retrospect. The crippling, energy-sapping demands on their time led those who were already taking drugs to depend even more on this stimulus. Don Henley confessed: 'We did a lot of work on drugs in the Eagles. Our schedule was just so gruelling. We didn't have the stamina otherwise. We'd go on tour, play a few gigs, then get on a jet and fly to Miami and start recording at 4 am, then get back on the plane at 4 pm to go do the next concert. So we took drugs.' They were running themselves ragged, but still had the resilience of youth on their side, as well as a real exuberance for putting together this new album despite the accumulating stress. They were actually learning to love the studio, where their ever-developing talent could let rip. 'We look for a marked improvement on the individual and collective level each time we make a record,' said Frey.

Henley was convinced that his personal strengths lay in writing and singing. He stressed: 'I've never been a particularly good drummer. I'm a good drummer for singers because I stay out of the way.' He was doing himself down unnecessarily, and his playing on tabla (small conjoined hand drums used in Indian music) articulated 'Too Many Hands', on which Frey nailed lead guitar along with Don Felder. On 'Hollywood Waltz', already ringing with the sound of Bernie Leadon on steel and mandolin, Glenn also introduced the harmonium, a keyboard instrument in which notes are produced when air is driven through metal reeds by foot-operated bellows.

A musician friend from the early days, Jim Ed Norman, assumed piano duties on 'Lyin' Eyes' and 'Take It To The Limit'. And while Leadon was responsible for lead guitar on 'Lyin' Eyes' and the contentious 'I Wish You Peace', this was the album on which Don Felder truly got the chance to come into his own as a lead guitarist. His work strongly dominated 'Visions', 'After The Thrill Is Gone' and most impressively on the hauntingly different 'One Of These Nights'. Felder revealed: 'Every time I write a solo, I think I'm a sax player. Horn players have to be melodic. One member of the jazz fusion band I'd had in New York played soprano sax. He and I played in unison, which helped my sense of phrasing and soloing.'

'One Of These Nights' had started out piano based, with Glenn Frey at the helm; he had also worked up harmony guitar passages for the number. But good though it was, the band knew the track could sound even better. Felder, therefore, devised interlocking rhythm guitar parts, which he added after the track was laid down. He recalled: 'Since "One Of These Nights" was a kind of rock version of an R&B style song, I figured the solo should sound like a sax. And since we didn't have a sax player, I did my best on guitar.' Felder's overriding memory of laying down the lead solo for this title track rests on a prank he and Bill Szymczyk played on Frey and Henley, who had taken time out to promote the upcoming album on a live radio show. It had been arranged that, at one point in the show, the DJ would patch through to the recording studio to do a down-the-line interview with Felder and the producer, prior to Felder then playing the solo for 'One Of These Nights' live on air.

For fun, Szymczyk and Felder set Frey and Henley up. Don Felder recorded a solo that began flawlessly. Then about midway, he deliberately hit bum notes and made glaring mistakes, which degenerated as the solo went on. They also recorded the impeccably executed one for the album. But when Frey and Henley came over the airwaves in the midst of their interview, announcing a sneak preview of this great solo, Felder and Szymczyk played the awful, error-laden version. Glenn and Don started out happily confident, praising their maestro musician to the radio listeners, only to stumble live on air, the more the dreadful mistakes clanged discordantly out. Horror turned to embarrassment, and maybe a spike or two of anger, before it dawned on the promoting pair that they'd been had and they creased up with laughter.

In hindsight, Frey and Henley hold differing views about the experience of making *One of These Nights*. To Glenn, it was unequivocally the most fluid and painless album the band ever made, whereas Don yearned for a time when making records did not demand so much time and energy. He felt that the Eagles had never had an easy time making albums.

The Eagles were aiming to move up significantly with this album, in which they had full confidence, and they were up for any form of eye-catching promotion. Before the album was released, therefore, in early summer 1975, they allowed themselves to be raffled off in a WCFL radio station contest as the prize for the high school in the Chicago region that exhibited the best sense of camaraderie and team spirit. McHenry High won, and accordingly secured a free Eagles concert. The quid pro quo was that the Eagles received prime time promotion when top US DJ, Larry Lujack, interviewed the band on his syndicated show, and premiered *One of These Nights*.

The high school gig was certainly different. It was performed in the sports gymnasium, a floor above the school swimming pool, and the Eagles and their young audience had to combat the soporific effects of oppressive humidity to get through the night. Despite the near sauna conditions, the band turned it on for the receptive youngsters and had them dancing in the aisles between the rows of bleachers.

A vastly different live appointment awaited the revved up Eagles in Britain when they flew into London to take part, on 21 June 1975, in a one-day music festival dubbed 'Midsummer Madness' at Wembley Stadium, before an audience of 72,000. Despite blistering sunshine, the crowd remained congenial throughout this 10-hour music marathon, at which the United States was well represented. After the opening act, Stackridge, next up was Rufus, a funk group fronted by the influential Illinois-born soul singer, Chaka Khan. And fresh from a triumphant American tour, second billing to headliner Elton John, were California's own Beach Boys. Mid-way through proceedings, Joe Walsh stormed on stage with his band and knocked everyone for six. Andy Childs, editor of the rock magazine *Zigzag*, enthused in his festival review: 'In my estimation Joe Walsh is one of the top five guitarists in America, and certainly one of the few who manages to retain the true essence of rock 'n' roll in his style. Until this performance I didn't realise quite how much strong and varied material he has at his disposal. He turned in a memorable set.'

It was the general consensus, however, that the Eagles – third top of the bill – took the event by the scruff of the neck. Andy Childs declared: 'The Eagles blew our heads apart and put them back together again! They were astounding!' Their ability to be near inhumanly perfect vocally and instrumentally shone throughout their spellbinding 15-song set, which kicked off with the ringing 12-stringers of 'Take It Easy', progressed through highlight numbers from their first three albums, and anchored with their chart-topping hit, 'Best of My Love'. However, also sewn into the set were two songs from the new album, 'Too Many Hands' and 'One Of These Nights'. By the time their set was over to tumultuous applause and delighted cheers, the Eagles had proved that they were tailor-made for outdoor stadium gigs.

The Eagles returned to America, poised to soar to new heights with the release of *One of These Nights*. Months of slog had gone into writing and recording this fourth album, which had racked up over $160,000 in production costs and exhausted from gigging, the band had had to make four cross-country trips to Miami during the course of its completion. But it all proved to be worth it when it seized the number one slot in the US album chart in July, where it reigned for five weeks. *One of These Nights* would also secure a number eight hit in the UK; clearly a mature and complex body of work, it became one of the biggest selling albums of the decade.

Scant trace now remained of their original country-rock leanings. Frey and Henley's vision of the world around them was shown through writing that had darkened appreciably, with cynicism, uncertainty, disillusionment and distrust all prominent. It neatly reflected the prevalent mood in America, and hinted at having flowed from personal experiences. Embroidered into it, too, was the influence of the drugs, which had led the pair through weird nights wavering on the edge of reality, and had played a part in producing the album's haunting quality.

With 'One Of These Nights', the Eagles cracked the UK singles chart for the first time when it reached number 23. But its impact in Britain was bigger than that: it proved to be a vintage year for singles that would permanently brand themselves onto the collective consciousness of that generation. 'Make Me Smile (Come Up And See Me)' by Steve Harley and Cockney Rebel, 'I'm Not In Love' by 10cc, Roxy Music's 'Love Is The Drug', Queen's 'Bohemian Rhapsody' and 'One Of These Nights' formed the backbone of those classic songs that provided the soundtrack of 1975. At home, 'One Of These Nights' also catapulted to the top, and that summer the Eagles became America's number one rock-pop band.

Overall, in *One of These Nights*, some of the most poignant lyrics explored the rife risk of disappointment in life, the emotional aspects of striving to find romance or stability, and the letdown that can follow when attaining one's goal does not provide the expected satisfaction. Don Henley, a master at expecting to be disillusioned, declared: 'It can be a woman, fame or peace of mind. What's important is how you feel about the prize when it is won.' Right then, elation was the only natural sensation to fill the Eagles. In an ephemeral business they had reached the top. Holding on to it would, in many ways, prove a tougher gig than getting there, and pressures would crowd in on them. But with plunging into a headlining world tour, commencing in America before rolling into Europe, the band's profile rocketed.

When featured in *Time* magazine as America's premier rock band – *One of These Nights* was enjoying its fourth consecutive week in pole chart position – it was projected that by the end of their 59-city tour, over 850,000 fans would have forked out $5 million to see the Eagles. And on 25 September 1975, the Eagles landed coveted front cover exposure in *Rolling Stone*. It was one adrenalin rush after another. Wherever they performed, they were greeted by ecstatic hordes whose unstinting enthusiasm lifted them to runaway heights, and the plaudits kept coming. Early on in the tour, after a gig before a record-breaking crowd at the Chicago Stadium, the band returned to their Holiday Inn accommodation, already exhilarated, to be met with a profusion of congratulatory flowers, gifts and telegrams from friends and spontaneous applause from hotel staff. While they had been wowing the crowd, on the nationally televised Rock Music Awards, 'Best Of My Love' had won Best Song, and the Eagles had been named Best Band of 1975, beating the other nominees, Led Zeppelin and the Rolling Stones. Glenn Frey quipped: 'Ah well, we can't be roguish underdogs anymore. We have to be gracious winners!'

Though buoyed up by this swirling success, the Eagles did not allow their feet to leave the ground entirely. For all his flippancy, Frey remained wary. He described negotiating the music world then as like walking through a minefield, and he seemed particularly sensitive to the power of facades. Glenn Frey was very much viewed as the quarterback of the Eagles, and in the mid-1970s his public persona was that of a vibrant, rakish and reckless character, ever up for a good time down in LA's hottest joints. Glenn was well aware that he was a figure of some considerable envy among young men. What he took time to tell his fans then was that what they didn't see were the long nights poring over lyrics, and the endless hours spent in a recording studio trying to get just one vocal exactly right. Frey was also determined to hold fast to his own sense of perspective, and he drew inspiration from seeing that performers like Paul Simon were continuing their careers successfully into their thirties.

Meanwhile, Don Henley was also taking stock from the top of the rock pile. With his propensity to fret, although he was proud of the Eagles' achievements to date, with being America's number one band, he knew the burning question was: could they keep bettering themselves? Looking around when at the top was fine until he glanced down. The band, however, would have no immediate fears on that score, and the next two cuts from *One of These Nights* were also hits. By November 1975, the cheating love-themed 'Lyin' Eyes' reached number two in America, and made number 23 in Britain. Then, before the year's end, the Eagles took number four in the US singles chart with 'Take It To The Limit', which peaked across the pond in early 1976 at number 12.

Glenn Frey's smooth vocal and Don Henley's distinctive rasp had come to epitomise the Eagles' addictive sound. But 'Take It To The Limit' showcased Randy Meisner's soaring falsetto, and both the song and its singer snared the music media's imagination, for no one really knew anything about this talented, but extremely shy home-loving star. Away from the stage, Meisner could go happily unrecognised, and no matter the media inducements, he still wasn't inclined to put his head over the parapet for praise, preferring to leave it to others to deal with the press. On the bass player's behalf, Glenn Frey did not hold back. Describing Meisner's lead vocal on 'Too Many Hands' and 'Take It To The Limit' as brilliant, he believed that his bandmate had come into his own. He said: 'In the group, Randy has always been phenomenal. Now, he's a changed singer in the solo vocalist category. Randy has always been the ribbon on our package.' Glenn likened Randy's high intensity voice to Gene Pitney's, while Don Henley admiringly declared that Meisner could hit notes only dogs could hear.

This triple triumph of hit singles complementing the chart-topping performance of their new album, exposed the Eagles to attack by that section of the music industry which loves to knock commercial success – the premise being that a financially rewarding product must automatically be artistically suspect. Such snobbery stems from jealous types who have never smelt great achievement, and Don Henley was immediately forthright: 'The way the record business is structured these days, if you don't have hit singles, you can forget it. You can work for ten years making eclectic and artistic underground albums, and maybe you'll get the recognition you deserve when you're half dead.' He pointed out that FM radio stations were increasingly playing chart music in order to survive, and bluntly added: 'Admittedly there's a lot of fuckin' rubbish in the singles chart. I won't mention any names. We all know who they are.'

Behind the pizzazz of success, however, the simmering trouble in the camp came to a head as 1975 drew to a close. The Eagles were flying higher than they ever had, but Bernie Leadon wasn't happy, and the reasons why were stacking up. For a long time now he had inwardly despaired of the band's musical direction. Artistic differences are normally a diplomatic euphemism for other, less edifying reasons. But in Bernie Leadon's case it was true. Don Felder made clear: 'Bernie's expertise was country. Musically, he wanted the band to go back into country. But everyone else wanted to move toward rock. Bernie lost the battle.'

Though major, that was just one aspect. Leadon hadn't liked the pace of life in the Eagles. So much time and effort was devoted to touring and recording, that he had begun to feel squeezed for chances to relax and let the creative juices flow naturally. Trekking countrywide had never appealed to him, and a recent bad experience when their plane had been badly rocked by a ferocious thunderstorm had left him uneasy about taking to the air. That same day, a plane had crashed with tragic loss of life, and it had felt like a case of 'there but for the grace of God. . .'

Leadon had been stressed at the length of time it took to record *One of These Nights*, and remained increasingly uncomfortable about the creative control exerted by Frey and Henley. It was difficult, in fact, to find a single aspect of Eagles' life that gave Bernie any sustained joy. Live concerts, he felt, had turned into business transactions, and he frankly felt a prat, riding to and from venues in stretch limousines. He believed such showy behaviour was tantamount to thumbing his nose at the band's audience. He had clearly reached a highly sensitive plateau. Yet publicly, in summer 1975, he was intimating that he felt good within the band. He agreed with Henley that the music around lacked finesse. 'It's just sexually oriented,' Leadon derided these inferior works, staunchly driving home that the Eagles were worth far more, and it showed.

Wistfully, Leadon claimed that all he needed for a great life was hot sun, crystal clear sea, fine wine, worthwhile music and his lady. But just as his relationship with the Eagles was dismantling, so his and Patti's relationship began to fray at the edges. The couple had begun to argue, often without a clear understanding of where their problems lay. It was around this time that Leadon came home frazzled one night, to find that Patti had taken peyote for the first time. By the time Bernie walked into their bedroom, his girlfriend, staring out of the French windows, was inhabiting another planet in her head. Dislocated from each other's consciousness, they must have both been very lonely. Lying in bed together later, when they could converse lucidly, Bernie confided in Patti that he was going to quit the Eagles.

Leadon had been so obviously discontented with the group behind closed doors, that it came as no surprise to the others that he wanted to leave. 'We'd had an indication over a year before that Bernie wasn't going to stay with us,' said Glenn Frey. Don Henley added: 'Bernie wasn't happy with the road. But then, he'd started his road map about six years before we began travelling.' Because the Eagles preferred to keep quiet about the schisms in the band, the exact details of Bernie Leadon's departure are imprecise. One colourful story circulated that Bernie, operating on a short fuse, lost his temper one night as the band gathered for a meeting in a hotel suite in Cincinnati, tipped a bottle of beer over Glenn's head and walked out. Years later Frey himself said: 'After months of discontent, Bernie went to the loo during a recording session and that was the last we saw of him.'

Whatever, Leadon's last gig with the Eagles came in late autumn as they wound up their US live dates by playing to 55,000 fans at the Stadium in Anaheim, California. Then, on 20 December 1975, came the official Eagles announcement that Bernie Leadon had quit. Music watchers were not too surprised at this development. They had talked of Leadon as coming over as a commercially successful musician with the guilty conscience of a purist. As an ex-Eagle, Bernie Leadon remained with Asylum Records and resurfaced in 1977, teamed up with singer-songwriter/guitarist Michael Georgiades to release *Natural Progressions;* produced by Glyn Johns, it peaked at number 91 on America's Billboard album chart. Leadon's long instrumental, 'Journey of the Sorcerer', from *One of These Nights,* was also later adopted as the theme tune to *The Hitchhiker's Guide to the Galaxy,* the 1981 TV situation comedy written by Douglas Adams. Bernie guested on a plethora of albums for other artistes for a period in the late 1980s, before joining the Nitty Gritty Dirt Band.

Since there had been a sense of inevitability about Bernie Leadon leaving, his departure did not destabilise the band, most of whose remaining members were totally tuned to becoming even harder musically. The venues that beckoned became bigger as stadium rock loomed on the horizon. And the Eagles wanted that fiery sound that could send sparks out over a vast sea of heads. Playing larger venues equalled bigger revenue, and they made no bones about the fact that they favoured chasing massive ticket sales. But developing a stronger musical style was the Eagles' chief motivating force. 'Glenn had always wanted to be rock,' said Don Felder. 'And Henley? He could sing the New York phone book and it would sell a million records. So he was really interested in that too.'

It is a testament to the musical strength of the Eagles that they did not suffer from the departure of such a talented musician as Bernie Leadon. While holding down his now well-proven lethal lead guitar role, Felder also assumed the task of providing any bluegrass influences required. But Frey and Henley were adamant that because of the instrumental demands of their songs, the Eagles could not go back to being a four-man band. The good thing was, for continuity's sake, that there was no doubt in anyone's mind as to who Bernie Leadon's natural successor should be.

Joe Walsh had been their friend for some time now, and had already indicated an interest in joining the Eagles. Walsh, of course, also had the advantage of sharing the same manager in Irving Azoff, and his producer was Bill Szymczyk. During some periods of discontented grumbling from Bernie Leadon, Walsh had often hung out with the Eagles. Don Felder, pre-Leadon leaving, once recalled: 'Joe often came around to smoke joints and jam after recording sessions. He told me, "If Bernie ever quits, I'd join you guys in a second."'

Joe Walsh did not muscle in on the Eagles, any more than Bernie Leadon had been ousted. It was Leadon's choice to go, and he decided when he had come to the end of the line with the band. Nevertheless, Glenn Frey had been pleased to learn of Joe's interest, and months earlier had sounded Walsh out about the prospect, in principle, of him becoming an Eagle should a vacancy arise. Joe's attitude had been that if it happened, Glenn should ring him. When Leadon walked out, then, there was no debate. Frey made just one phone call and Walsh was ready.

It seems strange to say, but Joe Walsh, one of rock's most colourful characters, made a low-key entrance into the world on 20 November 1947 in Wichita, Kansas. Raised for a time in Columbus, Ohio, where he attended Crestview Elementary, Joe was certainly musical from a tender age. His pianist mother steered him towards playing the oboe, and he was imbued with a strong appreciation for the classical works of Mozart and Beethoven. The Walsh family relocated to Montclair in New Jersey, where there was, as yet, no hint of the future chainsaw-wielding, piratical rocker. With sandy blond hair and a pleasant open friendly face, Joe blended in with his peers. 'I was the all-American boy, a child of the silent majority, playing third chair clarinet in my junior high school band,' he recalled.

In the harsher environment of this industrialised east coast state, the clarinet and oboe were quickly forsaken for acoustic guitar. Self-taught, Joe was good enough to make his public performance debut in eighth grade when, along with school friend Bob Ortman, he took part in a talent show. They performed 'Exodus', improvising their sound by using a Wollensack tape recorder as a PA system. With an irrepressible impudence that was beginning to shine through, Joe quipped of this one-off appearance: 'We sounded like Hank Williams sitting on a vibrator!' The future lead guitar wizard stuck with rhythm guitar for now, and soon formed a duo with another friend, Bob Edwards. Calling themselves the G-Clefts, they concentrated on playing instrumentals, very popular in the early 1960s. The Ventures were America's answer to the Shadows, and the G-Clefts tried hard to emulate numbers like 'Walk Don't Run' and 'Wipe Out'. At this point the pair played with more haste than grace, but their enthusiasm to be the next big thing in instrumental groups was insufficient, and they fell some way short of their target. Bluntly, Walsh owned up: 'We were terrible. But it was cool. I never got shit, because I only played rhythm!'

It was easy come, easy go at this stage, and by Joe's own admission his outlook on the world was remarkably innocent. 'I was really naive in high school,' he confessed. 'I didn't know anything about drugs or pussy.' All that would change, and so would his propensity till now to merely dabble in music. It was almost a given that the catalyst for Joe was his first exposure to the Beatles, when they burst onto US TV screens in 1964 on *The Ed Sullivan Show*. Joe has described the impact on him as: 'Fuck school! This makes it!' He became an overnight Beatles' devotee, absorbing the hysteria that this pop phenomenon engendered through his every pore, until music was suddenly an addictive force in his life.

On 15 August 1965, the Beatles kicked off their third US tour with a bedlam gig at the Shea Stadium in Flushing, Queens, New York. The record-breaking 55,600 crowd required a security force of 2000 men, and when the gig grossed $304,000, it set a world record for a pop concert. The 17-year-old Walsh was one of the faces in the audience that historic night; caught up in the delirium he, as he put it, 'screamed along with all the chicks'. Walsh hurtled out of Shea Stadium that summer night jet-propelled, determined now on his musical direction. He dissolved the G-Clefts immediately, and scouted out New Jersey's best answer to the Fab Four, the Nomads, whom he had learned were a man down. The vacancy was for a bassist, which didn't faze Joe. He blithely kept it to himself that he had never played bass guitar in his life, on the optimistic assumption that with only four strings, it couldn't be that difficult an instrument to master in a hurry. The bluff clearly was not beyond him, for he was invited to join the band.

For a high school prom gig with the Nomads, Joe got all dressed up one night as a clean-cut Beatles clone, complete with collarless jacket and Cuban-heeled boots. His parents were more than happy to frame a photo of their elder son playing at the prom, kitted out as a pseudo-Beatle. They were far less enamoured when they discovered Joe's ambition to concentrate on music. Joe endlessly tried to impress upon them that he was going to be a bona fide rock star, but their response was: 'Baloney!' Reasoned debate about this quickly degenerated into fevered argument, but the frustrated young man could not get through to his parents how vital this was to him. They were set on Joe going on to college. Inevitably, they won.

Joe had left high school in spring 1965; bowing to the inevitable, he now applied for a place at several small mid-western colleges. He was accepted by a few, but opted in the end for Kent State College in Ohio, where he enrolled that September. If his well-intentioned parents felt that they had made common sense prevail, they were wrong. It was the old adage: You can lead a horse to water, but you can't make it drink. According to Joe, he finally opted for Kent State because he'd read about it in *Playboy*, which had described it as more like a country club because it wasn't necessary to study in order to pass. Walsh believed this tongue-in-cheek description, and happily decided that Kent State College was the perfect doss he was looking for.

Not yet 18, Joe packed a suitcase and headed west to college, clutching a 12-string Rickenbacker. By now, he had avidly been teaching himself to play lead guitar and with his head full of nothing but making music, he fell straight away into the student bar scene. Study got scant attention. At every opportunity, he haunted the local clubs, drank beer, bedded the girls, played records and got into pub brawls. Little wonder that among his college tutors he became known as 'the phantom of Kent State'! It was becoming more and more obvious that inside the former innocuous all-American boy lurked an extremely colourful character. Like a lit firework that hasn't yet gone off, Joe was unpredictable. Just as he could look after himself in a fist-fight, he could also hilariously goof around and make friends dissolve into helpless laughter. Never a man to be easily overlooked, he was developing a unique personality.

He wasn't actually rudderless. He passionately wanted to be in a band again, this time playing lead guitar, and by the turn of the year he landed a place in a campus band called the Measles, in which his fast flourishing flair made him shine. The Measles rapidly became the hottest act on the circuit, with Joe Walsh recognisably the star. Joe blossomed both as a result of the four sets a night, three nights a week they played, and from being part of an energetic, enthusiastic and successful group. He called this period a secure and beautiful time. Being up close with audiences suited Joe, and he became as much renowned as an on-stage jester, prone to pulling extraordinary faces, as he was respected for his blindingly strong lead guitar work.

It had to be a casualty of this way of life that Joe's academic potential was squandered. Considering how seldom he attended class, it's amazing that he scored as an average student, but the writing was on the wall that he would fall by the wayside. The Measles felt like an outfit that could go places, and Kent State College's scholastic attractions couldn't hope to compete. Joe moved off campus into a condemned farmhouse on the edge of town to embark on three years of glorious freedom. He later classed these dying years of the 1960s the happiest time of his life. His parents, on the other hand, were appalled. His college attendance had been abysmal, his exam results less than adequate. They despaired from afar at his concentration on music, and in an attempt to steer him back onto the straight and narrow they withdrew their financial support. It backfired. It only became even more essential to Joe to nail pub bookings for this band. He said: 'Suddenly, I was totally self dependent.'

As the decade drew to a close, life soberingly darkened. Party atmospheres of free speech and free love, when high times were frequently gormless experiences, gave way to bad dope and serious social tension. Speed and heroin overtook LSD as the drugs of choice, and race riots were scarring America, fuelling student unrest. Joe later recalled: 'There were drugs all over the place, chicks were getting knocked up, and the race conflicts were getting worse.' After three idyllic years, it was a time of upheaval for Joe, too. First, the local city fathers evicted him from the dilapidated farmhouse, then the Measles began to splinter when one guy left to join the army. In early 1969, Joe was homeless, out of college, jobless and had quit what had been a promising band.

He wasn't adrift for long, though. In April 1969, he was approached by drummer Jim Fox and bassist Tom Kriss, two members of a Cleveland based rock band called the James Gang, with the offer of becoming their new lead guitarist. Not exactly hiding his light under a bushel, Walsh later claimed: 'They'd heard I was hot stuff.' Walsh's ability matched his ambition, but perhaps Joe felt that Fox and Kriss had inflated expectations of him. Moving to Cleveland, Joe threw himself into studying the guitar to a new level and genning up on the rock scene. He later confessed that at that point he didn't know who B.B. King was until he read an Eric Clapton interview and, for all his outward front, he was disconcerted when Jim Fox expected him to take on lead vocals in the band too. Joe wasn't keen, very self-conscious about his singing voice, which he classed as 'different'.

As a powerhouse rock trio, the James Gang soon attracted the attention of record producer Bill Szymczyk, who helped them to secure a contract with his then employers, ABC/Bluesway. The James Gang cut *Yer Album* which in November 1969 peaked at number 83. In January 1970, Tom Kriss quit, and bass player Dale Peters was drafted in. Since being thrown in at the deep end, Joe had taken to his role as lead singer and lead guitarist with gusto. Quickly bored with performing cover versions, he had begun to write his own music. Turning in high-energy stage shows, the James Gang began to build an enviable reputation.

As the band travelled around, Joe saw how the social unrest was worsening. Even so, he was in for a shock when he paid a visit to his old stomping ground of Kent State College. In every pocket of America where potential anarchy bubbled beneath the surface, the nervous authorities had adopted a policy of moving in swift and hard to quell trouble – sometimes with too heavy a hand. In early May 1970, things went tragically wrong at Kent State College when clashes between students and the Ohio National Guard turned ugly and left four students dead. Joe had just arrived on campus when he heard gunfire ring out. Everyone stopped dead in their tracks, knowing what they had heard but really unable to believe it. Joe later revealed how he saw a National Guardsman throw his rifle to the ground and sob: 'What the fuck have we done?'

In close-up Joe saw the frighteningly oppressive use of authority, and didn't like it. A curfew was imposed on the town. All bars were closed, freedom of movement was curtailed and deep shock set in. As soon as he could, Joe got the hell out and headed back to Cleveland. He wasn't there for long when he set out for Britain, along with the James Gang. His band had earlier opened for The Who in Pittsburgh, and had been invited to support the British band on a European tour.

Summer 1970 proved to be the high-spot of the James Gang's career, certainly for Joe Walsh. In September the single, 'Funk # 49', peaked at number 59. But the band's second album, *James Gang Rides Again*, released the following month, rose to number 20 and went gold. In June 1971, a single, 'Walk Away', petered out at number 51. But again, the new album fared better. Called *Thirds*, it got to number 27 in July, and raked in their second gold disc. Within a couple of months, 'Midnight Man' peaked at number 80, and by December 1971 *James Gang Live In Concert* claimed the number 24 slot and earned the band its hat-trick of gold albums.

With three gold albums to his name, one might have expected Joe Walsh to be on top of the world, but he wasn't. He felt that he was writing material that deserved even better texture than the James Gang could offer. He was penning songs that required harmony vocals that no one could provide. He knew that his songs could also benefit from piano accompaniment, yet no one could play keyboards on stage. It all led to the frustrating realisation that his creative growth was being stunted. Walsh was also uncomfortable with some of the changes that success had wrought. To him the emphasis seemed to have shifted away from creativity. It was purely a personal opinion, but Joe felt that the James Gang had become too preoccupied with big bucks. Joe admitted that he himself thought the money was great. He also said though 'But I felt like a whore.'

This strong sentiment was not an isolated downer. Joe had become bored with projecting the flashy, heavy metal lead guitarist and so, in late 1971, he quit the band. It must have been a big blow when Walsh walked away, and Joe became prickly about some aspects of the immediate fallout when, on the unreliable grapevine, he heard unsettling second-hand stories which appeared to misrepresent the reasons for his split. On leaving the James Gang, Joe had also quit Cleveland in favour of moving west to the wide-open space of Boulder, Colorado where, in a raw emotional state, he was loath to jump into another band right away.

When Steve Marriott asked Walsh in late 1971 to come to England and join Humble Pie, following Peter Frampton's departure to go solo, Joe declined. Usually a man who thrives on perpetual motion, it is indicative of how deep things had gone with Joe that he ran aground for a few months at this time. He was so sick of everything, he didn't even pick up his guitar. He just got drunk and lolled around until he felt creative and energised once more. This uncharacteristic inactivity came to an end in spring 1972, when Walsh decided to go solo, backed by a new band. Roping in bass player Kenny Passarelli and drummer Joe Vitale, with himself on lead guitar and vocals, Joe called the new outfit Barnstorm, and disappeared into Caribou Studios in Colorado to record an album with producer Bill Szymczyk.

Barnstorm was released on Dunhill Records in September. Described by *Rolling Stone* as 'ethereal', it was, however, too elusive, and bottomed out at number 79 in the album chart, while its only spin-off single, 'Mother Song', failed to register at all. Undaunted, Joe added keyboardist Rocke Grace to the line-up, and took to the road. It got the old adrenalin pumping. Walsh decided he wasn't best suited to the introspective singer-songwriter role. He was happier rocking again and he undertook a punishing schedule that saw him perform live gigs 330 days in one year, for part of it as support act to Stephen Stills. In that time, Joe wasn't too busy to acquire Irving Azoff as his manager.

In 1973, Walsh wrote avidly, and hastily returned to the recording studio, where he cut his second solo album, *The Smoker You Drink, The Player You Get*, which gave him a number six summer hit and earned him his first solo gold disc. In August that year, the riff-heavy single, 'Rocky Mountain Way', climbed to 23 in America and just cracked the British Top 40, deflecting a hint of paranoia that he was some kind of failure. After that success, Walsh felt that Barnstorm had run its course, and dissolved the band. In spring 1974, he quit Boulder for Studio City, Los Angeles. His single, 'Meadows', had recently been released with a whimper, lodging at a lowly number 89, but his sights were primarily set on making his next solo album.

Joe's need to interact with other musicians meant that as well as befriending the Eagles, he happily threw himself into session work with a variety of stars. Towards the end of the year he produced *Souvenirs* for Dan Fogelberg, which, with input from Glenn Frey, Don Henley and Randy Meisner, reached number 17 in America and sold over two million copies. Right then, Walsh preferred work to partying. He declared that LA was the place to go crazy if you weren't careful. He attached strong importance to his upcoming solo album, in which he hoped to exude new strength in his vocal range, playing and songwriting. *So What!* was released at the end of 1974, and secured the number 11 slot in the US chart, although 'Turn To Stone' barely crept into the Top 100.

So What! went gold, but Joe felt that he had arrived at another crossroads. There was no doubting his standing as a lead guitarist – Walsh drew the outspoken respect of Led Zeppelin's Jimmy Page and The Who's Pete Townshend, while Eric Clapton rated Walsh the finest lead guitarist to have emerged for a very long time. Though peer respect was pleasing, Joe was uncertain about how to plan his future. His following was such that he could book major concert venues with confidence, but that didn't always satisfy. He was also acutely conscious of the risk of merely churning out albums. He had tried carefully to guard against *So What!* resembling a warmed-over version of *The Smoker You Drink, The Player You Get*. He was debating his options, when he put together

…n Frey in the early 1970s. Both charismatic and dynamic, he was a pivotal force in getting …Eagles off the ground and ultimately was the glue that held the volatile band together.

…es' drummer Don Henley, pictured here in December 1974. Henley's innate sensitivity …ld emerge strongly when co-writing some of the Eagles' most memorable smash hits.

Bernie Leadon in Topanga Canyon, September 1973. A valuable component of the band, h
alternated between vocals, guitar, banjo and mandolin, helping to create the Eagles' unique s

Young Guns: Dressing up for a photo shoot at Shepperton Studios near London, December
1972, for their concept album *Desperado*. During downtime, the band staged quick-draw
competitions using real guns, loaded with blanks.

ndy Meisner in Topanga Canyon, September 1973. Even though he left the Eagles after the
tel California tour in 1977, Randy Meisner will always be remembered as the voice of
ke It To The Limit' and 'Try And Love Again'.

tured here in 1980, lead guitarist Don Felder was brought in to give the Eagles a harder edge.

Joe Walsh is one of rock's most colourful characters. Pictured here in the early 1970s, he was considered to be one of America's top five guitarists.

Timothy B. Schmit studied psychology before devoting his energies full-time to music. In 19 Timothy accepted the invitation to join the Eagles, stepping in for Randy Meisner whom he had also replaced in Poco.

tured here in a desert valley, Bernie Leadon, Don Henley, Randy Meisner and Glenn Frey,
original Eagles who headed to Colorado in late 1971 before recording their debut album.
the desert one night while tripping on peyote, they saw eagles flying high overhead and
k it as a good omen.

e Eagles, August 1974. The volatile personalities within the Eagles worked as much for as
inst the band. As their star rose, strain and pressure would take a heavy toll on their friendship.

When Bernie Leadon left the Eagles he was replaced by Joe Walsh. From left to right, May 1978: Don Henley, Timothy B. Schmit, Glenn Frey, Don Felder and Joe Walsh. In 1999 the Recording Industry Association of America included the Eagles in its elite Artist of the Century list and *Eagles: Their Greatest Hits 1971–1975* was certified as the biggest selling album in American recording history.

The Eagles performing on stage in 1975.

on Henley's distinctively rasping lead vocal would come to dominate the Eagles' sound. the 1980s he would go on to carve a highly successful solo recording career.

uary 1995, bass player Timothy B. Schmit and guitarist Glenn Frey play with the Eagles on ir Hell Freezes Over reunion tour. After a fourteen-year rift the band blazed back into the elight to massive commercial success for a second time around.

Maturity and experience may have mellowed them, but a volcanic unpredictability will alway characterise the Eagles.

Pictured here in 1978, Irving Azoff took over as manager of the Eagles in the mid-1970s. He was one of rock's most distinctive figures with an unparalleled style of doing business.

his backing band for the 'Midsummer Madness' gig at Wembley on 21 June 1975.

That band comprised keyboard players David Mason and Paul Harris, bassist Brian Garofalo with Ricky Fataar, ex-drummer with the Beach Boys. But this line-up would also disperse, especially when it began to seem that Joe was destined to become an Eagle. The two sides had been aligning for months. Joe had become attracted to the prospect of ditching the onerous responsibility that comes with being a solo act. Speaking of the pressures of being in charge, Walsh said: 'It completely fried every brain cell I had to finish an album.' He also described the ordeal of keeping a bunch of backing musicians happy and in order, as sometimes overwhelming.

There was no doubt that by the end of 1975, Walsh was ready for a change of scene. Don Henley later stated: 'Joe wanted to be in a band. He was tired of hiring bands, wearied with making all the decisions and writing all the songs.' When it was announced in December that Joe Walsh was Bernie Leadon's replacement, cries of indecent haste were heard. But Glenn Frey made it abundantly clear that the Eagles had not wanted a vacuum in which rumours could spread about the band splintering. For one thing, they were heading Down Under in the new year to complete their world tour, and it was essential to maintain public confidence. It would be a year before Frey confessed that as far back as the time of the Wembley June concert, they had known a change of line-up was on the cards, but had not wanted to talk about it.

The actual choice of Joe Walsh caught the rock world on the hop, which perhaps explains why most of the music media promptly suggested that Walsh wouldn't fit in. For a spell, Don Henley had a certain amount of private misgiving, which he took over a decade to divulge publicly. He said: 'When we brought Joe in, he definitely helped the band. But I think Joe had the attitude that he was doing us a favour. Later on, he became a little more gracious.' To those music journalists who criticised the introduction of Joe Walsh into the Eagles, Glenn Frey responded: 'Who are they to know anything? It's not their asses on the line.'

Joe Walsh made his live debut as a permanent Eagle on the resumption of the world tour in January 1976, when they played New Zealand, Australia and Japan, ending on 10 February. By the time this third new line-up returned to America, fans, critics and the band had had a chance to assess the blend. Don Felder was enthusiastic. He enthused: 'Not only is Joe a great player, he's a positive, humorous, great guy. People said it would never work, that Walsh was too heavy metal. But he backed way off and we gave each other plenty of room.'

In fact, the impressive collaboration between these two powerful lead guitarists was so breathtaking, it led *Rolling Stone* to declare: 'As a pure aural experience the Eagles are awesome. The Joe Walsh-Don Felder guitar attack could have saved the South at Gettysburg!' Don Henley approved of the far heavier sound the Eagles were now equipped to produce. With no disrespect intended to Bernie Leadon, Don described Bernie as never having really understood how to get that dirty rock sound, because his bluegrass roots had meant he hadn't been schooled in that area. Glenn Frey was in his glory. 'The guitar playing is much more to my liking now,' he said.

More than ever, the Eagles embodied an enviable wealth of talent. They had four different lead singers and three guys capable of delivering blistering guitar solos. The band was also now synonymous with skill in recreating studio perfection in a live setting, but that had not happened by accident. Musically and vocally, Glenn Frey's arranger's ear continued to be vital, and his willingness to surrender stage roles for the overall good of the group was ever apparent. Don Felder played banjo and a mean mandolin, which covered two bases left by Bernie Leadon's departure. When Walsh and Felder combined to make a formidable lead guitar force, Frey was largely content to alternate between playing a range of keyboard instruments and using his rhythm guitar skills to further anchor the bass and drum backbeat. While the soaring harmonies provided by Frey, Henley and Meisner were immaculately honed.

Frey's philosophy was that on stage the band should control every possible aspect. He spoke for them all when he said that the very worst the Eagles wanted to be, was great. Though able to play soft ballads practically in their sleep, the Eagles had been widening their range, and still sensitive to their being labelled a mellow country-rock outfit, Don Henley insisted: 'We play rock as good as anybody!'

Three of the four original Eagles remained in this new line-up, and the vast majority of the band's fans were unfazed by yet another change, and by the band's need to stretch. But they did occasionally get letters from grassroots devotees yearning to have the 'old Eagles' back. As Henley revealed, even before their newest recruit had played live with them, one fan had protested in a letter: 'How can you let Joe Walsh fuck up your harmonies?' With his wild facial contortions, Joe Walsh brought an aggressive edge to the Eagles, and his inexhaustible personality made him impossible to ignore. Don Henley recalled: 'Joe definitely caused some trouble. We used to laugh and say about Joe, "He's an interesting bunch of fellas!"'

Then again, the Eagles were just right for Walsh, for their own make-up was diverse. Publicly, they had assumed their recently earned superstar cloak with attractive nonchalance, but that volatile keg of dynamite was always there. The crosscurrents of their very individual personalities and their different lifestyles continued to be a vital force. Even the creative tension blistering around the surface was energising. As Glenn Frey, partial to sporting analogies, put it: on the field as a team the Eagles were invulnerable, but back in the clubhouse it was another story. They had recognised very firmly that they were each his own man, and there was no point in trying to change anyone to a different way of thinking.

Randy Meisner continued to do his job, then slip home, happy to be away from the limelight. He still could not be coaxed into giving interviews, preferring to stand back and let, as Don Henley admitted, 'Glenn and me shoot off our mouths.' That is not to say that Meisner just went with the flow. If he disagreed with something in the band, he did not hesitate to make his feelings known. He was also uncomfortable with some of the more colourful goings on behind closed doors, but considered that that was Frey and Henley's own business. Only occasionally subjected to the spotlight, Randy Meisner was nervous at ever putting himself on the line. As a dedicated musician, once he joined his wife and children, it was more his thing to hole up in his home studio and beaver away on ideas for the Eagles' next album.

The other homebird, Don Felder, had likewise had a recording facility built in his house, and when not devoting attention to his wife and family, he spent a great chunk of his free time slaving away, experimenting with sounds and knocking ideas into shape. He was primarily a musician, and had no interest in a madcap existence. He actively liked being 'anonymous', called himself a musical catalyst, and refused to become another neurotic statistic of LA, a chaotic city of self-obsessed types from which he ran the proverbial mile. By early 1976, Felder was considering relocating further up the coast.

Joe Walsh lived on the coast too, while Frey and Henley continued to haunt Los Angeles. Felder had a very sanguine attitude to the fact that the Eagles were a mosaic of varying personalities. 'Glenn and Don have no family anchors and they handle being rock stars very well,' he said at the time. In fact, Felder was glad that these two live wires *could* project such potent charisma. Every band needed one reckless dynamic lightning rod, and the Eagles had two. Frey and Henley lived the riotous LA scene on which they had made their mark by sheer dint of their personalities. There was, however, a sensitive side to both men that counterbalanced their wild image for women, drink, drugs and gambling.

In the past twelve months, the band had had a bit too much togetherness, since they had unavoidably worked hard to establish a platform of success after *One of These Nights*. For Don Henley, one consequence was that they hadn't had time to nurture long-standing friendships. He was aware of having neglected their bond with the likes of Jackson Browne and JD Souther. Their hectic schedule had left no room for many meaningful female encounters either. When Henley looked towards 1976, he envisaged re-opening old doors, touching base again professionally and personally.

As for Frey, he was acutely aware of having become caught up with being Glenn Frey of the Eagles, in the sense that he feared it had rendered him less sensitive to the needs of those around him. An innate team leader, Glenn always expected himself to keep his finger on the individual pulses around him. Frey knew he was viewed as the most rascally Eagle, always with something rash to say. But inwardly he was worried that he might have become so self-absorbed that he had failed to realise if Randy or Bernie had needed some confidence building. Poignantly, he wondered if his bandmates knew how much he liked them. Glenn was also conscious of the Eagles' position on music's totem pole. 'I figure the faster you go up, the sooner you come down,' he maintained, 'cause once you're up there, there ain't but one place to go.' Right then, though, the Eagles were set in only one direction.

For Frey and Henley the fast lane was rising up to meet them as they sped headlong into the wind, propelled too often by harder drugs. As some 1970s film and rock stars would later attest, right then it was 'snowing' in Los Angeles. 'Cocaine was everywhere,' concurred Henley. Night skiing, Frey called the use of a drug which can induce crippling paranoia. He later admitted: 'It's fair to say that cocaine may have brought out the worst in us.' Glenn's cocaine consumption was scary. At the height of this drug abuse a particular fix for Frey was said to be an 'eight ball', which was a staggering eighth of a gram of cocaine in a single line, which he would snort up in one go. If that was true, it would have marked a very worrying dimension to his use of this seductively addictive stimulant.

Don Henley took the view that drugs had their time and place, and sometimes friction set in over this. He revealed: 'I would get into fights with the other guys about smoking joints or doing coke before going on stage. Using drugs could screw up their voices and could make them sing out of tune. So I got nicknamed Grandpa.' Only later could this pair see what they were putting their tired bodies through. At the time, in their prime of life, they thought they were invincible, despite the fact that Frey joined Henley in developing a stomach ulcer. On tour, the band sometimes fell foul of the flu; they were especially susceptible because of how the combination of work and play was battering their individual immune systems. Regardless, after exhausting gigs they continued to relish staging their traditional post-concert Third Encore orgies of excess.

Touring, which had already been eventful, moved into another zone with Joe Walsh on board. Armed with a chainsaw – allegedly a Christmas gift from the equally unique Irving Azoff – over the coming years Walsh became a noted wildman who frequently caused outrageous damage to hotel rooms. Joe Walsh had already left his mark on his first tour as an Eagle by causing tens of thousands of dollars worth of damage to a single hotel suite before he carved into a painting the words, 'Party Til Ya Puke'. The shocked and irate hotel manager was fully recompensed when Azoff showed up pronto with a sizeable roll of hundred dollar bills.

Walsh also had the constitution of an ox, and all too often he was the only bright spark left bushy-tailed, the morning after the night before. While touring America and Canada around this time, one morning the Eagles were mainly flaked out, exhausted, with some suffering the bilious effects of having overdone it. It wasn't helped by stomach bugs felling people around them like ninepins. Feeling fine, Joe was irrepressibly on a mission to give his floored friends the benefit of his experience, which told him that in their condition, it was a bad mistake to freshen up by cleaning your teeth. He proceeded to regale them, despite their lurching stomachs, sheet-white faces and banging heads, with the gross tale of what had happened to him when he'd made that error before going on stage at the London Palladium, fronting the James Gang when they opened for The Who.

Said Walsh: 'Halfway through the first song I threw up and shit at the same time! I had to run behind the drums where, as I kept playing, roadies wrapped a towel around my waist so the audience couldn't see the brown patch!' Unable to voice a reply to this revolting tale, Don Henley moaned despairingly and collapsed back; Walsh stooped over him with the cheerful encouragement that their next tour pit-stop was bound to be better – Toronto, Joe claimed, was his lucky city, seeing as how he once met a girl there who *didn't* give him the clap!

In a friendly sense, the Eagles had much to put up with; their latest member acquired the nickname of 'Prince Roving Hand' from his disconcerting habit of goosing his bandmates when they least expected it. Joe also effortlessly extended his role as court jester by turning up at fancy restaurants or private parties in the guise of Metalhead, complete with aluminium foil stuck on him. Outrageous, unpredictable and fun, in these ways Joe Walsh kept people at bay from really getting to know him. His overt arrogance and over the top clowning were simple to read and to react to. Less easy to grasp was the real man beneath. Bill Szymczyk, who had known Joe for years, described him as the hardest person he had ever met to feel close to. Walsh used his larger than life personality to conceal a more vulnerable soul than people would credit him with.

From 1976 until the end of the decade, however, would be hallmarked by the most colourful and fraught aspects of life within the Eagles. For Don Henley, extra stress winged his way over a high profile, romantic on-off affair he had for a year or so with Stevie Nicks, the beautiful vocalist in Fleetwood Mac. Born Stephanie Lynn Nicks in Phoenix, Arizona, in 1948, she was raised in California. Nicks had been invited to join Fleetwood Mac in a phone call from Mick Fleetwood on New Year's Eve 1974, and by the time she and Don Henley became an item, they were both in busy bands. It was an era of conspicuous consumption for the rich and famous, but this glamorous couple still turned heads with the extravagant measures they adopted to make sure they could collide with each other.

Don Henley explained: 'I chartered a Lear jet and ran her to where I was, and for weeks I got a lot of shit about that from the band. If she had a couple of days off, she'd come and go on the road with us for a while. Then I'd fly her back in time for wherever Fleetwood Mac was supposed to be.' The other Eagles joked among themselves that it was a case of 'Love 'em and Lear 'em', but Henley defended this lavishness by pointing out: 'That kind of thing didn't happen every week.' Years later, Stevie Nicks would say that Don had taught her how to spend money just by watching how he operated. She recalled: 'He was okay with say buying a house or sending a jet to pick me up.'

It perhaps goes without saying that Henley's throwing money around was not a sign of him becoming a showboater. He didn't knock being wealthy. He'd never lost sight of how his father had worked himself into an early grave to provide for his wife and child. But Don saw fame's absurd side, and the quantities of cash he had, as an Eagle, sometimes concerned him. He feared things getting out of perspective. He would spend outlandishly, then feel silly about it afterwards. He felt a need to laugh off extravagance because, with his acquired pessimism, he fully expected the riches to dry up one day.

Henley displayed this kind of bald candour during press interviews. He and Frey were the main focus for journalists, and their complementary personalities still sparked off one another, making for some stimulating sessions. Unafraid to speak his mind, with his animated outlook Glenn was most likely to monopolise interviews. The quieter Don would bide his time, then at the opportune moment when Glenn paused, he would slip in and succinctly nut-shell the point his loquacious friend was trying to make. Despite their fame, there was nothing phrasey or phoney about these two. What you saw was what you got – often a full-on machismo. The much talked about 'Eighties man' wouldn't emerge for some years yet, and female rock writers sometimes left an interview not particularly pleased with the impression made. One wrote: 'Henley and Frey strike one as the kind of guys who will pick up girls and then drop them just to see how it feels, and then write about it. It's not attractive.'

Irving Azoff began to curtail access to the Eagles to protect them as their star kept rising, and when they did talk to journalists, the manager and band became wary of being misquoted. Suspicious of some journalists, Azoff was known to tape-record his charges being interviewed And their relationship with the press was not always easy. It had been a general decision within the band not to talk about Bernie Leadon's departure in any great detail, and some sections of the media had taken that amiss. Don Henley recalled: 'We had nothing to say, but a lot of people thought we were being stuck up.'

With touring over, the Eagles had their future to formulate, but not before the award season arrived. On 28 February 1976, at the 18th annual Grammy Awards, 'Lyin' Eyes' won the accolade as the Best Pop Vocal Performance By A Duo, Group or Chorus. *One of These Nights* had earned a Grammy nomination for Album of the Year, but lost out to Paul Simon's *Still Crazy After All These Years*. And 'Lyin' Eyes' missed out in the Record of the Year category to the Captain and Tennille number, 'Love Will Keep Us Together'. Ironically, as the Eagles contemplated a further move into rock, the Country Music Association in America nominated them for their Vocal Group of the Year Award. Industry recognition was very welcome, but even they had no notion of the extraordinary heights their next release would reach.

With no imminent prospect of releasing a new studio album, the Eagles culled ten tracks from their existing four albums, and in February 1976 released *Eagles: Their Greatest Hits 1971–1975*. Initially, media focus fell on perceptions of the band's seeming preoccupation with portraying death on their album covers. It was pointed out that the *Eagles* had sported on its sleeve a scarlet cactus flower surrounded by thorns; that *Desperado* blazoned a photo of the band as slain outlaws; that a snake had fallen victim to a hunting eagle on *On the Border*; that a cow skull adorned *One of These Nights*; and now this compilation album featured an eagle's skull.

What mattered to the band was that their greatest hits album shot to number one in the US chart, where it lodged for five weeks. Even that achievement though was a pale indicator of the colossal triumph ahead. In Britain it would zoom in at number two just a week later. But *Eagles: Their Greatest Hits 1971–1975* became the first album to be certified platinum by the RIAA, and today it stands as the biggest selling album in US recording history. Watching the album's rise throughout the year, Frey and Henley had interesting views. As to the striking album cover, Glenn was concerned that depicting an eagle's bald, shiny skull was not very good karma. Not insensitive to Native American Indian folklore, Don yet quipped that that's what the band members looked like after writing all those songs!

By the end of 1976, the album had sold five million copies and rising. Keeping grounded, a delighted Frey offset this success by telling himself that it was a different kind of buyer who went for greatest hits compilations. He was cautious in the extreme. Henley confessed that he wasn't really a great advocate of greatest hits albums. With his cynical view of record companies, he reckoned that these types of compilation were a relatively cheap but hugely profitable release for labels, from which they clawed in huge profit. The band also received a small amount of hate mail after their greatest hits album came out, accusing them of selling out.

The staggering ultimate success of *Eagles: Their Greatest Hits 1971–1975* could not be guessed at in spring 1976, but it was clearly a massively rewarding way in which to mark the end of the Eagles' first five years together. The material they had begun work on for their next studio album would knock spots off *One of These Nights*, and would showcase their creative development. But just as new heights beckoned, so did desperate, ultimately destructive, all-time lows.

CHAPTER 6

Decadence, Delight, Dope and Despair

BY SPRING 1976, the Eagles were the biggest selling band in America, which placed them, curiously, both in a comfort zone and a pressure pot. 'We had all those hit singles off of *One of These Nights,* and that gives you more room to breathe,' said Glenn Frey. In public performance, their laid-back confidence made them appear to be loitering casually on stage, but the challenge to surpass themselves was steep. Unlike some artists, the Eagles had no reservoir of spare material lying around after the completion of previous albums. They did save ideas, particularly for ballads, but they believed in starting afresh each time. At the outset of any album their view was the same, inasmuch as the work should ultimately have contrast and continuity. In the early stages of creating material they had a reliable system which nearly always kicked in – if they got beyond an eighth of the way into writing a song, they knew it had legs and would be worth wrestling with.

Work on material for their fifth studio album had begun the previous summer. The band's long-standing friend, JD

Souther, helped with two numbers, but each Eagle was intensely involved with the new creations, and when they returned to Criteria Studios in Miami, Florida, towards the end of March 1976 to commence recording, the first song to come together was 'Try And Love Again'. It was written by Randy Meisner, whose distinctive high register vocals provided the perfect plaintive quality to a song about the elusiveness of love captured, love lost and with Frey playing lead guitar they had got off to a sound start with a highly polished production.

'Try And Love Again' came in at over five minutes long, setting a pattern for lengthy numbers – potentially less radio-friendly, but that wasn't allowed to enter into the equation. In all, just eight songs formed the album (one duplicated as a short reprise), and the song to showcase Joe Walsh's arrival in the band was a number he and an ex-Barnstorm bandmate, Joe Vitale, had written, called 'Pretty Maids All In A Row'. Walsh played piano and synthesiser, accompanied by Frey, and Walsh also sang lead vocal. For some people, 'Pretty Maids All In A Row' was the cuckoo in the nest this time. *Super Rock* said: 'Though the song is surprisingly low-key, very moving and suggestive of Neil Young's style, it does not really fit in with the Eagles' sound. Time will more than likely erase any problems though, and Walsh will be a fully fledged Eagle.'

One of the Eagles' most insightful ballads was the moody 'Wasted Time', written by Don Henley and Glenn Frey. As the title suggests, it is a compelling ode to regret for the valuable time lost in life and invested in the wrong relationship. Its sensitively soulful sound was certainly by design. Frey dubbed 'Wasted Time' 'a Philly-soul torch song'. The sound emanating from Philadelphia had percolated into his bloodstream enough to inspire him to create his own soul song, paying homage to that influence. Branching out, the Eagles then gave it a lavish string production, for which they again enlisted the professional expertise of their friend, Jim Ed Norman.

For Glenn, however, the standout aspect of this song was Don's heartfelt vocals. Henley's range meant that the band could push back the boundaries. Dubbing Don 'Golden Throat', Frey likened his friend to Philadelphia-born drummer/vocalist Teddy Pendergrass, in the sense that Henley could 'stand out there, all alone, and just wail'. A kind of wailing would come from critics who chose to see 'Wasted Time' as yet another example of sexist songwriting by the Eagles. 'The singer blames a woman because she's unable to hold her man, while the man in question is the singer who's been deserted and left miserable,' denounced *Super Rock*.

A thread of mistrust and regret was already evolving in an album that would engender an apocalyptic vision. That was certainly true of the Henley/Frey collaboration, 'The Last Resort'. An evocative piece of storytelling, this was an especially sensitive ballad of extraordinary depth, airing such issues as power struggles, superficiality and questioned religion, hinting at the hypocrisy of some of those standing singing in church, while also addressing mankind's intrinsic greed and lack of appreciation for the land.

In the studio, 'The Last Resort' got the blood pumping. Frey later stated: 'Henley wrote most of the words and he really outdid himself.' Don knew it. For him, the lyrics stemmed from a deeply held belief that – were it possible – man could ultimately destroy heaven, because he had managed to ruin every heaven on earth. On his personal list of favourite songs, Henley would place 'The Last Resort' higher than any of the colossal hits to come from this album. A decade after its creation, he said of this song: 'I'm proud of it because I care more about the environment than about writing songs about drugs or love affairs or excess of any kind. The gist was that when we find something good, we destroy it by our presence. Man is the only animal on earth capable of destroying his environment.' His co-composer was on the same wavelength. 'The thing about 'The Last Resort' is that there are no more new frontiers,' said Glenn. 'You've got to make it here. Our job is to take care of this place.'

In the course of bringing this new song collection to life in the studio, an even stronger cynicism permeated their hearts and souls – or so it seemed, judging by the unvarnished view the lyricists, particularly Glenn Frey and Don Henley, were taking. The fickle nature of some women could do no other than rear its head, and to varying degrees it laced through all four of the remaining numbers. In the case of 'New Kid In Town', women's talent for letting men down was clearly dovetailed with the dicey reliability of fame. 'New Kid In Town' carried a three-way songwriting credit, with JD Souther joining Henley and Frey. Easily recognisable were the unsubtle brickbats about how the woman in the song is looking to pastures new the moment her guy's back is turned. But, evocatively, it also illuminated men's vulnerability in love, creating an unshakeable suspicion that the lyricists might be talking from personal experience – such was the pithy take on the central female character.

On the second level the song was, according to Don Henley, certainly personal with regards to their view of fame and the music business. He recalled: 'We were already chronicling our own demise. We were basically saying, we know we're red hot right now so we'll enjoy it while we may because it won't last for very long. We were always acutely aware that fame is fleeting and that you are built up, only to be torn down or self-destruct. They'll do it for you, if you don't do it yourself.' The Eagles were now masters at twinning the vagaries of the ruthless record industry with the fraught path of personal relationships. 'New Kid In Town', on which Glenn took lead vocal, was a prime example of this skill.

Accusations of being anti-women were hard to deflect when the Eagles came up with 'Victim Of Love', in which the singer is again the victim of loving an unfaithful woman. This song included JD Souther's second lyrical contribution, and Don Felder had teamed up with Frey and Henley to pen this raucous hard rock number. Henley's rasping, moody vocal highlighted a song that struck a blow against those who tried to claim that the Eagles were incapable of delivering authentic driving rock songs. 'It'll show people that we can play rock as good as Bad Company,' stated Henley; coincidentally, on this track he sounds eerily like gravelly vocalist Paul Rodgers, who had quit Free three years earlier to front Bad Company.

The lyrical content of a lot of rock songs during this period was, in the Eagles' opinion, pretty lightweight. To write a number like 'Victim Of Love' they felt was more difficult because as Henley inelegantly put it: 'It's hard to deal with a crotch rock tune.' Uniquely for a band that believed in overdubbing and careful editing, 'Victim Of Love' was a song with no overdubs. Don Felder revealed that 'it was recorded as a five-piece live stereo track'. They found this was a neat, uncluttered way of dealing with that one song. Like the spontaneity of a watercolour painting that either works or doesn't, cutting 'Victim Of Love' live was chancy, especially when the band was of a mind to let it stand as it turned out. But it turned out to be a powerful, blood-thumping belter to back 'New Kid In Town' as a single.

Although critics had tried to dismiss the Eagles, despite themselves they could never resist keeping an eye on the feisty band. And there was an almost voyeuristic interest in how much of themselves, their own life experiences, the Eagles' songwriters put into their material, how much the way of life of some members impinged on their work. By now both Frey and Henley were taking cocaine, and the drug's influence came to bear in a personal sense on Don during the recording of another composition, 'Life In The Fast Lane'. Penned by Frey, Henley and Walsh, this number would be dubbed one of the best drug songs ever written, and was described soon after its release as the hardest rocker the Eagles had produced, both lyrically and musically.

The song's origins alone were colourful. It started with

Glenn Frey coming up with the title. With his trademark candour, Frey has publicly revealed that he had been a passenger in a car one day with a drug dealer nicknamed The Count, heading to an Eagles' poker game. The drug dealer, behind the wheel, slipped into the left lane, and despite the fact that they had hit a treacherously twisty stretch of road, accelerated to over 80 miles per hour. A nervous Frey had urged him: 'Hey man! Slow down!' To which The Count had replied cavalierly: 'Hey! It's life in the fast lane!'

White-knuckled Glenn may have been at the maniacal car ride, but he still squirreled away the perfect song title. When he heard Walsh tinkering with a compelling new riff at rehearsal days later, he knew instantly that he had found a home for this title. Inspired by the obvious connotations in the title, the song lyrics began to tumble out. It was always wrong for critics to claim that the Eagles glorified the negative elements of California's richest or darkest inhabitants. On the contrary, they shone a stark light on the vacuous existence of many there. In 'Life In The Fast Lane' they brutally verbalised the bleak rootlessness and ultimate destructiveness of the so-called 'good life'.

Starting out with the depiction of a trendy, got-it-all couple who live for sex and drugs, the song sets a scene of reckless excitement and moneyed glamour in the rolling Hollywood hills and the Los Angeles basin. But as it develops, the debauched decadence begins to exact a merciless toll. It was a cautionary tale without moralising. 'That point gets missed a lot of the time,' stressed Don Henley. Rejecting the charge of championing a colourful lifestyle he was himself then pursuing, he maintained: 'I'm just trying to give others the benefit of my experience.'

Almost relentlessly, music writers tried to pin a target on the Eagles' collective back for making this wild decadence seem hotly appealing to thrill-starved, impressionable young guys aching to abandon their moral compass. But the band refused to bear that responsibility, arguing effectively that in that one song alone, they had clearly thrown into starkly telling relief the high price of such hedonism, and shown that it led to a most unattractive spiritual ghetto.

The Eagles could further argue that because they had wrapped up this cautionary tale in a potently thrashing rock context, teenage boys would be more likely to pay it attention. Henley was blunt: 'Get 'em in the crotch first. Their hearts and minds will follow.' Becoming deeply introspective, Henley also maintained that everyone has a dark side. He was not, he said, afraid of his. When it was on display though, as in this song, one unwelcome offshoot was that the forthright drummer received letters from religious zealots, keen to save his soul!

Although Joe Walsh wrote the distinctive opening guitar riff to 'Life In The Fast Lane', according to Henley it was Glenn and himself who wrote the rest of it. Henley also sang lead vocal. Recording the track, though, was a horrendous experience for Don Henley. Just a few years later he went on record to reveal that he could hardly bear to listen to the song as it came together in the studio, because he was getting high a lot and the song was making him ill. 'We were trying to paint a picture that cocaine turns on you. It messed up my back muscles, my nerves, my stomach, and made me paranoid,' he declared.

All that, though, did not prevent Henley, Frey and Felder from coming up with what millions of Eagles' fans consider the band's *pièce de résistance* – the title track, 'Hotel California'. Established as one of the most enduring rock songs of all time, it began life back on a scorching hot July day in 1975, as Don Felder recalled. 'I had just leased a house out on the beach at Malibu. I was sitting on a couch in the living room, the doors wide open. I was in a bathing suit and soaking wet, thinking the world was wonderful, when I started tinkling about with a 12-string acoustic and suddenly those 'Hotel California' chords just oozed out.'

Felder had a four-track recording deck set up in a spare back bedroom, and with the acoustic guitar clapped to his chest, he sped off to put these chords down before he forgot them. 'I also had an old Rhythm Ace,' he explained, 'and it was set to play a cha-cha beat. I played the 12-stringer on top of that. A few days later, I added electric guitar.' Excited by what he was creating, Felder couldn't leave it alone. Days after that, he came up with a bass line, at which point he mixed the whole piece of music together. Since Felder became an Eagle, he had consistently come up with demo tapes of instrumental tracks, which he then submitted to Frey and Henley. Normally, Felder's tracks did not prominently provide room for vocals, but this one clearly did. When Glenn and Don listened to Felder's latest ten-track tape one day on board an airplane, this particular one immediately snagged their attention.

Glenn and Don had been seeking fresh creativity. They had taken to driving out and about, occasionally revisiting the desert. Needing to throw off the trappings of their wealthy, comfy life, the two had even rented a hideaway, a small house in Idlewild, high up in the San Bernardino Mountains, to which they would escape, hoping to simplify their existence and unclutter their minds. The house was unfurnished, and so conditions were very basic. They literally camped in sleeping bags on bare hard floors, all in the quest of stimulating their minds into coming up with new songs. When they heard the track that became 'Hotel California', Henley got straight on to Felder, who recalled that 'Henley said: "I really love the one that sounds like a matador, like you're in Mexico!"' Henley and Frey gave it the working title of 'Mexican Reggae', but the song that had seeded from such a sunny outlook on life, ironically veered way off into intriguingly dark and complex realms.

This shift began with Frey's fertile imagination running loose. Felder later declared: 'Glenn is great at conceptualising.' No stranger to thinking in visual terms, this time Frey was eager to try writing in a daring new way, and he became consumed by conjuring up cinematic images – abstract cinema at that. He was thinking of filmmakers like Federico Fellini, whose work blurred the borders between fantasy and reality and absorbed in this, listening to Felder's music, Mexico now went out of the window. In his mind's eye, Glenn created the image of a lone guy who is almost hypnotised by the monotony of driving in the desert on a seemingly endless journey. Dead tired, he sees the light of some refuge in the distance and pulls in for the night. This is when he enters a weird world peopled by freaky characters, and is quickly spooked by the claustrophobic feeling of being caught in a disturbing web from which he may never escape.

To Henley it was a spine-tinglingly vivid tableau. He already harboured an attraction for the provocative ambience of places like old hotels and isolated motels – collection points where the paths of practically every kind of individual can cross for a transitory time. The film world had once been fond of churning out movies that used hotels as a dramatic device for corralling a cosmopolitan melting pot of people with problems, and Don bought into Glenn's disturbed direction. That wasn't particularly odd. The darkness of their thoughts had already surfaced in 'Life In The Fast Lane', and it was virtually inevitable that this new song would immerse itself in depicting the seamy side of life. Both Frey and Henley were all too awake to the frightening flip side of fame and caustic in their outlook, they set their feet on an almost irresistible road. They knew they had never written a song like it, and it would intrigue music lovers for generations.

Although they titled the song 'Hotel California', the state was an example for the whole of decadent American culture – a poignant statement, considering the nation was celebrating its 200th birthday that year. Said Henley in 1976: 'We figured since we are the Eagles and the bald eagle is our national symbol, that we were obliged to make some kind of bicentennial statement to try to wake people up.'

Nor did Henley shy away from admitting that the

hedonistic decadence they wrote about was something he was a part of at that time. 'We weren't on a pedestal passing judgement,' he said. 'We were living that lifestyle.' Frey was just as blunt. When asked if 'Hotel California' was anti-cocaine, he replied: 'It was anti-excess cocaine. We haven't always practiced everything in moderation.' Frey's expressed view on cocaine use was that if you used it when you had to, and not all the time, you would not get toxic. By his own admission, he was relying on close friends telling him when, or if, he was going too far. It was their support, he believed, that would prevent him from permanently screwing up his life. During this period, though, the truth was that if he was at a party he would, as he put it, 'go right fuckin' ahead'.

He and Henley had been able to step outside that decadence, to take a frank look at it. How they captured what they saw in song stunned them, and sparked spirited and varied debate worldwide for years. But it is hard to listen to 'Hotel California' and not attribute to it an unnerving sense of someone fleeing frantically from his inner demons, perhaps doomed to leave his soul behind in that wretched nightmare he had unsuspectingly entered. One of the most chilling lines in the song is the reference to being forever unable to leave. Don Felder said that in his view it 'was based on Jackson Browne's first wife, who committed suicide. In other words, you can die but you're still in the cosmos somewhere'. Immediately bombarded with questions as to that lyric and many others in such a complex song, neither Glenn Frey nor Don Henley was keen to demystify the work. Everyone's interpretation, they claimed, was as valid to them.

When they had dispassionately surveyed these eight songs, it was obvious early on that they had excelled themselves this time. Yet there were two ways of looking at their situation. Frey still felt that the pressure had eased because of the strong performance of *One of These Nights* and their greatest hits album. Henley continued to see the last successful yardstick as pressure to go one better. He acknowledged that that kind of expectation ensures that the songs are good, but as far as he could see, such perennial pressure was bound someday to have a detrimental effect.

Despite having this treasure trove of material to work with, recording the album would be an arduous experience, not least because over the coming months the Eagles would also be touring. Dividing their time and energies between studio and stage work made for an exhausting life, run to a crazy schedule. For Joe Walsh this was his first experience recording an album, Eagles style. He said: 'I had freedom to come up with some arrangements, which I did. And sometimes I was told what to play, which was fine too.'

Walsh stamped his influence on most of the songs. As Glenn played clavinet on 'Life In The Fast Lane', Joe took charge of lead guitar. He switched to slide guitar on 'Victim of Love' and his keyboard skills came as an unexpected bonus. A Hammond organ made its first appearance now on an Eagles' album, and Walsh's synthesiser, electric piano or organ work featured on 'New Kid In Town', 'Wasted Time', 'Pretty Maids All In A Row' and 'The Last Resort'. Randy Meisner played guitar one on 'New Kid In Town', while the electric guitar work fell to Don Felder, who likewise took charge of guitar on 'Wasted Time', in which Glenn Frey's piano playing already shone. While Felder's pedal steel graced 'The Last Resort', it was his lead guitar work on 'Victim of Love', and the solos with which he and Walsh punctuated 'Hotel California' that would stand out.

'Hotel California' had originally been written in E-minor. 'Just regular open normal chords in standard tuning,' explained Felder, and it was recorded for the first time in E-minor. It was an outstanding track that way – powerful electric guitar work and full-bodied 12-stringers in force, but after a week, Henley walked into the studio and flatly announced that it was in the wrong key. Felder recalled: 'It turned out it had to be in B-minor, which is a terrible key to play guitar in, and we had to re-cut it. It took us about twelve days just to get the basic tracks together.'

For guitarists the world over, the musical feature of 'Hotel California' was the landmark solo when Felder and Walsh trade back and forth with stylish power and astonishing precision. The breathtaking guitar duel took the two, sitting side by side, roughly three days to work out, and Felder has happy memories of this. 'I had a great time playing guitar with Walsh,' he said. 'It's easier for two people to share lead guitar than have one person carrying the burden.' Don Henley declared that 'Joe and Felder played some killer guitar. To me, it's like Duane Allman and Eric Clapton together.'

Felder and Walsh thrived on creating in the studio, and producer Bill Szymczyk was inspired when he came to combining takes. Felder revealed that he and Joe would learn from these compiled tracks, then cut it again. They also had other assistance. Said Felder: 'Glenn has written some great guitar licks just by singing them to us.' Perfectionism was everyone's watchword. 'The Last Resort' took 17 hours to mix. Henley admitted that by that time they were all driven crazy. Walsh, Meisner and Frey each sang lead on one song, leaving this task on the remaining five tracks to Don Henley. The distinction between Glenn and Don's lead vocal was no longer so apparent. According to Henley: 'Since I stopped smoking, it's become difficult for people to pick out who is singing what. My voice has altered.'

Although the album was clearly a major work, as 1976 progressed, recording had to be crammed into sessions carried out on spare days when the band wasn't playing live concerts around America. As had happened during the recording of *One of These Nights*, this time the Eagles were again jetting from stage to studio, recording through the night, then flying virtually sleepless to the next gig. When they could not physically be at the studio for a couple of mixes, Bill Szymczyk had to do the work, then join the band on the road to let them hear the tracks. It was a gruelling existence, which had some odd offshoots. For years, a story did the rounds that one night in Florida Don Henley, presumably under the influence of drugs, wrote a detailed memo several pages-long to one of the chambermaids at his hotel, apparently setting out his preference for the toilet paper in his en suite bathroom to be dispensed from the top of the roll and not from the bottom. Bewildering behaviour, but then the pressure was building.

Fractures within the Eagles became most destructive in the last three years of the decade, but the crack lines had started. Paranoia produced by Frey and Henley's cocaine consumption would fuel problems. And yet, the distorting distraction of dope and drink disguised looming rifts – for some of the time at least. For some, women too had only ever been an enjoyable vice. But Don Henley had split up with a steadier girlfriend, Loree Rodkin, during the time he was writing songs for the new album. Some critics, on reflection, wondered if aspects of songs such as 'Hotel California', 'Wasted Time' and 'Life In The Fast Lane' had been inspired by that break-up. As ever, though, Henley would not attribute a specific aspect of a song to a specific lady. It could only be speculation that some of these new bitter lyric swipes at women had come from this personal experience.

The fact that the road was getting bumpy possibly played a part in why Joe Walsh – himself no stranger to substance abuse – kept a corner of his solo career alive, despite being committed to the Eagles. In April 1976, he had released a live solo album called *You Can't Argue With a Sick Mind*, which reached number 20 in America and 28 in Britain. And at the end of the year, even when promotion was in full throttle for the Eagles' new album, Walsh would tell journalists that his solo projects would continue, that he was in the throes of sealing a solo deal with Asylum Records to release them. Walsh's candid opinion of the Eagles' lifespan was that they had another couple of albums in them. He highlighted, though, that it was getting harder for Frey and Henley to continue writing whole albums to the standard they and others expected. Privately, he could see it was difficult to keep topping the previous major achievement just to prove artistic development. Publicly, he praised the strengthening of the Eagles.

The Eagles' schedule was so packed that it was hard to imagine them having spare time to devote to anything except music and their career, but for some, politics was close to the heart. The US political map was about to change, and Don Henley had a burr under his saddle that apathy among voters was a pernicious enemy of democracy. The Eagles hoped to re-engage younger voters, to get them to believe that it was worth their time to go exercise their democratic right. And so, throughout 1976, they became involved in a number of political events. 'We got involved with Jerry Brown, the Governor of California, who was running for president,' explained Don. 'And we also got involved with the nuclear initiative to try to stop the building of nuclear power plants. We did benefits and tried to do some good work, tried to use our 'power' in a good way.' In the end, Jimmy Carter was elected President. Henley didn't kid himself that things could change overnight, but it was preferable to have a Democrat rather than a Republican ensconced in the White House.

By November 1976, with recording for the new album completed, the Eagles were all feeling the strain of the hard year they had put in. Still, they sidelined their stress and weariness when on stage, and through the summer and autumn, into winter they had found new nightly delights. In the cradle of the mid-1970s there was a significant rise in performers putting on highly theatrical shows, with laser light displays, exploding smoke bombs and ever more extraordinarily flashy clothes – even camouflaging their faces with stage paint in some cases.

The Eagles considered all that to be meaningless crap. Their way of electrifying a performance was to blind the audience with their ability. An ever increasing number of instruments accompanied them on tour, and it was established beyond doubt now that Joe Walsh's introduction had made the Eagles even stronger live. Henley felt that some of the band's early material sounded different with Walsh in there. But the drummer could still deliver 'Witchy Woman' every bit as evocatively as the first time he had performed it in concert. By the time they had been on the stump night after night, Don was growing tired of singing their playlist. Yet every evening there would be the odd song that somehow drew an extra response from him because of the mood of the crowd.

For his part, Glenn Frey was energised by the introduction into their live repertoire of some of Joe's solo material. He was excited to be getting stuck into the occasional non-Eagle number, particularly a hard rock number. More than ever it was clear that the Eagles had an impressive musical arsenal. There wasn't a guitar part that Frey, Felder or Walsh couldn't cope with. Randy Meisner's cameo moment continued to be when he took lead mike on 'Take It To The Limit'. As soon as he hit the high notes, the audience would leap to its feet and, at the end, give him a three-minute solid standing ovation.

Over their autumn gigs, the Eagles road-tested three of their as yet unreleased numbers: 'Wasted Time', 'New Kid In Town' and 'Hotel California'. They had worked these songs up for live performance with a pleasing ease, and were keen to gauge audience response. For now, Frey ruefully conceded that it was hard to lay songs on fans at gigs that they had not yet heard on radio or record. 'There has to be a repetition factor for some reason,' he admitted. The fans *were*, though, lusting after a new Eagles' studio album. It had been almost 18 months since the release of *One of These Nights*.

It was a time of massive anticipation for the band, too. This new album was not the Eagles' predictable next step, and Don Henley hoped that that would be acknowledged. Bearing in mind how much the Eagles had been knocked by critics, Glenn Frey was ready to make reviewers see that they had been wrong to dismiss them in the past. To Glenn the new album not only contained potential hit singles; he saw it as representing the whole world as something once elegant but was now corrupt. That slide from elegance into decadence was depicted on the album cover.

With hotels a big part of a band's life, it is rare for any one to stand out, especially one in the band's own backyard. But the Beverly Hills Hotel had become a focal point for the Eagles; having accommodated the rich and famous, whose behaviour had been the stuff of amoral Hollywood legend down the years, it was the perfect location for the album cover. Amid the luscious palm trees growing in towering profusion along the pavements of LA's most sumptuous suburb, the Beverly Hills Hotel stands at the junction of Sunset Boulevard and Beverly Drive. In 1976 it had pink rococo walls, and with its asymmetrical curves, scrollwork and decorative motifs it was elaborate in the late baroque 18th century style. It was *the* hotel in California. For the front cover of the new album, the hotel was photographed at sunset from a crane hoist 150 feet up in the air. The palm trees were darkly silhouetted against the night sky, which had a typically vivid Californian kind of rusty, smoky hue.

Don Henley found the Beverly Hills Hotel a romantic place in which to view all sorts, from well-heeled celebrities to phoney wannabes to wide-eyed tourists. But although the famous hotel was to be pictured on the front sleeve of the Eagles' new album, the band were not permitted to use the Beverly Hills Hotel name. 'We'd probably have been sued,' said the drummer. This is why on the front cover they superimposed a neon sign saying 'Hotel California'.

For the wide-angled inside cover shot of a crowded hotel lobby, the photographer was directed to an old hotel in Hollywood which had degenerated over the years. Once opulent with Castillian decor, it now had Formica surfaces, cheap wood-effect on the walls, even plastic chandeliers. 'That represented to us what has happened to California and the country in general,' said Henley. For the lobby scene, the

Eagles invited some friends along, but they mainly hired outsiders to come and be part of the shot. In an attempt to represent life's colourful tapestry they invited rich girls, office workers, surfers, hookers, pimps, fitness fanatics, slobs – it made for a surrealistic photo. Completing the theme of this symbolic sleeve, after outward elegance and inward decadence, the back cover of the album shows the same lobby of the rundown Hollywood hotel, now empty but for a solitary Mexican janitor who has been left to tidy up the trash left behind – the party is over.

Whether the cynicism behind the symbolism would register with the public, the party for the Eagles was ready to re-ignite when *Hotel California* was released in December 1976. Despite the band's hard labour, the album had missed so many deadlines during its creation that at one point Asylum Records had put it on the indefinite list. But its pre-release order book stood at one million copies sold, and it would go a staggering 16 times platinum. In Britain, the album was held at number two by *The Carpenters 1969–1973*. But in America, *Hotel California* provided the Eagles with their third consecutive number one album, and it stayed in the US chart for 107 weeks.

This was not just the band's next album. It was the vital start of a new chapter in the Eagles' career, and as such its message was to ask: where do we as individuals, and as a nation, go from here? They were aiming to say that a new set of values was needed, that the best thrills in life should stem from more meaningful things and have real substance. Frey felt that 'we'd accomplished the same kind of artistic desperation we had during *Desperado*'. Twenty-six years later, *Uncut* called *Hotel California* 'the Eagles' undisputed dark masterpiece, nothing less than a requiem for the end of the American Dream, painting a picture of fractured hope, lost innocence and corrupted ideals'.

In 1966, the Mamas and the Papas had had a classic hit with the sunny, sentimental 'California Dreamin'', which was meant to epitomise the mid-1960s, west coast style. A decade later, the daring precision of *Hotel California*'s lyrics was far more than a sharp commentary on a single state, but the subtlety of using California as a microcosm for the whole country, even the world, eluded the understanding of many critics, who failed to see beyond the album title. 'I was a little disappointed with how the record was taken, because it was meant in a much broader sense,' said Don Henley. 'We were looking at the self-indulgence of our entire culture.' Throughout 1976 the Eagles had toured the US almost constantly, and along the way had produced an album that made them the most powerful band on the planet. 'In any band's career there's one album that is the zenith of their productivity. *Hotel California* was ours, and we knew it,' said the drummer.

The Eagles were truly flying closest to the sun, but at the height of this success they once again had ambivalent feelings. Henley maintained that they had started out hungry for fame and fortune, and now that they had both, they were still starved of something. To Frey, if being a commercial success was all the Eagles amounted to, that would be a vacuous existence. Transferring soul and emotion onto vinyl was an art form in his view, and he feared ever losing the passion to be able to do it. Glenn was also ultra conscious of how intense an experience it was, being feted as America's biggest band by fans and the record company. The building pressures and fatigue strains showing behind the scenes worried him. He had never lost the 'coach' mentality, and viewed staying together as a bigger challenge. Bands broke up ten a penny. It took more guts, he believed, to find a way of hanging in there. Frey did not deny the risky pace at which he led his life while carting his dreams, confessing that he liked the fast lane. 'It's very stimulating, but you can get trapped,' he said. Don Henley, meantime, took the view that though you're in the fast lane, you can get out. The trick was getting out before losing it, and with your wits intact.

At the end of the year there was, as yet, no public sign of the trouble brewing in the Eagles. Don Henley was pronouncing to journalists that there were no power struggles, no fighting, no problems over musical direction as there once were, and that the band was happier than it had ever been. Certainly the band's two main spokesmen still gambolled about in informal interview situations. Reporters given access to Frey and Henley couldn't fail to note that Glenn was forever surrounded by the sports sections of newspapers from cities scattered across America, to assist him in placing telephone bets with his bookmaker. When asked: 'What's it like now being an Eagle?' Glenn would grin and quip: 'It's a pain in the ass!' Henley, poised to seriously point out the exigencies of being top of the heap, would instead fall about laughing. It was a light-heartedness with which they could keep deeper probing by outsiders at bay.

The band's media interviews to promote the new album were conducted at one of the bungalows at the Beverly Hills Hotel, in the presence of Irving Azoff's people, there to help and to keep an eye on the journalists. Before settling down for one particular session, Henley remarked that Paul McCartney had just that morning checked out of the bungalow. Frey joked irrepressibly: 'Gee! Maybe he left some marijuana!' Apart from the banter, tales of drugs parties involving the most colourful Eagles never ceased to float around, and seemed to be underpinned when Don Henley told London's *Evening Standard*: 'I don't know how much longer I can physically keep going.' Just as the new year dawned, the Eagles had contributed a new catchphrase to the English language with 'life in the fast lane'.

At the end of January 1977, the chart-topping *Hotel California* won the trophy for Favourite Album in Pop/Rock at the annual American Music Awards held at the Civic Auditorium in Santa Monica, California. The following month, *Hotel California*'s first spin-off cut, 'New Kid In Town', became a Top 20 hit in Britain, but took pole position in the US singles chart. Backed by 'Victim Of Love', it was a double A-side in all but name, and was on its way to becoming a million-plus seller. In early March, the unstoppable *Eagles: Their Greatest Hits 1971–1975*, which continued to rack up mind-boggling sales, won the award for Album of the Year with the National Association of Record Merchandisers (NARM) – all of which gave the Eagles an enviable springboard from which to launch a world tour.

The month-long US leg kicked off on 14 March 1977 at the Civic Center in Springfield, Massachusetts. Four nights later, when the Eagles played New York City's Madison Square Garden, during the encore Rolling Stone Ron Wood joined them on stage. Mick Jagger and Bill Wyman remained in their seats. The Eagles flew straight to Britain, where they were committed to eight sold-out gigs. Four years earlier, they had performed in Scotland, supporting Neil Young. On their first return visit, they filled the Glasgow Apollo Theatre for two nights. They likewise wowed capacity crowds twice over at Bingley Hall in Stafford, but the lion's share of the UK tour took place at the Empire Pool, Wembley, where they played four dates.

Commencing on 25 April, they set out to shine. Sartorially, they remained satisfyingly workmanlike in denim jeans and rolled up shirt-sleeves. But they had effectively jazzed up their stage setting with a neon 'Hotel California' sign on either side, and just as they were about to start on opening night, the backdrop slowly rose to reveal a classic pinky-red Californian sunset, with palm trees silhouetted against the skyline. Never garrulous on stage, Glenn announced: 'We are the Eagles from Los Angeles.' For the next two hours, their sound was tight and the acoustics were perfect, which was not always achievable in a venue which, in the mid 1970s, was often described as a great hollow barn. Hitting their enthralled audience first with 'Hotel California' to resounding whistles, cheers and applause, they delivered an energised set, switching back and forth with ease between country-influenced numbers and heavier rock songs. Their arrangements were flawless, and they brought in a string backing for 'Wasted Time' and 'Take It To The Limit'.

In terms of musicianship, the Eagles' unique power was evident when four guitars were to the fore playing the rocker, 'Already Gone'. Jim Evans for *Record Mirror* wrote of the Eagles' opening night at Wembley's Empire Pool: 'Joe Walsh yelled at the audience, "Bring out yer dead!" Walsh was bouncing with energy and wielding a mean axe. Though at no stage did he out-blow Don Felder.' Evans summed up: 'The Eagles are a supergroup but they don't remain aloof from their fans. They were as knocked out by the warmth of their reception as the fans were by the music. The Eagles have well and truly taken off!' On their final night at the Empire Pool, Elton John sat in on piano for an encore of the Chuck Berry number, 'Carol'.

The Eagles then headed through Europe, playing places in Germany and France they had never visited before, eliciting universal enthusiasm at each pit stop. By now the single, 'Hotel California', had followed 'New Kid In Town' to the number one slot in the US chart – again a million-plus seller. They could not know it, but the song, which made number eight in the UK, was destined for classic status; for many, 'Hotel California' has become the song forever most associated with the Eagles.

Along with the adrenalin rush of a blisteringly successful tour and the racking up of chart triumphs, the off-duty partying now reached new heights of excess. Don Henley later stated: 'We reached our saturation point with drugs around 1977–78.' It's been said that there was so much cocaine going around that the Eagles' road crew had a standing joke that you had to sleep four hours a week, whether you wanted to or not! Roadies would circulate at gigs, issuing Third Encore passes to the prettiest girls clamouring to be invited to the after-gig shenanigans. This tour, giggling groupies competed to be captured for posterity on 8mm home movie camera, cavorting with the footloose among the Eagles.

By this time, Don Henley actually had to have a special orthopaedic mattress delivered to every hotel room he stayed in. His drug use had affected his back muscles now to an even more painful degree. It was an ailment that must have made drumming for hours on end a nightly agony. The European dates ended mid-May at the Scandinavium in Gothenburg, Sweden. Back in California, at the end of the month the Eagles joined Foreigner, the Steve Miller Band and Heart for two gigs at the Oakland-Alameda County Coliseum Stadium in Oakland before a 100,000-strong crowd. A fortnight later, in mid June, the second US leg of their tour kicked off at the Civic Center in Roanoke, Virginia.

In Britain in summer 1977, it was nigh on impossible to escape the impact at street level of punk rock music, with the Sex Pistols grabbing most of the headlines. After their *Anarchy in the UK* release in late 1976, a new furore erupted in June over the single, 'God Save The Queen'. Grossly offensive to many, the Sex Pistols couldn't help but get right up the nose of talented musicians, and although the Eagles had decided to back off from public comment on this nihilistic musical trend, in private they still had contempt for punk rockers. In a Santa Monica bar one summer's evening, a punk rock band began thrashing out a cacophony which was irritating the hell out of Don Henley, sitting with Glenn Frey, some friends and a couple of journalists. Eventually, amid the rowdy crowd while the band plunged into the Sex Pistols' new single, Frey called out that these aggressive punks didn't look that tough to him.

Henley, however, couldn't keep his seat, and at the end of the band's set he strode over to the group stepping down. Since the whole ethos of punk was to push aggression into peoples' faces, proponents of the music could expect to bring on clashes. Henley had his say privately, but clearly heatedly. The spiky-haired singer who had projected an on-stage violence, promptly sized up to the Eagles' drummer and the threatening atmosphere tightened palpably until, squinting past Don Henley's shoulder, the punk saw Glenn Frey now approaching. The prospect of facing two fuming Eagles proved too much, and he hastily beat an ignominious retreat.

By the end of June, the third single release from *Hotel California*, 'Life In The Fast Lane', peaked at number 11 in America and by the time the world tour concluded in late summer, the Eagles had performed to close on half a million people, and had grossed $2.8 million. By that time, however, life was turning darker. The start of the major burnout had been inevitable, and was the result of several factors.

'Making all this money just turned our heads around,' confessed Don Henley. But it was not so much egos running amok: crippling tension and stress from over-work, unending partying and the paranoia induced by taking drugs had made nerves brittle in the band. Add in their incendiary cocktail of personalities, and the lid was beginning to rattle ominously. It didn't help that they were shattered. 'The rock business is like cramming 60 years into 30,' said Frey. 'We live twice as fast as normal people do.' As he also pointed out, sleep had become a planned activity.

Back in 1975, Randy Meisner had reckoned that the reason there was so much strain in the band was because they were so close. He had said then: 'There's tension among us *because* we give each other second thoughts. But we remember the Beatles. Since Lennon and McCartney split, they have never been as productive. The Eagles are staying together.' Two years on, the struggle to do that was tough. In spring 1977, Frey declared that 'part of the depression, is keeping this band together'. And Henley later concurred: 'Keeping the Eagles together was a full-time job.'

It must have been a significant blow, then, when after years of a close bedrock friendship, Glenn and Don had a blazing row that made it impossible to continue sharing a house. When they had moved into Dorothy Lamour's old Hollywood mansion, with its glinting swimming pool, basketball court and stunning panoramic views, the pair had nudged each other, rubbed their hands and gleefully declared: 'It doesn't get much better than this!' On the downswing now, they couldn't stand to live so much in each other's pocket. 'There was so much turbulence about,' Frey recalled. 'Perhaps a lot of it was bluff.' It is possible that neither man truly knew which spark lit that particular fuse, but Henley went to lodge for a while with Irving Azoff. Looking back on the strife, Henley admitted: 'It had been great for a while. Then the demons reared their ugly heads.'

Two of those demons, perhaps interlinked, were drugs and guilt. Henley recalled: 'I used to get accused in the Eagles of being a perfectionist for all the vocal punching [dubbing over existing vocal tracks] and stuff. But that was done out of necessity, because there was so much grass and other illegal substances being ingested, it was the only way we could get decent vocals going.' The guilt stemmed from their colossal wealth and success. Henley found it a hard area to get to grips with. 'You know you don't deserve it,' he maintained. 'You get too much of everything when you're too young, and it comes really quickly. It messed me up for a while.'

Every Eagle was aware that, in the scheme of things, an artiste has a limited time in the sun, followed by a longer stretch of living in the shade. In their quest to prolong their reign at the top, Glenn Frey and Don Henley had been dubbed 'The Pressure Brothers', which sat ill with trying to run the band as a democracy. The fractures and fallouts could only worsen. Though, for the time being, they were determined to hang in there. Or rather, four of them were. Randy Meisner decided to call it a day with the Eagles, and in September 1977 he quit. Just as the band had been loath to discuss Bernie Leadon's departure publicly, the reason for their bassist leaving was again deemed to be a private issue, 21 months on. It was a very rocky time, and there have been claims that at one gig in Knoxville, Tennessee, at the end of the Eagles' tour,

Meisner had felt unable or unwilling to return to the stage to sing 'Take It To The Limit' as an encore.

Allegedly, Meisner told the others that he felt unwell, which, it is claimed, Don Henley had some difficulty believing at the time. As tempers backstage flared, the story goes that accusations flew back and forth, and the bass player threw a punch at Glenn Frey, at which point security had to pile in to save one musician from the other, and it was the end of the line. Offsetting this colourful scenario, Don Felder much later maintained that 'We pleaded with Randy not to leave the band, but he felt it was time for him to attend to his personal life.'

Randy Meisner had conscientiously devoted his spare time to his family, hightailing it home to Nebraska at every opportunity. But he had inevitably missed out on some important aspects of his wife's life and his children's growing up. According to Felder, the band offered to slow down their hectic work schedule if he would change his mind and stay. But it didn't work. Felder said of Meisner: 'He'd reached a point where his heart told him to stop.' Years later, in a rare interview, Randy himself opened up: 'I'd been thinking about leaving for a year. We were touring so much, it was really getting to me. It was kind of sad, nobody was smiling much backstage.'

If there were hard feelings in 1977, though, time out from the madhouse of the demanding whirlwind that was the Eagles, would tease away the wrinkles; both Glenn Frey and Don Henley provided backing vocals on the title track of Randy Meisner's 1980 solo release, *One More Song*, a number written by Jack Tempchin, appearing to eulogise Randy's final days as an Eagle. As Meisner left to recuperate with his wife and kids, and to contemplate his musical future, the sense of uncertainty within the band got a little to Don Felder. 'When Randy quit everything was real insecure,' he said. And yet Randy's replacement was very quickly lined up. Bearing in mind what Meisner had brought to the Eagles, in their quest to fill that void the band could see no further than Timothy B. Schmit, an immensely proficient musician-songwriter with a high-register singing voice. With a twist of fate, Schmit had replaced Meisner in Poco, when Randy had left to join the Eagles.

Timothy Bruce Schmit was born on 30 October 1947 in Oakland, California. His father, Danny Schmit, was a musician who played violin and bass, and Timothy's formative years were spent living in a trailer van in which the family constantly travelled around, searching for gigs. To keep body and soul together, Schmit senior picked up casual daytime employment wherever he could, and played bars and small clubs in the evenings. Music was a passion that he passed on to Timothy, who became inured from birth to a musical and itinerant way of life.

When Timothy was 10 years old, his father secured a full-time post as a musician in the house band of a club in Sacramento, California, and so finally the family dropped anchor. By now he had been taught to tap dance, and was good enough in 1957 to come runner-up in a local talent competition. The winner was a rock band, and watching the older boys do their stuff that day provided Timothy with his first attraction to playing music. Over the years, his father had taught him to play the violin, but Timothy now trained his sights on learning the trombone, then the ukelele, which led him on to bass guitar. Timothy recalled: 'The first guitar I owned was a Harmony tenor with four strings and tuned to fifths. I really wanted to play the tenor guitar. And everything I saw on stage or heard on the radio influenced me. When I started the guitar I was into folk music.'

Acts such as Peter, Paul and Mary, the Limelighters and the Kingston Trio appealed to Timothy in his early high school years. By the time he turned 15 in 1962, he joined forces with two Sacramento school friends, Tom Phillips and Ron Flogel, to form the folk trio Tim, Tom and Ron. The Californian music scene at the dawn of the 1960s, with LA clubs like the

Rainbow Gardens, the Cinnamon Cinder and Pandora's Box on Sunset Boulevard, was a world that the young Schmit could as yet only gaze upon from afar. But he *was* knocked out by the new musical phenomenon coming out of California, when the Beach Boys burst onto the radio airwaves; when 'Surfin USA' hit the number three slot in America in May 1963, Timothy was bitten by the bug.

Tim, Tom and Ron changed their name to the Contenders and promptly ditched folk music to become a surf band, hammering out their versions of Beach Boys songs. There were many flourishing bands around Sacramento, some with very talented musicians. Schmit did everything he could to study the bass players, absorbing what made any one stand out from another. At home, he would then try dedicatedly to emulate the best of the best. He was heavily into the electric guitar sound, and once the Contenders enlisted drummer George Hullin, the band felt more substantial. At their first rehearsal as a four-piece electric band, they knocked out over a dozen surf instrumentals. The scene was swiftly shifting shape, though, and once the British Invasion landed in America with the Beatles in 1964, surf fell foul of flat out pop music. Along with the new re-style, of course, came another name change – Tom Phillips, Ron Flogel, George Hullin and Timothy B. Schmit now became the Beatles-style band, New Breed.

Playing bass guitar, Timothy was also New Breed's lead vocalist, and with an average age of 17 they played the bar scene, building a steadily swelling grassroots following which was prepared to form a travelling support as New Breed gigged around northern California. Seeing Timothy become so immersed in music pleased Danny Schmit. One evening, just before his son was due to leave home for a high school gig, Danny looked at him all dressed up like a Beatle, and offered him two pieces of advice if he was planning a music career. He told Timothy to ignore any hurtful press criticism – 'just be glad you're important enough to be written about' – and never to trust a living soul in the business.

Not quite ready yet to adopt a cynical view of the world, the teenage Timothy left high school and enrolled at a Sacramento college to study psychology, while relentlessly pursuing his music. For seven years he grew with his fellow bandmates, evolving through each incarnation and responding to the times. New Breed was, briefly, the Breed, and by 1968 had become Glad. Regular gigs were one thing, but Timothy's aspiration of making the leap into the proper music world was given a boost when that year ABC Records offered Glad a deal to record an album.

Recording took place in Los Angeles, and produced *Feelin' Glad*. Its sleeve was very much in the flower power style, although for now Timothy wore his dark hair very short. For all that, he was a distinctive looking 21-year-old. With a strikingly strong facial bone structure, he had a wide, fresh smile that reached his lively eyes. The happy expressions on the faces of Glad, however, belied their disappointment when ultimately they failed to make any money from the album.

At the end of the decade, at a crossroads in his life, Timothy faced re-evaluating just where he was going. Although psychology intrigued him, it was music that nourished him, though he was loath to continue down his current road. Then fate intervened. While in Los Angeles to record *Feelin' Glad*, a friend had introduced him to Richie Furay, guitarist/vocalist with Poco, who now offered him an audition to join the band, since bassist Randy Meisner was leaving. The time was right for Schmit. His Sacramento friends renamed Glad, Redwing, and became a country-rock outfit that cut a handful of albums and enjoyed sturdy regional popularity. In February 1970, Timothy dropped out of college and officially joined Poco's line-up. Ahead of him lay another seven-year cycle, this time with a band for which strong live performance would be more of a feature than consistently achieving high chart placings.

Poco's debut album, the 1969 *Pickin' Up The Pieces*, had stopped at number 63 in the US chart. *Poco* managed to reach five places higher in 1970. Timothy was thrown into the deep end when, four months after joining, Poco appeared on 3 July before 200,000 people at the Second Atlanta International Pop Festival, held at the Middle Georgia Raceway in Byron, Georgia. Other acts on the bill included Jethro Tull, Rare Earth, B B King and Jimi Hendrix, making one of his last live performance appearances before his sudden, shock death ten weeks later. Timothy Schmit's experience of playing in prestigious company continued just a month later, on 6 August 1970, when Poco joined Paul Simon and Janis Joplin, among others, in a 12-hour anti-war 'Concert For Peace' gig at New York's Shea Stadium, marking 25 years on from the bombing of Hiroshima.

Between 1971 and summer 1977, Poco would release nine albums, the highest charting being the 1971 live offering, *Deliverin'*, which reached number 26 in America. Poco made their live UK debut performance in February 1972, playing at Loughborough University, before staging two gigs at London's Rainbow Theatre. In August the following year, the band grabbed attention with a notable concert at San Francisco's Winterland Ballroom, but by 1976, Poco were still playing support gigs to bands like Stills & Young.

Timothy had thrived, however. Enjoying Poco's country-rock roots, he had settled in easily and developed apace. Poco had been losing its original line-up. In a three-year period, both Jim Messina and Richie Furay had quit. Furay's departure had thrust Timothy into a more prominent role, and he had seamlessly become Poco's spokesman on stage. He also shared lead vocal duties and had flourished as a songwriter, credited by the time he was 28 with having penned some of Poco's most popular songs.

Timothy's style of bass playing had changed too. He had started playing bass with his thumb, then began using a pick. 'It wasn't until I joined Poco though that I used my first two fingers,' he recalled. 'At first, I was terribly clumsy, but I forced myself to play that way. It gives me a little more control.' Schmit saw bass as a root instrument, very much integral to a band's rhythm section, but his professional admiration was reserved for Chris Squire, the London-born bassist with the progressive rock band Yes. 'His playing is way beyond me,' Timothy declared in 1976. 'Squire plays bass like a lead instrument!'

Although Poco's album chart performance hit a low that summer, when *Rose of Cimarron* creaked to a halt at number 89, Timothy Schmit continued to keep the faith. He felt that each album, though commercially unsuccessful, had nevertheless been valuable in terms of artistic development. What most appealed was how much the songs and their production values were totally their own achievements. He enjoyed involvement in the production side of things, and adored performing, whether on a public platform or privately in the recording studio. He was acquiring very much his own increasing profile within the band, but his dedication to Poco was solid, and for a while his plan was to hang in there, in the belief that major success would come.

In July 1977, *Indian Summer* managed a slightly more respectable chart placing of number 57, but Schmit was now unsettled. Undergoing yet more personnel upheavals, Poco was changing, and a consequent shift in musical direction was under way. Timothy was not so sure anymore that his path lay with Poco. It was propitious then when, in September, Glenn Frey called him to say that Randy Meisner was leaving the Eagles. Would he like to fill the post? For Timothy, it was a no-brainer. He once said: 'I loved Poco. It was as democratic as a band could be.' But when he joined the Eagles, he would not have been surprised to be offered a salary. 'They could have kept me out of the corporation,' he said, 'but that's not the way they do things.'

With long flowing hair and a gentle manner, Timothy's hippy demeanour led to him instantly being nicknamed 'Woodstock'. Don Felder said: 'Timothy brought a great personality into the Eagles.' In sharp contrast to Randy

Meisner's retiring nature, his replacement patently brought a full-on energy and enthusiasm for the stage – someone who loved the limelight and was eager to engage with the audience. This fresh injection, however, did not relieve the Eagles' privately deepening tension. Schmit later confessed that it hit him straightaway that all was not well. 'When I joined, I guess the band was getting very shaky,' he said. 'I chose not to pay attention to it. I thought it was just part of the deal. In bands there's conflicts – you work them out.'

Though privately riven with problems that would only worsen, publicly the Eagles were soaring. By the end of 1977, they remained firmly America's premier recording and performing rock band. And the following February, the Eagles collected two Grammy Awards when 'Hotel California' won Record of The Year and 'New Kid In Town' took the coveted trophy for Best Arrangement for Voices.

Another kind of collective voice that continued to be obstinately *un*appreciative, though, came from the critics. The Eagles were in a no-win situation with this body of people. They had long since been blindly bashed for supposedly commercialising sunny California. Now, critics interpreted the darkness of *Hotel California* as the Eagles exploiting what was happening in society! There were even those who, since the Eagles had very firmly come to represent southern California, still complained that none of the original members was a native Californian. 'Principal songwriters Frey and Henley constantly pepper songs with references to outlaws and heroes. They celebrate the values of the Old West with no real sense of irony, no sense of distance,' accused *Super Rock* in December 1977 while *Rolling Stone* picked up on the Eagles' reputation among rock writers for seeing the world with a misanthropic disdain. The old sexist chestnut, also, would not die a natural death.

'We got slammed for all kinds of stuff,' said Don Henley. 'Accusations of misogyny would come up every so often, which I think is completely ridiculous. But people are always seeking something to jab at.' The nitpicking did border on the absurd. 'Hotel California' rates as one of the most intriguing and complex songs in music, yet one critic's jibe was to point out to the songwriters that wine was not a spirit!

Some of the critical barbs glanced clean off the Eagles, but others dug in and created a festering sense of grievance, provoking Don Henley to state openly that their songs were being underrated. He pointed out that the Eagles' songs had more to do with what was happening at street level than Bruce Springsteen's songs. East coast critics in particular, who could not see beyond the New Jersey-born singer-songwriter, positively rushed to take up arms at such utterances. Glenn Frey agreed with Henley's long held sense that there was a whiff of personal vendetta among certain critics. Glenn was said to have begun compiling a little black book with a difference – noting the names of those critics with whom he would like to take issue over their comments. What Frey certainly had was disdain for those who took a hipper-than-thou attitude. 'What they're so pissed off about, is that it is *us* in this situation!' he declared.

The Eagles are not alone in feeling aggrieved in this way. As Def Leppard frontman Joe Elliott states on behalf of rock bands in general: 'If we did what the critics wanted, we'd please them and piss off our audiences. Criticism can hurt when it's personal or spiteful, and it often feels as though if you're talented they want to knife you. Def Leppard has had "One star, bin it" slaggings off in reviews when the album they're talking about is selling millions! It's some guy in an office, drawing a wage wishing he was a rock star! But really, critics' effect is limited in music. Percentage-wise they don't have a lot of clout, I'm afraid!'

Disappointment, deep hurt, intense anger – the Eagles ran the gamut of emotions over what they saw as the critics' refusal to give them a fair shake of the stick. Since the Eagles did not have, as Don Henley put it, 'too many highfalutin' ideas' about themselves, they felt maligned. 'It made us lash out against the critics sometimes,' recalled Don, 'which is always a mistake, since they have the last word.' While that is unarguably true, in 1978, however, the Eagles came up with a unique way of literally hitting back.

CHAPTER 7

The Mean Machine

FOR SEVERAL WEEKS throughout spring 1978, the Eagles and critics for *Rolling Stone* traded colourful insults via the rock magazine's Random Notes pages. It seemed that no aspersion on their respective individual masculinity was deemed below the belt, and as to which side was the more offensive, the honours were pretty evenly split. With both the band and the pen-pushers determined to cut deepest, it could have gone on interminably, but eventually they decided to settle their differences on the sports field. The Eagles would play a team put together from *Rolling Stone* in a professional game of softball – a modified form of baseball, played on a slightly smaller field. The place and date was fixed – Sunday, 7 May 1978, at the Dedeaux Field on the USC campus, Los Angeles – and the tension increased several fold. This wasn't a celebrity challenge; this was a grudge match, and neither side denied it.

Charles M. Young for *Rolling Stone* declared: 'We could not get the Eagles to take our criticism. So we wanted to teach them a lesson that would make musicians everywhere quake if they had thoughts of back-sassing our reviews.' Don Henley recalled: 'As game day approached, the threats in Random Notes grew more ridiculous. Glenn's already tenuous relationship with Charles Young was rapidly approaching switch-blade and tyre tool proportions!'

The Eagles' manager, Irving Azoff, and *Rolling Stone*'s publisher/editor, Jann Wenner, were little better. Both vivid personalities with strong characters, Azoff and Wenner had had long-distance bawling matches down the telephone over the friction. Indeed, when it was decided that the loser would make a $5,000 donation to UNICEF's world nutrition program, although both businessmen supported this charitable scheme, they feared this wager arrangement might dilute the fact that the respective teams were out for blood!

Seventy-two hours before match day, the east coast contingent arrived in Los Angeles, hell-bent on further stirring the already boiling pot. Until then, tossing insults coast-to-coast had had to suffice. Now Charles Young maintained that an intense desperation had set in. Let loose on the Eagles' turf, the feisty, fearless critics were soon up to no good. According to Mikal Gilmore for *Rolling Stone*, the visiting team, worse the wear for drink, made post-midnight flying raids on the respective homes of both Frey and Henley and finding the musicians out, they poked inflammatory notes through their letterboxes. Someone clearly with a sick sense of humour, also left a note containing a threat against Glenn's beloved cat, Charlie.

On Saturday afternoon, the day before the game, as the Eagles had their last practice session at Dedeaux Field, Jann Wenner sat hunkered down low on one of the top bleachers with a couple of his team's players, on a spying mission. They were grim-faced enough as it was, when they spotted Don Henley sauntering onto the field perimeter carrying baseball shoes which sported steel spikes. Springing to gimlet-eyed attention, Wenner discovered Glenn Frey was wearing similarly lethal looking shoes. Unable to put it past the Eagles inflicting eye-watering damage on his journalists, Wenner stampeded down the rows of bleacher benches to hotly confront a fiendishly pleased-looking Azoff.

Jann demanded that the Eagles put rubber cleats on the spikes, or the game was off! Irving argued that his boys were only wearing regulation softball footwear. 'Someone might get hurt!' hollered Wenner. 'How exciting!' declared Azoff. After spirited haggling over the issue, the Eagles conceded and agreed to sheath the steel spikes in rubber cleats. Although such was the rock-bottom trust between the two sides, that Jann Wenner sent out that evening for metal spiked shoes for his team. And in a late night team talk session, he and his players discussed the merits of wearing them for the match.

When Sunday afternoon arrived, the crowd in the scorching hot sun at Dedeaux Field was unevenly divided. The spectator benches for the Eagles were packed to capacity, and included celebrity supporters such as Joni Mitchell and comedic actor Chevy Chase. Apart from some cheesy sweet cheerleaders seconded from Hollywood High School, the support bleachers for the critics were embarrassingly sparse of people. The emcee for the event was none other than Joe Smith, chairman of Elektra/Asylum Records. Smith showed no partisanship towards the colossally high-earning Eagles, however, and in the pre-match build up commentary, booming around the arena, he showered verbal abuse on both teams. 'Joe seemed to hate everybody equally,' Frey later recalled.

The Eagles' team wore black and gold, while their opponents had opted for red and white, their shirts displaying a design of a clenched fist emerging from a dagger. Irving Azoff's jersey had printed on it in conspicuous lettering: 'Is Jann Wenner Tragically Hip?' Over the tannoy system, Joe Smith announced the line-ups, then keeping up his pithy denunciation, addressed the expectant crowd: 'The first thing you'll ask yourselves about these teams is: how could either side possibly win? And Jann Wenner and Irving Azoff are undersized egomaniacs!' he added.

The Eagles' national anthem was 'Life In The Fast Lane'. No one can recall the other anthem, for the tension on pitch was too gripping. Later, the rock critics conceded that that softball game in front of an agog crowd was the nearest any journalist would ever come to taking part in something like the World Series. Then came the order to 'Play ball!' First up to bat was *Rolling Stone* team captain, Charles Young, sporting a bandage on his right arm. Speculation flew around the Eagles' dugout that this was proof that Young had come off worse in an encounter with Frey's cat the other night! As the two teams tensely joined battle, it became obvious that the critics were better at character assassination than physical attack – the east coasters were destined for a drubbing.

Nerves got the better of some players, which was understandable when one considers that the Eagles' team wore the aggressive looking under-eye dark face paint more associated with American football players. Even Jim Dunning, reckoned to be the rock magazine's best player, succumbed to the jitters. And when the Eagles came to bat in the bottom of the first, their newest recruit, Timothy Schmit, wearing a Samurai headband to hold back his long hair, was patently uneasy. With his hippy style and placid demeanour, Schmit had not seemed much of a threat to the *Rolling Stone* team. Charles Young later confessed: 'Appearances are deceiving. I figured, "Easy out!" and Schmit hit a line drive so hard it took off the third baseman's glove!'

At the end of the first inning, the Eagles were leading 3-0, but by the top of the third, the *Rolling Stone* team had tied the score at 3-3. Said pitcher Don Henley: 'We realised we had to tighten up our defense.' The Eagles scored three in both the third and fourth innings, but failed to score in the fifth. Glenn was unhappy. A 9-3 lead to him was far too skinny. He roused the troops, pounding it into everyone that it wasn't enough. Coach Frey in full throttle demanded no more quiet innings.

Rolling Stone's match report later revealed: 'In their half of the sixth, the Eagles responded by sending ten men to the plate to bombard losing pitcher Tim Reitz with consecutive singles by Felder, Walsh and Henley, followed by consecutive doubles by Schmit, Frey and Peter Cetera (bass player with Chicago).'

It was when the score stood at an embarrassing 15-3 that the drowning critics wheeled out their secret weapon in the eighth inning, in the form of shapely relief pitcher Lucie Gilburg. Preying on the Eagles' Achilles heel reaped dividends; the band were so busy getting an cyeful of Lucie that she managed to put them clean off their stroke. She put out three Eagles in a row. Triumphantly punching the air, Jann Wenner lunged forward in his seat and gleefully crowed across the field to Irving Azoff that that alone was worth every cent of the $5,000 that he knew, by now, he was going to have to fork out.

Despite further flurries at a *Rolling Stone* revival, the match ended 15-8 to the Eagles. UNICEF's world nutrition program got their donation from the rock magazine, plus proceeds from bleacher tickets that had been sold to various record companies in blocks.

When the Eagles held a post-match celebration at Dan Tana's Italian restaurant, Glenn magnanimously praised the band's vanquished opponents. *Rolling Stone* critics conceded that the west coast superstars were not, after all, sissies. Although mulling over what had happened with the fragrant Miss Gilburg, Frey queried drolly if he was somehow a sexist symbol – something girls felt a need to trounce.

Curiously, in time, some of the Eagles' most cutting critics would become friends with the band. Right then, with this distraction over, the once close friends in the Eagles went back to confronting the strained state they were in. Recording for their new album had already begun back in March. This time they utilised both Bayshore Recording Studio in Coconut Grove, a suburb of Miami, Florida, and One Step Up Recording in Los Angeles. Work became a tortuous, long drawn out process. Their hearts were struggling to be in it, and over an 18-month period matters would worsen. Sometimes they headed home to write, other times they'd try to create on the mike. And recording, as ever, had to be interspersed with touring duties.

This new song collection would ultimately lay bare the disintegrating relationships within the Eagles. Despondency weighted down nearly all ten numbers, and the running themes exuded hurt, desperation, confusion, loneliness, biting cynicism and regret. Some songs spoke poignantly of lost dreams and attacking the phoney sincerity prevalent in the world, they mainly had a grim overlay. There was a single exception – 'Heartache Tonight'. Frey had started the rock number when he had a visit from his friend, Bob Seger, who usually called by whenever he was in Los Angeles. Said Glenn: 'I was showing 'Heartache Tonight' to Seger and we began jammin' on electric guitars. Then he blurted out the chorus.' After Bob Seger left, Don Henley and JD Souther collaborated with Glenn to complete it. 'The song is what it was intended to be – a romp,' said Frey.

Souther joined Frey, Henley and Joe Walsh to compose 'The Sad Cafe', a song soaked in sorrow, which years later *Uncut* described as a 'manifesto of defeat'. And JD teamed up with Glenn and Don for 'Teenage Jail', by which point, according to Henley, the Eagles' mood had become real sick. 'In The City', a dark depiction of the mean streets, was the work of Joe Walsh and Barry de Vorzon. Otherwise, the Eagles kept it in the family, Timothy Schmit making his Eagles songwriting debut with 'I Can't Tell You Why', a hauntingly ambiguous ballad written in conjunction with Frey and Henley.

Technically proficient as always, this time the band found the meticulous precision of singing the same few words a dozen times over, to get a handful of syllables just right, went for their fraying nerves. Out on the road, the Eagles managed to conceal their crippling strain from the fans who flocked to their stadium gigs. As summer 1978 rolled out, they performed around America with the Steve Miller Band as their opening act. Playing live in vast arenas did it for Frey, who has declared: 'There's nothing more exciting in the world than when you take a jet helicopter from Manhattan, fly around the Statue of Liberty and over to Meadowlands Stadium and see 90,000 people waiting to hear you play. No drug in the world will get you that high!'

On any given night, the Eagles would take to the stage just before 10.00 pm for a two-hour set of their greatest hits. Incorporated in their playlist would be a handful of Joe Walsh songs from his James Gang days and Timothy Schmit would add in a song from his time with Poco. Grassroots fans, loyal to the Eagles from the beginning, had only Glenn Frey and Don Henley to hold on to as original members. But the newcomers had successfully blended in, and Timothy Schmit quite obviously enjoyed taking a more visible role live than his predecessor bass player had.

The rascally clown on stage was undoubtedly Joe Walsh, with his propensity for pulling piratical faces to match the buccaneer-style headscarf he wore. Joe remained as unpredictable as he had always been; before a live audience, while his bandmates stood their ground and played, he would dash about, jumping off the risers, projecting harmless missiles into the crowd. He had a homemade device that he said could fire telephones from hotel balconies! His infectious sense of humour was a crowd winner.

In one concert review, however, *Record Mirror* wrote: 'The sound that makes the Eagles unique, the one that makes you want to weep over your lost youth, emanates from the throat of a skinny guy walled off behind his drum kit. The audience can see only a small part of him and are mystified about whom to clap for on the Eagles' best material.' Something the fans still did not know, was that to get through demanding performances, Don Henley had to have daily acupuncture treatment on his spine.

Although very much an Eagle, Joe Walsh had gone ahead and signed a separate solo recording deal with Asylum Records, and in June 1978 he released the satirical single, 'Life's Been Good', which reached number 12 in America, two places higher than its best in Britain. Its parent album *But Seriously Folks...*, produced by Bill Szymczyk, stopped at number 16 in the UK but climbed to number eight that summer in the US, earning Walsh his first platinum disc in his own right.

Glenn Frey called roadwork 'the decadence festival', and in late July the Eagles launched another round of live gigs, beginning in Edmonton, Canada, before disappearing back into the recording studio, where they toiled with no great progress. In December 1978, the Eagles surprised their fans by releasing a Christmas single. It was their cover version of the bluesy Charles Brown number, 'Please Come Home For Christmas'. Backed by an Eagles song, 'Funky New Year', it made number 18 in the US chart and gave the Eagles a Top 30 hit in Britain before the year ended.

At the dawn of 1979, it was two years since the release of *Hotel California*, and Asylum Records was growing very nervous. Chairman Joe Smith made no bones about the fact that the label now needed the Eagles' new offering as soon as possible. Smith candidly confessed that Asylum Records fell $15 million short in its company projections through not having had an Eagles' album release in 1978. Joe Smith was also concerned that the passage of time had allowed a host of emerging bands to capture the media's attention and the public eye. And he was patently not sure how deep a new Eagles' album would penetrate the radically changing music market. Asylum had to hold its nerve, and so did manager Irving Azoff.

Azoff's relationship with Asylum Records was as stimulating as ever. Smith stated: 'Irving uses terror and high volume to achieve his goals.' Azoff admitted that he would light a fire under any record label to ensure the Eagles got what they deserved. Certain other aspects of the ever-expanding record business became a source of intense irritation to Irving Azoff. He considered the touring side an area ripe for sizeable fraud from ticket scalping. He worked out that if a band in the late 1970s grossed $200,000 from one of those big, prestigious venue gigs, double that sum of money had in fact changed hands. Caustically, he declared that he just might consider selling the one thousand top-priced seats for Eagles' gigs direct to the scalpers for $20 each, and give the remaining $9.50 per seat to charity. 'I've tried everything else to beat them!' he growled.

As a highly motivated, dedicated personal manager, Azoff was fully aware of the need for strong fiscal management. The music business had quadrupled just as bands like the Eagles hit it big. Irving revealed: 'If you handle the Eagles, their road crew and families, you become responsible for 55 people and you're running a multimillion dollar business. If you don't handle it [the money] right, the government will take it away from you.'

In April 1979, the Eagles were roughly 14 months down the recording track, and the slog was no easier. At One Step Up Recording in Los Angeles, Don Henley had invested five hours in overdubbing bass drum work on the rhythm track for 'Heartache Tonight'. It was rare to quit the studio before sunrise. They did occasionally take a break, however, when they went all out to 'monster', which in Eagles' parlance meant letting off steam and relaxing. It seemed an apt term as far as Glenn Frey was concerned – he pointed out that when a guy was doped up and drunk, he did tend to look somewhat different! While in LA, Frey bolted from the recording studio to the Troubadour, where knocking back the Budweisers among friends, he happily surveyed the beauties sashaying by the club. Openly ogling one particularly curvy mini-skirted lady, Glenn groaned: 'Look at that! The buns of doom!' Where others his age fretted about leaving their twenties behind, Glenn, recently turned 30, decided he liked the wider scope it now gave him. The young ladies looked deliciously younger and the older women, not so old!

Carefree interludes became a less effective release, however, as the pressure on the band drastically increased.

Back in Coconut Grove, Miami, the mood in the studio was bleak. Joe Walsh revealed: 'We ended up with the tapes running but nobody knowing what was going on. We lost perspective. We kinda sat around in a daze for months!' Frey confirmed that for him and Henley it was an extremely fraught situation. 'We were at a stage where there were no positive thoughts about the work. Don and I would sit across from each other for hours, not saying a word. We'd sit, trying to write, but we were both afraid to suggest a lyric or a chord, in case it wasn't perfect.'

Caught in that web of confusion, haemorrhaging confidence and lacking creative spark, the band suffered an ordeal on several levels; only later could they see that they ought not to have put themselves through the mill that way. A decade on, Henley confessed that songs such as 'Teenage Jail' and 'The Greeks Don't Want No Freaks' were by-products of how morose they had become, and that frankly the entire album was not worth the grief they endured to make it. Pernicious resentment festered about which songs were selected to go on the album, and personal rivalries were worsening. Plainly, they were quite simply sick of each other. Frey and Henley's once impregnable bond was crumbling. The drummer was also increasingly exasperated by Joe Walsh, and was quoted as dubbing the wild guitarist 'a troublemaker'.

At the root of it all they felt that they had nothing to say, just when the record company was looking for them to surpass the classic *Hotel California*. Looking on, Joe Smith found nothing to cheer him. The band's massive success made them all extremely wealthy young men. So, from the record label's point of view, it could not depend on the Eagles seeing a financial incentive to get their act together. It wasn't that the Eagles stubbornly wouldn't do so – they couldn't. For some, cocaine consumption exacerbated the mounting problems. Don Henley saw the wider dilemma. 'Drugs aside, we were burnt out physically, spiritually and creatively,' he declared. 'We needed a break but the machine wanted more. There were contracts to fulfil, concerts booked. We had to feed the monster.' Henley called making that album one of the most miserable experiences of his life.

Each Eagle tried to eke out some pleasure where he could. In Don Henley's case he had become romantically involved with 32-year-old actress Lois Chiles. Having graduated from the University of Texas, Austin, in 1969, before becoming an actress the dark-haired stunner from Alice, Texas, had been one of the top models of the 1970s. Said Henley at the time: 'I like beauty, but that isn't enough. I want someone with brains too.' When it was put to him that in celebrity circles, partnerships were frequently becoming a commodity exchange – status for looks – Henley denied that that applied to himself and Lois Chiles, revealing that she hadn't known who he was when they met.

It would have taken more than the romantic entanglement with a vivacious beauty, though, to offset the inexorably encroaching bad thoughts plaguing Henley. He found much to be dissatisfied with in a political and environmental sense. But also, festering resentments from way back to his school years over religion and the like were helplessly seeping to the surface, haunting his restless dreams and carving a furrow in his young brow by day. As Don brooded, so Glenn struggled to chill out by drawing on a succession of joints. Nicknames for individual Eagles came and went. In the late 1970s Frey's attachment to marijuana led him, within the band, to be called 'Roach' (after the roll of card which forms the butt of a cannabis cigarette). And it was hard for him not to be in reflective mood at times.

Randy Meisner in Nebraska had signed a solo recording contract, and Bernie Leadon, still living in Topanga Canyon, was also recording demo tapes when not surfing. The changes in line-up had unquestionably strengthened the band, and Timothy Schmit was telling journalists how he felt real blessed to be in the Eagles, describing the band as the closest one he had ever work with. Which was fine – none of the Eagles relished washing their dirty linen in public – but the strain and pressure just would not go away.

Frey missed his friendship with Henley. Glenn, who was by now involved with a woman from New Mexico on a more solid footing than usual, spoke publicly of how in a weird (and strictly *not* homosexual) way, Don was his 'longest successful "romance" – almost eight years now'. Frey maintained that the key was to be able to agree to disagree. Right then, in reality, that was hard to practice. It was also not the healthiest time for the band. Visitors to the Bayshore Recording Studio in Coconut Grove, Miami, were treated to the sight of stacked boxes of antacids. Frey would be shovelling multi-vitamins down his throat, and too often a pasty-faced Henley looked ready to throw up. Right up to the wire, the Eagles slaved on an album that had torn the guts out of them. Even when some friends gathered at the studio for a playback party, as the waiting guests got sloshed, Frey, Henley and Bill Szymczyk were still in the control room, thrashing out minute details into the early hours.

The album was to be appropriately titled *The Long Run*. After over 18 months of work, and at a cost in excess of $800,000, at just before 6.00 am the following summer morning, Glenn and Don finally joined the Eagles' inebriated guests. Bleary-eyed and bone-weary, they announced that the album was complete. There was no euphoria, excitement or energy. The only recognisable emotion was relief.

The album's artwork was very funereal looking, and when *The Long Run* was released in September 1979, critics dismissed it as mediocre. Having already sold two million copies before release, however, *The Long Run* seized the number one slot in the US album chart. In a year-long chart run, this sixth studio album from the Eagles would rack up nine weeks at the top – one more week than *Hotel California* had reigned supreme – and it ultimately went seven times platinum. *The Long Run* was the Eagles' fourth consecutive number one album in the US, and would reach number four in Britain by October. 'Heartache Tonight', with Frey on lead vocal, was the lead-off single; in November 1979 it became a US chart-topper, selling in excess of a million copies, though only reaching the UK Top 40. This success, however, pitched the Eagles back into vogue, and the band featured once again on the cover of *Rolling Stone*. The title track, sung by Henley, did not capture British hearts, but early in the new year 'The Long Run' would chalk up a number eight hit at home.

Towards the end of the year, politics swung into focus once more. In September, Joe Walsh announced that he intended to run for President in 1980 on a platform of 'Free gas for everybody', although he did have a serious disgust with his country's current government. On 21–22 December 1979, the Eagles, along with Chicago, Linda Ronstadt and others, performed two benefit gigs at San Diego's Sports Arena and the Aladdin Theater in Las Vegas, raising around a quarter of a million dollars for the presidential campaign satchel of California Governor, Jerry Brown.

Despite their loyal support of the Democrat cause, the Eagles' own internal politics remained their most intense worry. How much longer the strife could be kept under wraps was debatable. Yet for now, outward appearances were wreathed in glowing success. Their six studio albums, documenting and bookending an amoral decade, were among the biggest selling albums in rock, not to mention their ever soaring greatest hits volume. The Eagles were the largest selling US rock band of the 1970s. This was augmented in late February 1980, when 'Heartache Tonight' took the Grammy Award for Best Rock Vocal Performance By A Duo or Group.

Springtime saw the release of two singles from *The Long Run*. 'The Sad Cafe' unfortunately failed to fly, but in mid-April 'I Can't Tell You Why', featuring Timothy Schmit on lead vocal, notched up another US Top Ten hit for the Eagles. It is perhaps only hindsight that lends ambiguity to this ballad's lyrics but they seem to allude poignantly to the fragile state of the band who, despite everything, had by now embarked on another tour.

Financially, the Eagles were living up to being America's biggest band by still earning a staggering $1 million per show, but they were in a blindingly bad way, and from their viewpoint the tour had disaster written all over it. The fans went home nightly, having been thoroughly entertained, completely oblivious to the fact that they might never see their heroes on stage together again. Bad blood was boiling over behind the band's public facade, pitting one Eagle against the other, often for reasons that no one could comprehend. The atmosphere was so aggressive that they had begun to communicate through intermediaries on their frazzled staff, who were walking on eggshells.

Everything was a source of intense irritation, and Don Henley now found the more raucous band antics grating on his nerves. He had never been one for making a public spectacle of himself. So, come early summer 1980, his tolerance levels had plummeted to zero. He later revealed: 'I'm not a priest or anything, but we had a bad enough reputation in rock as it was. I think, when you get on an airplane, go to a hotel or restaurant, you should behave like a human being.' The 'I'm not a priest' part was more than ever true. A free agent again, Henley was accruing an almost legendary reputation in Hollywood for his charismatic sexual prowess. A striking-looking, intense man of intriguing depth, he was even more a magnet for the ladies. But the tiring life was exacting a merciless toll. Henley called this period the darkest years. And certainly the Eagles nosedived to earth with a resounding thud as this latest tour came to a violent end.

After returning to the west coast of America, where they played a week-long series of shows at the Santa Monica Civic Auditorium, the Eagles' last concert that tour took place on 31 July 1980 at the Long Beach Arena, and was a benefit gig for Democrat senator Alan Cranston. That night the tenuous hold they had on their tempers disastrously snapped. Friction between Frey and Felder had been worsening before stepping out on stage, but as the gig progressed the atmosphere darkened so seriously that they began hurling abuse at each other. Glenn owned up: 'We were on stage and Felder looks back at me and says, "Only three more songs until I kick your ass, pal!" And I'm saying: "Great! I can't wait!" We were out there singing 'Best of My Love', but inside both of us were thinking – as soon as this is over, I'm gonna kill him!' The descriptive threats of just what each intended inflicting on the other after the gig grew so unrestrained that sound engineers hurried to switch off Glenn's vocal microphone to stop the audience from hearing what a beating up Frey and Felder wanted to mete out to one another. It wasn't bluster.

The audience applause was still echoing in the emptying arena when, having quit the stage, the two enraged Eagles flew at one another. Fists connected and complete mayhem ensued as the other Eagles piled in. In seconds, the entire band was embroiled in a bloody pitched battle of searing venom. Jaws cracked, knuckles bled and valuable instruments were wrecked in the violent eruption. Bill Szymczyk later remarked: 'The Eagles showed me the fine art of turning expensive acoustic guitars into kindling wood.' But that quip belied the profound shock backstage at the band's total loss of control. It eventually took dozens of hands to pull the wild-tempered, evenly matched men apart. In terrible turmoil, the five went their breathless, bruised and livid separate ways that night, each trying to avoid acknowledging what their shaking road crew now knew – that the writing was on the wall for the Eagles.

Indeed, it quickly became obvious that that violent release of stoked-up tension had not resolved a thing. They were not going to be able to put it behind them and paper over the cracks, which more resembled yawning chasms, and further pressure was set to worsen matters. The Eagles owed the record company one more album. Obviously, in the crippling climate, creating a new studio offering was out of the question, and so they decided to put together a live album with cuts taken from their recent tour, and from an LA Forum gig in 1976. Even collaborating on this project was extremely difficult.

When Henley, Felder, Walsh and Schmit headed to Miami in late summer 1980 to begin studio work on this live album, Frey remained resolutely in Los Angeles. According to Irving Azoff, Asylum Records tried dangling the carrot that if the album could just contain a couple of new Eagles' songs, they would stump up an extra $2 million advance. But Frey still wasn't tempted into the fold. Don Felder revealed: 'Glenn refused to participate as a group member. We flew tapes back to LA, and he went into the studio with his own engineer. He did his part, then mailed the tape back.' Bill Szymczyk later remarked that the three-part harmonies had come about 'courtesy of Federal Express'.

The *Eagles Live* double album was released in November 1980. *Melody Maker* said of it: 'The halcyon days of *Hotel California* are over and *Eagles Live* only serves to reinforce that observation.' The fans, though, were not prepared to concur, and the new release reached number 24 in Britain, but number six in America; like *The Long Run*, it went multi-platinum. In their fragmented state it was, however, impossible for the Eagles to draw any joy from this success, and Don Henley had his hands full of unexpected trouble when he found himself under arrest.

Henley was apprehended in his Hollywood home when, in the early hours of 21 November 1980, police arrived to discover a naked 16-year-old girl suffering from a drug overdose. At the party the cops also found a quantity of various drugs; Don was charged with possession of marijuana, cocaine and Quaaludes, and with contributing to the delinquency of a minor. He was fined $2,000, given two years' probation and ordered to attend a drug counselling scheme, but the incident was just too juicy to die down quietly.

Initially, Don refused to comment publicly on the bust, deeming that what went on within the walls of his home was his sole business, provided he was not harming anyone. But this attitude only sparked more interest in the event, and eventually he spoke out.

According to Henley the truth of what happened never came out. Although loath to go into precise detail, he spoke to journalists about how, curiously, some fire department officers had first turned up at his house that night. These people said that while, strictly speaking, they were obliged to take the girl to hospital to be checked over, if he would take care of her they would leave it at that. The firemen apparently also said that they were not out to get anyone busted, and Don was adamant that the 16-year-old was fine by the time the firemen turned up. Henley would have preferred not to give this episode any oxygen of publicity, but bluntly he confessed: 'I had no idea how old she was. I had no idea she was doing that many drugs. I did not have sex with her. Yes, she was a hooker. Yes, I'd called a madam. There were roadies and guys at my house.'

Not long afterwards he admitted that, emotionally, he had been at the bottom of the barrel when that bust took place. And why? A combination of reasons, but primarily because by then Glenn had telephoned, telling him that he was quitting the Eagles. Frey had then gone on to let the rest of the band know. Said Felder: 'Glenn didn't want any more to do with us.' Frey had not come to this momentous decision lightly, but he had known for some time before the fisticuffs backstage at the Long Beach Arena, that he could not take much more of the way the band had become.

Things had changed too much, and the pressure he felt was enormous. 'Don and I didn't have time to enjoy our friendship,' said Glenn. 'We always had to worry about doing this or living up to that.' Frey described himself and Henley as living 'in mutual darkness' at that time, and revealed that it had, unsurprisingly, become harder to write together.

Within the Eagles, Frey had been a kind of director of player personnel, but latterly, the effort that took did not seem to be appreciated. He revealed: 'I couldn't understand all these disturbances from the others in the band, because I was subordinating myself. Why couldn't somebody else see their way to taking a step back? That really grated on me. They didn't make subordinating myself worthwhile anymore.'

Glenn went round in circles about quitting the band in which he had been such an engine. But in the final analysis he looked forward at the start of the 1980s, and could not face a whole decade in which the Eagles might bash their pan in to produce maybe three albums – not when making albums debilitated them so much. Frey frankly needed more involvement with music than he had allowed himself for a long time now. Friends were constantly approaching him to produce their records, and a variety of projects seemed vastly more appealing than being locked into working with one outfit, however precious it had once been to him. The thought of going solo stimulated him, and the prospect of letting go of the task of dealing with band tensions and intrigues considerably lightened his heart. The Eagles had had one of the most intense internal band relationships in music, and that lit powder keg was a burden Frey needed to be rid of. 'I realised the Eagles were running my life,' he later said.

Deep down, Don Henley knew that his long-time close friend had had, as he put it, 'a belly full' of the strife in the band. For all the strain and pressure, Don could not hold back on revealing how selfless Glenn had always been. Describing his songwriting partner as a great captain, Henley spoke publicly years later about how Frey had forever encouraged band members to flourish, to come to the fore – something that eventually had drained him of too much. Don declared: 'Glenn was sacrificing a lot of his creativity to placate other people's egos.' According to Henley, an extraordinary amount of time, thought and energy had gone into keeping the Eagles as democratic as possible – a great deal of metaphoric hand-holding, caring for everybody's emotional wellbeing. And that had squeezed out time and energy to be musically creative.

He said: 'Glenn didn't get the chance to express himself artistically, and after a while that began to bother him. And we both grew tired of babysitting the other guys' needs. It's the burden of leadership – eventually your subjects hate you, even if they're living real well.'

The Eagles were exhausted from the crazy demands brought on by their worldwide fame and the punishingly decadent way some had lived the high life. The acrimony between them as they split up became legendary. Henley recalled uprisings he considered to have been generated by some of the guitar players, admitting that at times it drove him wild. He acknowledged, too, that it had been significant once he and Frey were no longer so firmly on the same side, but he insisted categorically that the Eagles' split had *not* primarily occurred because of the rift between himself and Glenn. There were, he bluntly admitted, rifts and factions throughout the band.

Although *The Long Run* was a strong commercial success, at the back of the Eagles' mind throughout its creation was the weight of expectation on them to better *Hotel California*. Inwardly they knew that they had seen their finest hour, and that as both collaborators and friends they were drifting inexorably apart. But still, Glenn Frey's defection came as a bombshell. Said Don Henley: 'I just wasn't expecting it. The group splitting up really sent me over the edge. I was shocked and hurt, and I was lost for a while, drinking heavily, doing a lot of drugs.' Two decades on, the drummer spoke candidly about the part drugs had played. 'They brought out the worst in our personalities and eroded our objectivity. But I've never been so down that I couldn't get up.' Henley admitted that back then, in their twenties and thirties, they had revelled in the darkness. 'We weren't afraid of it. Dark and light, yin and yang. Without one, the other is meaningless.'

While the Eagles constituted a powerful unit to which each

member brought a wealth of talent, when Bernie Leadon and Randy Meisner had quit, they had been replaced. Yet when Glenn Frey decided to walk, the band broke apart, and it is hard not to acknowledge that he was the glue that had held them together.

Like Henley, Don Felder was completely floored when Frey called time on his involvement with the Eagles. 'I remember how devastated we all were,' said Felder. 'It was like getting hit in the face from out of nowhere. The bottom dropped out of everything!' Felder and Frey had fought ferociously on the night it all caved in at the end of their last tour, but despite the heartfelt spleen at that time, Don Felder clearly hadn't decided that the Eagles were over. Once he stopped reeling from the shock that Glenn wanted to go solo, he put his head together with the others. Felder admitted: 'We were all clinging to the hope of changing Glenn's mind. We figured he'd do his solo record, then consider re-forming the band.'

It is Felder's opinion that the feuds in the Eagles had never been rooted in individual egos clashing, but rather in concerns for the quality of work being produced. He confessed that many conflicts had erupted over what was the best artistic way to proceed. The Eagles had become so big that the weight of their own success was almost frightening. To Felder, fear of not forever excelling themselves had restricted them, creating a tendency to play it safe, which in turn stifled creativity. They had always set themselves incredibly high standards, but in doing so had built a mountain that was difficult to climb in such strained circumstances. It was a self-perpetuating pressure that Felder described as 'often unbearable'. Years later, however, he so missed the other Eagles, he once quipped: 'It's like a divorced guy, missing his ex-wife', meaning you only nostalgically remember the good times.

Joe Walsh had always kept one foot in his solo career, and so had a less intense view of the disintegration. He was fully aware, though, that *Hotel California*'s colossal popularity had made the Eagles 'very paranoid'. Wherever they turned, people seemed to bombard them with questions as to how they were going to top that.

Timothy Schmit, meantime, knew there was now no hiding place. He rented an enormous plush house in Los Angeles and had been looking forward to becoming independently wealthy. He had optimistically chosen to overlook the obvious strains in the Eagles when he had joined them in 1977, but in truth had watched the band crumble around him. 'I watched it chip away,' he recalled. 'People's personalities got in each other's way. Being in a band is sort of like being in kindergarten. It's a struggle for power and dealing with each other's personalities.' That said, on the subject of the Eagles actually grinding to a halt Schmit admitted: 'It was a bit of a shock to me. I was just starting to enjoy the fruits of my labour with the band.'

Possibly the only person not to be shocked was Irving Azoff. The manager had watched one mini explosion follow another in the Eagles. On occasions, the fallout had resulted in a personnel change. When the boat had rocked, he had settled for stepping discreetly back and waiting for it to steady again. This time, though, was different.

It is perhaps no surprise that Don Henley seemed to take the break-up the worst. Over the years he was certainly the one who spoke remarkably emotionally about it. He admitted that although the Eagles' separation in the early 1980s turned out to be a good thing in the end, at the time he felt his life was over. 'I'd had this other half all those years,' explained Don, referring to Glenn. 'I felt very alone. I was wondering how I was going to replace him in my creative life.' Don Henley, of course, went on to carve a very successful solo career, but he couldn't see it right then. By his own admission, his consumption of whisky increased, and life went from bad to worse. In fact, 1980 was a dreadful trail of depressing events for Henley. He had no special girlfriend, the Eagles were split up, he had the run-in with the law, and he was almost killed in a private plane crash in Colorado. John Lennon's shocking murder on 8 December also had a profoundly negative effect on Don.

The private pain, strain and confusion suffered by the band remained concealed, however. On 30 January 1981, at the American Music Awards held at the ABC-TV studios in Hollywood, the Eagles took the trophy for the Favourite Pop/Rock Band, Duo or Group, and *Eagles Live* clinched the award for Favourite Album in the Pop/Rock category. 'Seven Bridges Road', written by Steve Young, the only song not to have previously appeared on an Eagles' studio album, was released in America as a single and reached number 21 in early February. But it couldn't be business as usual.

Timothy Schmit couldn't envisage the Eagles taking flight ever again. 'I never thought lightning would strike twice,' he said. Glenn Frey later told journalists starkly: 'There will never be a Greed and Lost Youth tour'. And when asked what were the odds on the Eagles ever getting back together, Don Henley, almost a recluse in the early 1980s, famously declared that hell would freeze over first. The public would not know it officially until spring 1982, but the Eagles were over, and it looked terminal.

CHAPTER 8

Spreading Their Wings

IRVING AZOFF KNEW that the Eagles had definitely dissolved, at least for the foreseeable future, when Glenn Frey and Don Henley separately came to him in early 1982 with their respective solo albums. Each man exuded an air of not needing the band anymore, and through listening to these individual works, Azoff gleaned a poignant glimpse of the differing ways in which the two stars had fared in the previous two years. In Glenn's case it was clear that walking away from the Eagles had indeed been an act of self-preservation. After the brawl backstage at the Long Beach Arena in 1980, he headed fast for the house he owned on Kauai's north shore in Hawaii, not for the first time desperately hoping to heal in idyllic surroundings. In 1982 he revealed: 'The whole time the Eagles were together I can count the number of two-week vacations I had on one hand, and all of those weren't holidaying, so much as hospitalising myself on a beach.'

Any public utterance flying around about the Eagles had tended to feed the sense of acrimony between the former friends, but Frey preferred to shut his mind off to the dark phase they had gone through towards the end. 'I don't look back in anger,' he maintained, 'because I'm trying to not look back at all!' Frey had always believed in quitting when at the top, and had determinedly needed to lighten up – to get enjoyment out of music once more. Although he'd been the dynamo within the Eagles and was inherently a team player, he was also a schemer, and since he had quietly contemplated a time ahead when he could go solo, it was a task he'd set about with relish at the dawn of the decade. He had linked up with longstanding friends, songwriters Jack Tempchin and Bob Seger, to help him come up with a blend of mid-tempo rock numbers and infectious ballads that spoke eloquently of love cherished and love lost, of deceit and anxiety.

When Glenn had marshalled his most promising musical ideas, he had called together some musicians and cut a few demo tapes. Each song took three takes, and work spread over only two days. He came away with somewhat rough versions, but they served their purpose. The last thing Frey wanted was to immerse himself in one obsessive task. So he broke away from nurturing the seeds of this potential album to produce records for Karla Bonoff and Lou Ann Barton. Of the latter artiste he explained: 'I ran into Jerry Wexler in New York, and he got me involved in that album. I scouted her in Dallas, loved what I heard and spent the summer of '81 working with Jerry and her down in Muscle Shoals.'

The actual environment of the famous Muscle Shoals Sound Studios in County Sheffield, Alabama, made a lasting impression on Frey, as did the rhythm musicians he met there. Glenn declared these guys to be the best in the business, and he made up his mind to record his first solo album at Muscle Shoals. He was also inspired to write two more tunes, specifically with the studio's rhythm section in mind, and was burning with enthusiasm when he re-teamed with Jack Tempchin in Los Angeles.

Once he had a clutch of ten numbers, Glenn headed back to Muscle Shoals and settled in with drummer Roger Hawkins, bass player David Hood, guitarist Duncan Cameron and others. In the Eagles, Don Felder and Joe Walsh had latterly dominated the intricate lead guitar work so synonymous with the band, but Glenn Frey was no mean lead guitarist. With style and taste, he'd handled solos that had embroidered the Felder/Walsh hurricane in the Eagles, but he had stepped out of that particular limelight on purpose. Now with his own album, he nailed all the lead guitar parts himself. Modestly, Frey confessed to not having what he termed 'the greatest quiver' as a rock lead guitarist, saying he did not always bend the strings absolutely the right way, but he got the job done. Yet his lead guitar solo in 'I Volunteer' on this solo album was hailed as expressive style at its best.

Seeing the album take shape gave Glenn a sense of satisfaction. It had a decided R&B flavour, contained classic rockers such as covers of the Huey Smith and John Vincent song, 'Sea Cruise', and 'I've Been Born Again', by Don Davis and James Dean. Frey opted for a Spanish guitar lilt for 'She Can't Let Go', one of the five songs he and Jack Tempchin co-composed. Backing vocals for the raw, energetic 'Partytown', were provided by a motley crew of celebrities and Frey's friends, including John McEnroe, Jimmy Buffett and Irving Azoff. According to Frey, Azoff didn't clap his hands like the others. 'He slapped his wallet!' insisted Glenn. 'True – I couldn't make that up!' 'All Those Lies' was the only solo Glenn Frey composition; it was a song whose lyrics smacked of paranoia and desperation. To avoid such negative emotions infiltrating the recording studio, Frey set himself a hard and fast rule to work in two-week bursts, then break away and live a little, to ease any tension.

He was all too familiar with how being cocooned in a studio begins to wear, and it was essential to him to keep a spring in his step. Making a record, he declared, 'should be uplifting, not a drag'. At the same time, once in the studio his concentration was total, and the fact that Muscle Shoals Sound Studios was in a dry county contributed to this work ethic. There was zero nightlife. Glenn discovered he would have to drive miles into Tennessee to get even a mixed drink. So it was get up, work, home and bed with no – or few – distractions. Frey remained upbeat. The man who had had inexhaustible energy gradually recovered the enthusiasm that had been smothered latterly in the Eagles. He had also shaken free of the obsession with making perfect records, realising he could rely on his own judgement. 'I know what sounds good,' he said.

When asked if he consciously wrote commercial material, with his trademark lack of pretentiousness Frey replied: 'You bet!' He'd no interest, he said, in making records of limited elitist appeal. He was highly competitive in a cut-throat business. That said, he retained the highly critical ear that had been invaluable in the Eagles, and he was ruthless with material. If a song did not do anything for him after a couple of weeks, it was jettisoned. For this first solo album he roped in Jim Ed Norman and Allan Blazek to help him co-produce. 'Producer is such a nebulous term,' said Frey. 'I found out when producing that the more the artiste knows, the less you have to do.' As a skilled arranger, Glenn knew exactly what he wanted when he went into the studio, but he was flexible. He had a game plan, but 'I can coach during the game too,' he said.

Throughout this whole spell, it impinged strongly on Glenn that he was in a new cycle. Ten years earlier, he had been a gimlet-eyed 23-year-old, seeking to take the music world by storm. At 33, in 1981, he'd been there, done that. 'I was a good solider of nine years. Fuck that!' he declared. 'I want a saner life, where I'm more in control.'

When his album was ready, Frey pondered long over its title – his irrepressible sense of humour making him toy with *Prelude to Obscurity* or *Do You Know Who I Used to Be?* In the end, he opted for *No Fun Aloud*, and Frey's first foray as a solo artiste was launched on the Asylum Records label in late May 1982. On the one hand, he didn't think the album sounded much like an Eagles' effort; on the other, he hoped to have created a sound that would make people feel that they knew this guy.

No Fun Aloud made number 32 in the American album chart and went gold. The first single from it, the touching love song, 'I Found Somebody', went one place higher than the album in July. Near the end of the year, 'The One You Love' rose to number 15, marking Frey's best placing, since 'All Those Lies' would stop just outside the US singles Top 40 a few weeks later. It was a respectable solo debut, but most important to Glenn, he was thoroughly enjoying life, especially being his own boss, and by autumn 1982 he was talking of touring. He had no illusions of packing outdoor giant stadiums like the Eagles had; his sights were more modestly set on 3000-seater halls.

By the time Frey was becoming invigorated at the prospect of fronting a road band for live gigs as a solo artiste, Don Henley's first solo album had hit the shelves. But his path back into the public eye had been vastly more fraught. Having been numbed by the Eagles' break-up, Henley's reclusive attitude had initially shrunk his world. It took a while, but eventually he admitted that Glenn had been right. It *had* been time for the band to fold. Right then, though, Don was disturbed by it. He had concentrated literally on the home front – for one thing, having a new house built. It was designed in a sturdy, stucco Mediterranean style, and the perfection that went into every aspect meant it took almost two years to construct to Henley's satisfaction. He also read avidly, and took to spending a lot of time in his home state of Texas.

But music had been in Henley's veins for too long for him to just turn his back on it, and ideas had begun to stir in his head. The problem was, he had never planned on being a solo artiste, and so had never given any thought as to how he would go about it. Plus, when immersed in music, it had never ceased to be a round-the-clock worry to him. He would even fret in his sleep. He had to ask himself: did he really want to go back to worrying about material, its quality, its performance, how his peers would see it? He had had a belly full of feeling criticised, maligned and even misunderstood as an Eagle. The merciless scrutiny that falls on any star branching out solo from a successful band was daunting; Henley had to wonder if he was ready for it yet.

In a sense, Don dipped a toe back into the water when he briefly linked up professionally with ex-lover Stevie Nicks to duet with her on the ballad, 'Leather And Lace', which reached number six in America in January 1982. But an important component of Henley's future came in the shape of veteran Los Angeles session musician, Danny Kortchmar, who had enjoyed a long and successful professional partnership with singer-songwriter, James Taylor. 'It was lucky for me that Danny came along,' admitted Don. 'He helped me to define myself as a solo artiste.' Kortchmar became Henley's new creative partner, going some way to filling the void left by Glenn Frey.

Henley's ideas had been formulating more tangibly throughout 1981, although songs were as yet in the embryonic stage, but he decided to set up jam sessions at his home. Danny Kortchmar later recalled: 'Don rounded up the usual suspects – anybody who could write or play. I thought Don could get a lot funkier and meaner. The Eagles had always been very controlled. It was a stretch for Don, but he was ready for it.'

Similar to how Henley and Frey had operated, when this new team settled in, Kortchmar created music tracks and Henley wrote lyrics over them. Danny quickly discovered that Don looked for immediacy. Something either hit the spot with him, or it left him cold. 'He flies by the seat of his pants!' declared Danny. It was a tricky, nervy time for Henley. In Danny Kortchmar he had made a fruitful connection, though not always a plain sailing one. Henley valued what became a musical brotherhood of two, which lasted for the decade ahead, but he would describe their professional relationship as 'sometimes blissful, sometimes stormy'. Apart from that, despite the boost provided by having a new cohort, Henley's self-confidence was still low. 'I was floundering at the beginning,' he revealed.

That very insecurity, however, provided a pain that prompted Don creatively to put together an urgently stark song collection. Though including some infectious ballads, overall it adopted an aggressively acerbic lyric tone. Henley co-composed two songs with JD Souther, and one with Bob Seger, but the lion's share of songwriting collaboration was with Danny Kortchmar and cynicism, poignancy, vulnerability, regret and animosity hallmarked the album.

Social commentary stamped a new wave style number called 'Johnny Can't Read', while in 'Them And Us', Henley pushed to the fore the threat to the world from weapons of mass destruction. 'The Unclouded Day', written by J K Alwood and J F Kinsey, and arranged by Henley and Kortchmar, was a throwback to cowboy-country rock. 'Talking To The Moon', penned by Henley and JD Souther, which conjured up a sleepy Texas town and a lonely guy struggling to get over a broken romance, was wistful vintage Eagles. Henley included a Celtic pipes/woodwind instrumental called 'La Eile'. One of the two standout tracks was 'I Can't Stand Still', about a man riven with jealousy, tormented by imagining his woman in the arms of another guy which exposed Henley's continuing mistrust, in song, of women. 'Dirty Laundry' was the other, a withering anti-media rant in which Don's incisive wit shone from beginning to end. No one could accuse Henley of not saying what he means and meaning what he says.

Drafting in Greg Ladanyi to co-produce with himself and Danny Kortchmar, Henley headed into Record One Studios in Sherman Oaks, California, where, over time, he was joined by two ex-Eagles. Timothy Schmit played bass on 'Nobody's Business', and sang backing vocals on four numbers, including 'I Can't Stand Still' and 'Dirty Laundry'. Joe Walsh played guitar on the future hit single, which attacked the media. Don Felder was not involved in this solo album, and Don Henley and Glenn Frey had not seen one another in over a year.

Although Henley had begun to edge out into the limelight again, he went through a very tough time. Putting together his first solo work gave him 'a reason to go on'. Unfortunately, some of the fuel came from the bottle. 'I drank a lot of Scotch making *I Can't Stand Still*,' admitted Don – not that that surprised him. He called it a habit of his to go a bit crazy when embarking on an album. He had finally come to acknowledge that he would deliberately create turmoil for himself in order to force all his feelings, however frighteningly raw, to the surface, so that he could feed on them, draw creative inspiration from his own anguish. Don did not have his troubles to seek. It later emerged that the lady in his life at this time, Maren Jensen, was suffering from the debilitating effects of Epstein-Barre Syndrome, from which she has since recovered.

Ten years younger than Henley, the blue-eyed, brown-haired Maren had been born in Glendale, California, into a non-theatrical family – her father was a physician. After majoring in theatre arts for three years at UCLA, her beauty and stunning figure had drawn her into modelling. As a top fashion model, she had graced the front covers of *Cosmopolitan* and *Seventeen*. Just before becoming involved with the ex-Eagle, Maren had moved into acting, having landed a role in the popular late 1970s TV series, *Battlestar Galactica*, although her talents also spread to writing and playing music. Maren had sung back-up vocals for Don on 'Johnny Can't Read', and as Don had helped nurse her through her illness, he held on to the hope that she would recover. In 1982 he told journalists that as soon as Maren was well, he hoped they would start a family together.

Domesticity was playing heavily on Henley's mind that spring. He owned a farm, and around his lovely new home he envisaged planting a garden, but come mid-August, he launched himself back into the media spotlight with the Asylum label release of *I Can't Stand Still*. It hadn't come easy, but Henley was proud of his solo debut. He said: 'After the album was completed I figured – yeah, I *can* do this!'

I Can't Stand Still reached number 24 in the US album chart. The first single release, 'Johnny Can't Read', stood outside the US Top 40 in September, and four months later the title track stalled at number 48. The release in between, 'Dirty Laundry', though creaking to a halt at number 59 in the UK singles chart, gave Henley a massively popular number three hit at home. 'Dirty Laundry' became a million seller, and went on to earn Henley a Grammy nomination for Best Rock Vocal Performance/Male. He had come out of seclusion with a bang. With debut solo albums from both Frey and Henley going gold, the focus inevitably settled on the other ex-Eagles.

Bassist Timothy Schmit had been caught off guard by the Eagles splitting up, and initially he went into session work. In 1982, his vocals could be heard harmonising on the Crosby, Stills & Nash album, *Daylight Again*. He recorded a cover version of the Tymes' song, 'So Much In Love', for the soundtrack to the 1982 teen comedy, *Fast Times At Ridgemont High*, starring Sean Penn and Jennifer Jason Leigh. Don Henley, Don Felder and Joe Walsh likewise had songs featured on this soundtrack album. Felder had also contributed a solo composition to the soundtrack to the 1981 comic strip/science fiction cartoon, *Heavy Metal*. Like Schmit, Felder would take time to spread his wings into releasing a solo album. Joe Walsh had always maintained that form of independent outlet.

In summer 1980, Joe's solo song, 'All Night Long', had cracked the US singles Top 20, and in May 1981 he'd released another solo album, *There Goes the Neighborhood*, on

Asylum Records. Of its eight tracks, Joe had solely composed five numbers, having linked up with old friends, Joe Vitale and Kenny Passarelli, for two songs. 'Rivers (of the Hidden Funk)' was a collaboration with Don Felder. 'A Life of Illusion' made number 34, and the self-produced album reached number 20.

Eagles' fans watching these individual machinations were hawklike in gauging individual chart performances. It was only ten years since the band's initial creation, and not so long since two of the original four members had left. Interest in what Bernie Leadon and Randy Meisner were up to, therefore, had not completely waned. Leadon seemed to have retrenched, re-teaming with old friends. In 1982 and 1984, he backed ex-Byrd Chris Hillman on a couple of releases before going on to form a Christian bluegrass band, called Ever Call Ready, with Hillman, Al Perkins, Jerry Scheff and Dave Mansfield. In 1985, the group issued an eponymous album on the A&M label. Randy Meisner, on the other hand, had ventured further into solo territory. Following on his 1980 album, *One More Song*, on whose title track both Glenn Frey and Don Henley provided backing vocals, the bass player released *Randy Meisner* on Epic Records in August 1982.

Flying solo came far from naturally to Meisner, who had preferred as much as possible to be the invisible man during his tenure with the Eagles. Talking of that painful shyness, he said: 'It was a hard thing to get rid of. Nowadays, I'm taking a stand, growing up. I had to stick my neck out and give it a shot. That's how I will learn.' Randy picked off a Top 30 hit with 'Never Been In Love' from that eponymous album. Meisner's solo work was clearly reminiscent of the Eagles' sound. But the nearest that fans got to having their band together again was when Asylum Records released *Eagles Greatest Hits – Vol 2* in October 1982. Disappointingly, it dropped anchor at number 52 but, over time, this compilation would go 11 times platinum.

This indication of the continuing strength of the Eagles' popularity had the record label practically gnashing its teeth that the band had broken apart. No matter what each Eagle could achieve individually, they were always going to be stronger together. Unsurprisingly, the band was bombarded with highly lucrative offers to reunite, an issue that grew to be hugely frustrating for some of them. In 1983, Don Felder explained: 'We've been offered millions to do shows again. Henley, Walsh, Timmy and I are all for it. We'd like to get back together, make a record and do a tour. But then we call Glenn about these offers and he doesn't want to know. We're on hold, waiting for Glenn. We can't do it without him.'

The maestro musician was equally candid publicly about the fact that Frey had consciously thrown up an invisible but impregnable firewall between himself and the other ex-Eagles. According to Felder, those four talked to one another, but there was a serious lack of communication between them and Frey. He also made it clear, however, that he would like to regain contact with Glenn. Felder, in fact, continued to think long of his former bandmates. He wasn't wearing rose-tinted glasses. He had not forgotten that there had been what he termed 'some awful stuff', but he never allowed that to erase the good elements of having been in the Eagles. He fully expected, were the band ever to reunite, that there would be battles. But it still stimulated him to anticipate a time when they could stage a comeback.

Throughout 1982 and into 1983, Felder burrowed away recording in his home studio between guesting on albums for the Bee Gees, Diana Ross, Stevie Nicks, Joe Walsh and others. At first he was reluctant to record a solo album. Taking responsibility for a whole album was something he confessed he was afraid of. Talented as he is in his own right, it spooked him not to have Frey and Henley to rely on. But if Felder believed he needed that crutch, Irving Azoff was keen to disabuse him of the notion. It was the manager who enthusiastically coaxed and badgered Felder into trying out his solo wings.

Eventually coming round to the idea, Felder knuckled down with the guiding principle that he did not want to make a 1983 version of an Eagles album. What he came up with was very much a solo effort, in that out of the eight songs created, only two were written with a collaborator. He wrote 'Never Surrender' with Kenny Loggins, and 'Night Owl' with bassist George Perry and drummer Joe Vitale. Timothy Schmit sang backing vocals on 'Night Owl', as well as on 'Winners', 'Haywire' and 'Who Tonight'. When it was complete, Felder had put together a powerful, guitar-oriented pop/rock package that he titled *Airborne*. In advance of this debut solo album's release, he firmly knocked on the head any suggestion by the music press that he had waited so long to emerge with this work because he had felt intimidated by Frey and Henley launching new careers. 'I'm not comparing my album to theirs', he insisted. He also said that he had not produced a solo album for the money, revealing that financially he had done very well in the Eagles. This turned out to be fortunate, for when *Airborne* was released on Asylum Records in November 1983, it crash-landed at number 178 in the US album chart.

Five months earlier, Joe Walsh had released *You Bought It, You Name It*, which had stopped at number 48 and spawned a single, 'Space Age Whizz Kid', that didn't quite make the Top 50. After this, Walsh produced Ringo Starr's album, *Old Wave*, in 1984, the year in which Timothy Schmit at last made his debut in the solo arena. Timothy had toured with Jimmy Buffett, playing bars and providing back-up vocals. He had also featured on Buffett albums. In spring 1984, Schmit had then rejoined his old band, Poco, who that summer released the album, *Inamorata*. Its dismal chart performance, peaking at number 167 in America, hardly convinced Schmit that he was moving in the right direction. Unfortunately, when he struck out on his own later that same year, the signs were no more encouraging.

To put together nine tracks, Timothy had worked with a number of songwriters, including JD Souther, Josh Leo and Vince Melamed. Rita Coolidge sang vocals on a number called 'Gimme the Money', with Joe Walsh guesting on guitar. Walsh's distinctive playing also featured on 'Something's Wrong', on which Don Henley drummed and sang backing vocals. Henley also lent his percussion skills to 'Lonely Girl'. On release in October 1984, the clutch of songs embracing a wide range of musical styles did not catch on with the public, and *Playin' It Cool* was frozen out at number 160 in the US album chart before slipping into oblivion, dashing Timothy Schmit's hopes of making his mark.

In terms of solo endeavour, the success story throughout 1984 centred once again on Glenn Frey and Don Henley. At the same time, Frey was coming under fire from various angles for continuing to be the fly in the ointment regarding an Eagles reunion. Frey inimitably told *Billboard*: 'If the Eagles were to fart in a bag, the label would've tried to get a stereo mix and ask me what I wanted on the B-side!' Frey was being fingered by music magazines as the guy who recently rejected two lucrative US Festival offers for an Eagles reunion. He confirmed: 'The US Festival *did* twice offer us a lot of money, but money is not an issue. If the Eagles were to get back together, it would have to be for the right reasons.'

Journalists, too, were beginning to niggle at the man they had regarded as the Eagles' quarterback, about why he and Henley were not communicating. Glenn publicly praised Don, and made no bones about the fact that he greatly respected the drummer, but he said: 'The reason Don and I don't talk so much is because the Eagles were our common interest, not because we had any falling out.'

One potent reason why attempts to rope Frey into re-forming the Eagles failed was that he still enjoyed his freedom, and didn't hide his feelings on that score. 'I discovered that trying to guide people is more trouble than it's worth,' he said bluntly. 'It's a lot easier now that I'm running my own dictatorship, as opposed to being in a struggling democracy.' Flippantly, Frey quipped that his songs grew on people 'like warts'. But he held firm views on what an album's make-up should contain – 'action, tension, love scenes and places to relax'. He hoped he had come up with all these ingredients when putting together his second solo album, *The Allnighter*, a ten-track mix of styles ranging from the Memphis soul of 'I Got Love', to the chilling edginess of 'Smuggler's Blues'.

This time around Frey had co-composed two songs with Hawk Wolinski, but his main co-lyricist was again Jack Tempchin, with whom he had developed a sturdy rapport. 'I don't like writing alone,' said Glenn. 'I don't trust myself. You don't have to have the conversation with yourself: Is this good enough? Jack and I are completely honest with each other as far as criticism goes.' While Frey found it valuable to solicit other opinions, he is intrinsically a guy who trusts his gut instincts, and he was happy with this latest solo work. He was knocked back, however, when Asylum Records, now under new management, passed on *The Allnighter*, saying that it was not contemporary enough.

Asylum Records' decision puzzled music watchers. Frey's *No Fun Aloud* had, after all, gone gold, but then Glenn owned up that he just might have brought that rejection on himself because of a letter he had written to Elektra/Asylum chairman Bob Krasnow. Krasnow had been giving press interviews and, according to Frey, had told journalists: 'The label is not going to be a country-rock graveyard. This is a new company.' Feeling that the guy lacked a sense of history, Frey contacted Krasnow. Glenn stated: 'I photostatted a copy of that interview and wrote on the front of it: "Dear Bob, Don't ever come to LA or your fuckin' ass is mine!"' With some understatement, Glenn conceded that this move might have prejudiced Krasnow against him.

MCA quickly picked up the outspoken ex-Eagle's second solo album, and released *The Allnighter* in June 1984. It reached number 37 in America, and the following summer went six places higher in Britain. The first cut from it, 'Sexy Girl', peaked at number 20 in the US singles chart in August, although the title track bottomed out towards the end of the year at number 54. In January 1985, however, 'The Heat Is On', already picking off a number 12 hit in Britain, delighted Frey by rising to number two in America. The song had undoubtedly benefited from its inclusion in the rough-edged action comedy movie, *Beverly Hills Cop*, starring Eddie Murphy, one of the top grossing box-office draws of 1984.

In November 1984, another single from *The Allnighter*, 'Smuggler's Blues', went to number 12, but it had an impact on Frey's life that went beyond music, inasmuch as it sparked an acting career for him. In 1984, *Miami Vice* was a new US TV cop series in the pipeline. Created by Michael Mann and Anthony Yerkovich, and due to star Don Johnson and Philip Michael Thomas, the show would be one of the first TV series to use chart music as a central element, and shot in a rock video style. The makers of this trendy cop show contacted Frey when he was shooting the video for 'Smuggler's Blues'. Glenn explained: '*Miami Vice* was filming its first episode, and they wanted to get the show somehow involved in my video. They offered footage from the show at one stage, but in the end we were too rushed to work something out.'

Despite this missed opportunity, Mann rang Frey and invited him to lunch at Le Dome in Los Angeles. He had a proposition in mind. 'I went for the blue suit routine,' Glenn recalled, 'so he wouldn't think I was a rock 'n' roll weirdo, and I'm sitting at the bar awaiting the arrival of *Miami Vice's* executive producer, and in walks this guy in white Levis, sandals and a Hawaiian shirt!' According to Glenn, Michael Mann didn't ask him if he had ever acted in his life. Instead, Mann explained straight off that he had the concept for an episode of the show based on 'Smuggler's Blues', and told Glenn he would be perfect for the role of Jimmy Cole, a spaced-out junkie pilot.

Frey jumped at the chance, and subsequently made his acting debut playing Cole in the *Miami Vice* episode called 'Smuggler's Blues', which was screened on NBC-TV across America on 1 February 1985. This one acting experience gave Glenn food for thought. He queried: 'How long am I going to be able to go out on stage and play rock music and look young and vibrant? Acting is something I could do until I die.' Frey would have another connection to the popular cop show when Michael Mann asked him for a song for the opening episode of a new series. Frey wrote 'You Belong To The City', which gave him his second number two domestic hit single in September 1985. By that summer, he was back on the road in his day job, having left acting behind for now.

Rock Magazine declared that *The Allnighter* had 'truly established Glenn Frey as a serious solo artiste'. In 1984/85, Don Henley also confirmed his standing with the release of his second solo album, titled *Building the Perfect Beast*. On the one hand, Henley maintained that by the time he'd made this new album he had reclaimed some of his previously lost confidence. On the other, he admitted: 'There's part of me that would like to just go away and disappear tomorrow and *never* come back.' His attitudes were based on a mosaic of conflicting feelings, but he was adamant that he had shed the 'I'll show you' attitude, and that he didn't carry around quite so much anger anymore.

The legacy of the Eagles was still strong. 'The Eagles is a two-edged sword,' said Henley. 'I'm not trying to divorce myself completely. The songs I'm writing now are extensions of songs I wrote then.' Yet he continued to have difficulty thinking of himself as a solo performer. He had always been comfortable in a group. Even something so imbued in Don as songwriting was a baffling process to him. It might be argued that he had a tendency to over-think things, but when he completed a song he didn't really know how he had got there. 'It comes literally out of the air,' he maintained. 'It comes through me and it comes a lot from my subconscious.' Don described having a lot of 'brain chatter', which got very cluttered at times. So it was hardly surprising that he felt great relief whenever he was satisfied with a song.

Unlike when he and Frey had sat together to write, now Henley frequently liked to be left alone with material that a co-composer had come up with. He preferred to write with people who were content to give him a cassette tape of their offering, then leave him to it. For this new album Henley's collaborators were Danny Kortchmar, JD Souther and three members of the Heartbreakers, who had backed Tom Petty: guitarist Mike Campbell, keyboard player Benmont Tench and drummer Stan Lynch.

Henley's biggest hit from *Building the Perfect Beast* was 'The Boys Of Summer' and he recalled how the song almost wrote itself. Mike Campbell had given him a track that he played in his car, and inspiration had simply oozed forth. 'It came *screaming* out of me,' said Don. 'I was jumping up and down because I *knew* I had something there!' Before booking studio time, Henley always had to sing for a couple of weeks, to warm up his vocal cords. He called it beating them into shape, claiming he had one of those singing voices that the worse he treated it, the better it sounded.

His new record deal was with Geffen Records, and after stimulating studio sessions, *Building the Perfect Beast* was released in November 1984, peaking in the new year at number 13, one place higher than its UK best. In 1985, three singles, 'All She Wants To Do Is Dance', 'Not Enough Love In The World' and 'Sunset Grill' reached numbers nine, 34 and

22 respectively. But it was 'The Boys Of Summer', released in December 1984, that brought Don Henley most attention. The ballad, awash with the protagonist's memories of a very special girl and his inability to move on, hit number 12 in Britain, but number five in America, and won Henley the Grammy Award for Best Rock Vocal Performance/Male. The video for 'The Boys Of Summer', directed by Jean-Baptiste Mondino, went on to win Best Video, Best Art Direction, Best Cinematography and Best Director categories at the 2nd annual *MTV* Video Music Awards held in September 1985 at New York's Radio City Music Hall. *Building the Perfect Beast* stayed in the US album chart for over a year, and sold in excess of two million copies.

The success of this sophomore solo work nudged Don Henley into taking to the road. The prospect of doing live solo concerts both exhilarated and petrified him. His touring backing band contained all fresh faces. He had gone to LA clubs and spread the word that he was recruiting. Swamped with applicants, he had held a month-long series of auditions, during which he said his search for a lead guitarist was 'excruciating'. In the end he was happy, though. Henley was also pleased to be travelling with less exuberant types than he'd been used to. Said Don: 'They didn't get on airplanes and start throwing ice and shit.' His problems came from coping with his nerves about being the main focus. 'I'm not Mr Showbiz,' he said. 'Some nights I'd catch myself out front and go: "Jesus! What the *hell* am I doing? This isn't me!"'

In February 1986, when Henley picked off his first Grammy at the 28th annual Grammy Awards, Frey was also one of the nominees in the category Best Pop Vocal Performance/Male for 'The Heat Is On'. With Glenn and Don flourishing solo, it looked less likely that the Eagles would ever be birds of a feather again; moreover, it had been a lean time for the others. In summer 1985, Joe Walsh had released a solo album, *The Confessor*, which stalled at number 65. Don Felder switched focus entirely, to hosting and acting in *FTV*, a children's television variety show. He was also writing music for another children's programme called *Galaxy High*.

In the meantime, in spring 1985, yet another compilation, *The Best of the Eagles*, had charted at number eight in Britain, as the band's back catalogue went from strength to strength. Fame was fine, but the way in which celebrities were becoming increasingly venerated was worrying to a star community that was still stunned by John Lennon's senseless, cold-blooded murder. As far as Don Henley was concerned, a vastly disproportionate importance was being placed on stars. When one journalist put it to him defensively that Bruce Springsteen was worshipped because of his immense sincerity, Henley (who has nothing personally against Springsteen) replied: 'Fine. As long as they remember that he's also just a guy and he puts his pants on, one leg at a time.'

Henley's other grave concern was the lack of effective police protection provided to stars. This worry climaxed for him in the mid 1980s, when a disturbed guy rang him, having somehow got hold of his home telephone number. To Don, the young man was clearly doing a lot of drugs and going off the rails. He fixated on Don, found out where he lived, and started camping in the area outside his home. It was unsettling enough behaviour even before the night the guy telephoned to say that he was coming to get Don. Over the years, Henley had had his life threatened on several occasions, but he took special heed this time and called the police, who told him there was nothing they could actually do until the guy did 'get' him. 'That makes a lot of sense!' Don rapped back acerbically. 'I'll call ya when I'm fuckin' dead!'

By the end of 1985, Henley was at his ranch in Aspen, Colorado, where he held a New Year's Eve party that later drew much attention when it was claimed that at this busy bash the future Democratic presidential candidate, Gary Hart, first met his alleged mistress-to-be, Donna Rice.

Glenn Frey also had a home in Aspen, and by 1986 he was choosing to spend most of his time there, along with Janie, the lady in his life. Janie ran a gallery in Aspen, and Glenn was proud to praise it and her publicly. 'The gallery's called Janie Biggs' Fine Arts Limited and it's taken the town by storm,' he told journalists. 'Her last show exhibited a selection from Jack Nicholson's private collection – Chagall, Matisse, Picasso. Janie has taught me to appreciate art.' Settled into domesticity with Janie, the once rampant ladies' man had been altering his ways. He maintained that – leaving music out of the equation – everything of value he had learned in life, he'd learned from women. Moreover, now aged 37, he had renounced all abusive activities in favour of a clean living existence.

Frey was starting to toy with ideas for a third solo album. But what seized the attention of Eagles' fans and the music media in spring 1986, was the notion that a tiny chink might just have opened in Glenn's armour about the band reuniting. Glenn had admitted that, after the recent *MTV* awards, he and Don Henley had stayed up all night talking about getting together to write some songs once more. Maybe it was the party atmosphere, the Roederer Cristal champagne copiously flowing, or plain old-fashioned nostalgia, but the pair got up a head of steam imagining going back to collaborating as once they'd used to – catching a buzz, beer in hand, side by side at a piano.

Frey fuelled these enticing rumours by revealing: 'I think enough time's passed that the pressure wouldn't be as great as it once was. I really miss working with Don.' He also complimented Henley by confessing that he aimed someday to make a record to rival *Building the Perfect Beast*. But hopes of the Eagles taking flight again were dashed when Glenn equally claimed that to get back together would most likely dilute their achievements – their legend even. He didn't see himself in his forties, still singing 'Take It Easy' for the millionth time.

In 1987, Timothy Schmit released his second solo album, *Timothy B*, which sank at number 106 in America. Likewise, that August, Joe Walsh's *Got Any Gum* peaked at 113. Exactly one year later, Frey's third offering, *Soul Searchin'*, managed number 36, while in September 1988 the first single from it, 'True Love', charted in America at number 13. 'Living Right' petered out at number 90 in March 1989, and 'Two Hearts' didn't chime with the public at all.

In 1989, though, Frey's attention had again diverted to acting when he landed an extended guest role as Bobby Travis in the CBS-TV series, *Wiseguy*, created by Stephen J Cannell and Frank Lupo, starring Ken Wahl. By this time, Glenn had become so health conscious that he was now inspirational poster material at health clubs and gyms. Don Felder, having retreated from public view, devoted his time to his family, while one wondered if Timothy Schmit had taken a backward step by playing with the reunited Poco for their album *Legacy*.

For Don Henley, come 1989, fortunes were decidedly mixed. On 30 January, he had surprised many at the American Music Awards by stepping in to drum for Guns 'n' Roses when their drummer, Steven Adler, came down with the flu. Having completed his third solo album, *The End of the Innocence*, he declared that he was feeling real good. It had taken him eight years, he said, to get over the Eagles, but he'd got there, and had made what he termed 'the frightening adjustment' to being a solo artiste.

But the intervening years since the release of *Building the Perfect Beast* had held their personal turmoil, in that he and Maren Jensen had split up. He'd thought they were destined to commit to starting a family. 'I was evidently wrong,' he said. Yet, if marriage wasn't yet on the menu for Don Henley, he didn't necessarily count that as a bad thing. He'd watched some of his friends get hitched and promptly lose their creative edge because of their contentment. Don was definitely keen to discover a way of not having to go through hell in order to stay sharp and as ever, he wasn't afraid of the dark side he'd viewed so often now.

He did not advocate staring into a psychological or emotional abyss. He felt that living somewhere between deficiency and excess was the answer, but he continued to battle a deep-seated sense of insecurity. He maintained he was always reminded of Paul Simon's 1968 song, 'Fakin' It' – meaning, you think someday somebody is going to find out that you're not as good as your hype. It was strange. With his building solo track record, Henley ought to have exuded confidence, but getting the right mindset to come up with *The End of the Innocence* had been difficult. Out of this soul-baring he had emerged with one of his most revealing songs – 'The Heart of the Matter'. Usually so non-committal as to specific lyrical inspirations, he admitted that this number was extremely personal. It was wrought out of the break-up of his long, serious relationship with Maren Jensen. The words had had to be wrenched out of him at times. 'It took a few cocktails to get some stuff out, but I felt a lot lighter afterwards,' he confessed. He knew that it wasn't going to change a thing, but he had needed to get his raw feelings out in the open.

The End of the Innocence was released in June 1989. It lodged at 17 in Britain, but gave Henley a number eight hit at home. Released as a single, the title track likewise rose to number eight in the US in July. 'The End Of The Innocence' also brought him another Best Rock Vocal Grammy Award, while the album went multi-platinum.

Since the Eagles' break-up at the start of the decade, the course of each ex-member's fortunes had been interesting to track. But throughout, the question of whether the five would ever gell again had never gone away. Frey still did not want to know, and the others clearly didn't feel that they could go ahead without him.

Although Glenn Frey and Don Henley were each perfectly capable of successfully functioning separately, a kind of invisible umbilical cord seemed to exist between them. Henley stated frankly: 'He and I just happen to be a great combination.' As the 1980s began to evaporate, it didn't seem so certain that the Eagles would not, after all, take wing again.

CHAPTER 9

Rumour Has It...

IT MUST BE SAID that the signals emitting from Frey and Henley in the last quarter of 1989 about a possible Eagles reunion were decidedly mixed. Don revealed that he had renewed his offer to Glenn for the two of them to write songs together again, and Frey's response was that they should just stay in touch and see what happened – friendly, but non-committal. At the same time, Henley also declared that a reunited Eagles would not be the same, observing that 'you really can't go back and recreate that'. For all that, there were reports of studio try-outs taking place very quietly.

In the meantime, each Eagle carried on with his solo career, and Henley was in expansive mood. He declared: 'I've been doing this long enough that I'm starting to feel like an elder statesman, like I've done a pretty good body of work and that feels good.' Henley was certainly the most visible, having launched a major US solo tour in early August, on the back of *The End of the Innocence*. The tour reportedly cost in the region of $600,000 before even staging the first show, but Don was calmer than he had been in years. Introspective as ever, he spoke of being done with publicly testing his limits. 'I've got to a point in my life where I'm through with jumping off cliffs,' he said. 'The space I have to conquer now is inside me.'

Commencing in St Louis, Henley gigged all over America, taking in Cincinnati and Detroit, Frey's birthplace. Whereas Glenn was avidly pursuing a conspicuously healthy lifestyle, Don was still prone to the odd savage hangover on tour. The 1980s fitness craze encouraged people to treat their bodies as temples to worship and nurture. Creeping gingerly to his tour bus one morning, as if one wrong move would shatter him into a thousand tiny pieces, Henley quipped about abusing his body with the previous night's piss-up: 'It's my temple! If I want to tear it down, I will!'

Seven weeks into his solo tour, at the end of September 1989, fans flew into a fluster of excitement when Glenn Frey joined Henley on stage during a concert in Los Angeles. It was the first time the pair had performed publicly together since the Eagles split, and the reunion rumour mill immediately ground into action. Ignoring this rife speculation, Henley was more interested in raising the consciousness of the American people at large about what they were doing to the planet. He had always been sensitive to such issues, but in the 1990s he would become a high-profile environmentalist. He declared: 'This entire country is going to have to wake up to the fact that we have severely fouled our own nest – and it has to stop.'

Henley already belonged to the Texas wing of a nature conservancy group, and had thrown his weight behind the battle against the construction of a toxic waste incinerator near his hometown of Linden. In February 1990, he joined Paul Simon, Sting, Bruce Springsteen and others for a Rainforest benefit gig at the China Club in Hollywood, which raised over $1 million. One of Henley's strongest passions, however, was the Walden Woods Project, a non-profit organisation that he founded in 1990. It is dedicated to preserving the forest area surrounding Walden Pond in Massachusetts, where the 19th-century Concord-born writer, Henry David Thoreau, lived and worked. Don became immersed in Thoreau's writings when as a young man he had struggled to come to terms with his father having developed heart disease. 'Walden Woods is widely recognised as the cradle of the American environmental movement,' he said, 'and Henry David Thoreau is recognised as the father of that movement. I was appalled when I first heard that the place was in danger. You assume these places are protected.'

The project raised millions to enable the purchase of environmentally sensitive land around Walden Pond; fulfilment of its aims kicked off in 1990 with the successful acquisition of a 25-acre site known as Bear Garden Hill, which had been earmarked for the construction of a large condominium unit. Throughout the decade, further tracts of land were steadily bought up, thereby thwarting developers and real estate moguls. The groundswell behind the Walden Woods Project quickly gathered pace, and in 1994 Henley's 'baby' scored an important victory when the residents of Concord voted to shut down a landfill situated across from Brister's Hill. By 1996 the Walden Woods Project had purchased 96 acres of preserved land.

On 24/25 April 1990, as part of his solo tour, Don Henley played two benefit gigs for the project at the Centrum in Worcester, Massachusetts and over the two nights he attracted star support for his cause from the likes of actors Ed Begley Jr., Carrie Fisher and Don Johnson. But the huge talking point was that Henley was joined on stage by Glenn Frey and Timothy Schmit for an eight-song set. The sight of *three* ex-Eagles now performing together sent speculation of a fully-fledged reunion soaring sky-high. In July 1990, Schmit released another solo album, *Tell Me the Truth*, on which Henley was one of the producers. Prior to that, Joe Walsh began the new decade working as a DJ on New York's radio station, KROQ. During 1990, Walsh linked up with his former James Gang bandmates, Jim Fox and Dale Peters, for a television special in Cleveland called *The Class of 1970*.

The only reunion that the music media continued to fixate on, however, was an Eagles one. Again it emerged that Henley had raised the idea with Frey of their collaborating on a couple of songs for a possible new Eagles greatest hits compilation. Glenn visited Don for a meeting-cum-get-together, at which relations were pretty good. Afterwards Henley would only divulge: 'This Eagles thing is a day at a time. I wouldn't venture to make any predictions.' Journalists couldn't directly prise a cheep out of Glenn Frey on the subject, and when they turned to Irving Azoff, he told them: 'Glenn wants to conduct his on-again/off-again relationship with Henley in private,' adding tantalisingly, 'but on Glenn's behalf, I would say Don and he are speaking.'

By the end of the year, both Frey and Henley received honours. The Rock 'n' Charity Foundation recognised Glenn for work he had avidly undertaken to help prevent Aids and cancer. Don received the People For The American Way's Spirit of Liberty Award, at Los Angeles' Beverly Wilshire Hotel, cited for his anti-censorship and pro-environmental efforts.

For Frey, life had been steadily changing, and in 1991 he became a father with the birth of a daughter to his wife, Cindy. In April, his solo song, 'Part of Me, Part of You', reached number 55 in the US singles chart and featured that year in the offbeat Ridley Scott feminist road movie, *Thelma and Louise*. About the same time, Joe Walsh produced his latest solo work, *Ordinary Average Guy*. Then in May he played two acoustic benefit gigs in his home town of Wichita to help raise money for the area's Tornado Relief Fund. For Eagles' fans focused on the band re-forming, solo endeavours spilled frustratingly into 1992.

Timothy Schmit joined Joe Walsh along with Todd Rundgren, Dave Edmunds and Nils Lofgren on Ringo Starr's All Starr Band tour, and Walsh released the album, *Songs for a Dying Planet*, in August 1992. Meantime, Don Henley joined Mojo Nixon on stage to perform Nixon's song, 'Don Henley Must Die', at a Mojo Nixon gig at the Hole in The Wall in Austin, Texas. Referring to Henley's nerve at participating in such a provocatively titled song, Nixon declared: 'Henley has balls the size of church bells!'

Glenn Frey released his fourth solo album, *Strange Weather*, which he promoted with a tour in late summer 1992. Come October, he was happy to be back in Detroit to play at the Palace, marking his first performance in his home city for seven years. Though reporters queued up to ask him when he would re-form the Eagles, Frey made no bones about enjoying the experience of taking his solo act on the road. 'Touring is different nowadays,' he stressed. 'I'm more interested in sleep and gold, and less interested in staying up late and making a name for myself.' He also plainly believed in delivering the goods to the fans, faithful from the first. 'A fair portion of the show is Eagles' songs,' he said. 'People want to hear them and it's not fair to be so self-indulgent as to say, "I'm not in the Eagles, so I don't do Eagles' songs now."'

Away from the stage, Glenn was happy in his private life, and still invested a good portion of his time in charity work. Through an organisation called the Grassroots Aspen Experience, he and his wife particularly gave their free hours to helping underprivileged children to visit the wilderness. Glenn said at the time: 'It's taken about three and a half years to reorganise my life, but a lot of good things are happening for me.' Frey had never lost his touch as a born communicator, and it was a natural extension of that gift when he took on the role of temporary tutor at UCLA in Los Angeles, lecturing on songwriting over a two-month course. His wife was pregnant with their second baby and he wanted to stay close to home.

Ronnie Rubin, director of UCLA's entertainment and performing arts department, was thrilled when the ex-Eagle agreed to take the weekly songwriting classes. Said Rubin: 'Glenn was very concerned about having a manageable sized group. He wanted people who were seriously committed to writing songs, as he wants to have an impact on their lives.' Frey was an unorthodox, enthusiastic and highly motivating teacher, and because his class size was limited to 20, he could devote individual attention to everyone. He told his students upfront: 'You can't teach creativity, and you can't show somebody how to summon inspiration. It is a pretty unpredictable set of circumstances that leads to the creation of a song. But there is a lot to have in your mind, so that you are ready when the time comes.'

In spring 1993, Frey was ready to go out on a twin-billed US tour with Joe Walsh, performing to sell-out crowds. In July, *Glenn Frey Live* was released, having been recorded the previous summer at the Stadium in Dublin, Ireland. It didn't chart, and Frey's sporadic acting career suffered an embarrassing setback in 1993, when a TV show flopped in which he had the lead role. The TV drama series, *South of Sunset*, had been created by Stan Rogow, and was to have been a vehicle for Glenn Frey as Cody McMahon, a film studio security chief who starts up The Beverly Hills Detective Agency. Frey's co-stars were Maria Pitillo and Aries Spears, but the show was cancelled after only one episode when its debut received a 6.1 Nielsen rating – believed to be the lowest debut in major network television history. Glenn did care about the mishit, but in 1993 he found more than enough joy at home when his first son was born. In time, he was followed by another son.

On the political front, things by now were looking up, and both Frey and Henley had reasons to be cheerful. After their two decades supporting the Democrats' cause, Bill Clinton had swept into the White House in November 1992, ousting Republican George Bush. The charismatic, dynamic young president held his Presidential Inaugural Ball in Washington D.C. in January 1993, and Don Henley was one of the special guest performers.

For several intensive months, Henley had had his rampant environmentalist hat back on, and on top of his passionate commitment to the Walden Woods Project, he had founded the Caddo Lake Institute, a privately operating, non-profit, scientific foundation formed to protect Caddo's wetlands ecosystem. Caddo Lake, where Don's father had taken him fishing as a small boy, straddles the northeast Texas and northwest Louisiana line and as the only naturally formed lake in Texas, it is home to hundreds of species of plants and animals. The lake also has the largest variety of fish in a Texas body of water. Everything from alligators to bald eagles make their home at Caddo Lake, which is named after the Indians of the Kadohacho tribe, who inhabited the area in the 16th century.

This cause did not enjoy the same high profile as the Walden Woods Project, but was no less dear to Don Henley. 'Caddo is much more significant as an ecological treasure, regardless of my childhood attachment to it,' he said. 'This lake is always under threat from exploitation. It's a common treasure that belongs to everyone.' In 1993, Caddo Lake was officially designated a wetland of national importance by Bruce Babbitt, the Secretary of the Interior.

It would have been easy to believe that all these environmental, charitable and solo endeavours had suffocated the prospect of the Eagles ever re-forming, regardless of the regular rumours over the past many years. But in fact, it was a charity album to benefit Walden Woods that started the ball rolling towards the long-awaited comeback. The album was *Common Thread: The Songs of the Eagles*, released in November 1993 on Irving Azoff's Giant Records label. Some of America's hottest country music stars, including Clint Black, Suzy Bogguss, Alan Jackson, Tanya Tucker, Vince Gill and Travis Tritt, sang cover versions of classic Eagles' hits as their tribute to the legendary band.

If anyone had doubts as to the continuing strength of the Eagles' popularity, this album put paid to them. It took the number one slot in *Billboard*'s country chart, and won the Country Music Association Album of the Year Award. *Common Thread* also hit number three in America's pop music album chart and sold in excess of three million copies.

The appetite for the real Eagles to re-emerge grew the strongest yet and fans' hopes and expectation reached fever pitch.

Industry rumours of a reunited Eagles rocketed in December when it was discovered that Glenn Frey, Don Henley, Don Felder, Joe Walsh and Timothy Schmit had gathered on the Hollywood set of the filming of Travis Tritt's video for his rendition of 'Take It Easy'. It was extraordinary that this was the catalyst that brought the Eagles together, virtually just like that! Offers of millions of dollars had been waved under their noses, and had failed to bring these disparate, explosive characters back close to each other again. Yet the country singer's manager had lifted the phone and asked, and the individual answers had all been 'Yes'.

Frey later reflected: 'Timing is everything. The writing was on the wall between the *Common Thread* album and the Travis Tritt video, and also where each individual's life course was. It was the right time to do it.' This gathering for the video shoot was the first time that all five had physically been in the same room in 14 years, far less performed together. Felder recalled wondering if it would be possible for them all to stand in the same room, smile, play and have a good time – or was it going to be too weird?

The success of the country stars' tribute to them had had an extremely uplifting effect, however. 'I think we had a heightened appreciation of what kind of legacy we'd created,' confessed Henley. 'They had instruments set up and we started jamming. We played some blues, 'Rocky Mountain Way' and 'Take It Easy', and we kind of liked it.' According to Don Felder, they only played 'Take It Easy' a couple of times before launching into that full scale, invigorating jam. It was fun, like a bunch of high school rock band members back together for a 20-year reunion. Felder felt the whole thing had something akin to a sense of innocence about it. It was like a throwback to the days before colossal success had brought with it such intense pressure.

A myriad emotions enveloped the five, and shortly after that momentous day, in early 1994, telephone calls began bouncing back and forth between them. In February, Frey, Henley and Walsh performed at the Double Diamond Club in Aspen, Colorado, to benefit the Grassroots Aspen Experience organisation. The packed crowd were wildly enthusiastic, energising the ever-watchful Irving Azoff. *Common Thread*'s success and the remarkable Travis Tritt video shoot sent Azoff into fifth gear. Personally, he had never given up hope of a full-blown Eagles' reunion and sensing they were ripe for that final nudge, he invited all five to lunch with him in Aspen to discuss the prospect in earnest.

Over fine wine and good food, Frey, Henley, Felder, Walsh and Schmit found a version of that old camaraderie. Each knew that comebacks are a big step. They are notoriously fraught and risky – failure to shine can snuff out the past lingering light. But, never shy of challenges, they decided to go for it. The buzz in music circles grew into a cacophony, and fans were thrilled and excited. What remained to be seen was whether the Eagles could soar to the same heights again, more than two decades after they had first taken flight.

CHAPTER 10

When Hell Froze Over

WHEN IT FINALLY HAPPENED, 'reunion' was not the word the Eagles wanted used to describe their re-forming as a band. They preferred to see it more in terms of simply picking up where they had left off. There had been precious little benignly simple about the intervening 14 years. Still, as if to brook no argument on the matter, in his gravelly Detroit growl Glenn Frey would barefacedly declare: 'For the record, we never broke up. We just took a fourteen-year vacation.'

Like the thought of a phoenix rising from the ashes, there was a genuine stir of excitement about one of music's biggest bands re-forming, and not just among the Eagles' worldwide legions of fans. Irving Azoff, a pure master of the PR game, faxed a stark alert to the mass media: 'Hell Has Frozen Over', piquing a music press that had had its run-ins with the feisty band in the past.

For the band, it was an incredibly momentous time. Frey, Henley, Felder, Walsh and Schmit ran the gamut of emotions, anticipation being the foremost. 'There's something magical about a band,' Henley admitted. 'None of us in our individual capacities was as big a deal as we are together.' Looking back, Glenn Frey said: 'In some ways, we were prepared for a sleigh ride from hell!'

They took the first concrete step towards their public comeback on 25 April 1994, when they gathered at the Warner Brothers Studio soundstage in Burbank, California. They were filmed performing two live 22-song concerts before an invitation-only audience for an *MTV* special to be dubbed 'Hell Freezes Over', and aired in six months' time.

At times it was a strange experience for the five; they almost felt they had never been apart. Each had long ago taken charge of his own life, become master of his own domain – a vastly different thing to operating as a unit. Yet despite the passage of so many years, the Eagles clicked back into their individual roles in the team, and were remarkably relaxed, judging by the ribbing and easy laughter in rehearsal, when Henley twice fluffed his lines singing lead on a particular song.

The set list for both shows was a blend of classic Eagles' hits, a peppering of songs from each member's solo repertoire and four new compositions specially written for the upcoming album. 'We couldn't have gone out and just recycled the old stuff,' said Frey. 'We had to have some new tunes. That's why we were excited about writing.'

It must have been a delicate balancing act initially and learning from past mistakes, the Eagles knew it would not be wise to set themselves an intense schedule. They needed this new phase in their career to be painless, if possible. One essential component was that Frey and Henley had gravitated back to something like their former close bond. It was Glenn's contention that any true friendship worth having inevitably goes through and survives extreme pressure.

The album to accompany their comeback tour would consist largely of selections culled from the live *MTV* special, to which the four new numbers would be added. And a diverse quartet they made. Only one song was a non-Eagle composition – a weepy ballad, 'Love Will Keep Us Alive', the work of Pete Vale, Jim Capaldi and Paul Carrack. Frey had collaborated with Jack Tempchin to come up with the country-tinged 'The Girl From Yesterday'. While working with Stan Lynch, Henley had penned an introspective number, 'Learn To Be Still'.

The only Henley/Frey composition was an anthemic number, 'Get Over It'. Henley had given Frey a book titled *Nation of Victims: The Decline of the American Character*, which Glenn absorbed to the point that when Don had showed up at his house and simply said he had the beginnings of a song called 'Get Over It', they were immediately in tune like old times. 'We started batting back and forth,' said Henley. 'It was great.' 'Get Over It' poured forth as a nakedly biting attack on the 1990s rampant victim/compensation culture. It was irking Henley intensely to see the rising trend of people refusing to take responsibility for their own actions. He said at the time: 'You see all this whining every day on TV. It's become an industry.' The energy and precision in 'Get Over It' was proof that the songwriting symbiosis between Frey and Henley had not withered. Coincidentally, in May 1994, the pair received recognition as lyricists when they were honoured with ASCAP's Founders Award at the organisation's 11th Pop Music Awards, held at the Beverly Hilton Hotel in LA.

By that time, their focus was firmly on the Eagles' vital comeback tour, about to launch at the end of that month. Don Henley felt there was no reason why at this juncture they couldn't be the Eagles, and also solo artistes when the spirit moved them, without it causing schisms. 'We could have done that in the first place,' he mourned, 'if we hadn't been so overwrought about everything. Since Glenn and I are getting along, the spark feels rekindled.'

The worry was that a different sort of spark could ignite. Writing together and recording an historic TV show as a band had been challenging, but the real test would be going on the road together. They had once been a highly flammable mix, and although each Eagle was now well into his forties, they could still be an incendiary combination. Patently aware of the risk, Glenn bluntly revealed: 'This tour is like driving a truck full of nitro-glycerine from Los Angeles to New York, and you don't get paid till you reach New York, and there's no insurance!'

So? Was the motivation money, asked the more intrepid journalists? Henley put them straight: 'This is about friendship. If we weren't getting along, there's not enough money on this planet to get us to do it.' On the subject of money, the Eagles came under fire from the rock press over ticket pricing, which ranged from $100 to $120, the latter often with parking charges included. Frey pointed out that these ticket prices were competitive with those to see the Rolling Stones or Pink Floyd. He also vehemently argued: 'Why shouldn't *we* make the money?' (as opposed to the ticket scalpers). While he was at it, Glenn growled that they had turned down offers of lucrative sponsorship deals. That this was not about greed was further underscored by the fact that, although they had intended to keep quiet about it, a sizeable portion of the tour's proceeds would be going to various charities.

The sell-out Hell Freezes Over tour kicked off on 27 May 1994 at the Meadows Amphitheater in Irvine, California. Over the next six months, the Eagles crisscrossed America, pitching up mid-tour in Toronto, Canada, in July and every step of the way they set out to light up their enthusiastic, loyal audiences with nightly powerhouse performances. Throughout the summer, indeed, the Eagles vied with Barbra Streisand for the top slot in the weekly concert gross chart compiled by *Amusement Business*, and invariably the Eagles won.

Despite the risks involved, it quickly became apparent that they had pulled off a triumphant return, but as American fans lapped up the Eagles live, UK supporters had to bide their time. In the absence of British gigs, a new compilation album, *The Very Best of the Eagles*, was released in Britain in July, charting at number four.

The tour was flying along Stateside until October, when it had to be interrupted because Glenn required hospitalisation. He suffered from a recurring gastro-intestinal problem, and surgery had become necessary to alleviate the pain this caused him. He successfully underwent abdominal surgery at Los Angeles' Cedars-Sinai Medical Center, and required a period of recuperation. Upbeat as ever, Frey declared: 'It gave us an opportunity to step off the Eagles' fast track just long enough to take a good long look at what we were doing, where we were going.' Glenn also saw the enforced hiatus as making the band appreciate what they had. The public at large got the chance to appreciate the Eagles when, on 26 October 1994, *MTV* premiered 'The Eagles: Hell Freezes Over'. Millions of viewers tuned in for the dynamic special.

The following month, the long-awaited album, *Hell Freezes Over*, was released on the Geffen Records label, and despite a fourteen-year absence, such was the Eagles' phenomenal popularity that it debuted in America straight at number one. In Britain, it made number 18, quickly going gold, and the multimillion selling album proved to be a global smash hit. *Hell Freezes Over* shot in at number two in Canada, went platinum in Sweden, Norway, the Netherlands, Finland, Germany and Italy, triple platinum in Japan, six times platinum in Thailand, and remained in the Australian Top 100 for seven solid months. It also spawned 'Get Over It', which reached number 31 in the US singles chart.

Basking in this success, the Eagles, off tour, could pick up the reins of their respective personal lives. For Don Henley that meant making some changes. In 1994, the Northridge earthquake had destroyed his Los Angeles home, prompting him to move back to his home state of Texas. With him went Sharon Summerhall, whom he had met about two years earlier and to whom he was by now engaged. Sharon had been a model, had lived for a time in Paris, and studied art history. Don described her as 'a good, warm-hearted sensitive Texas girl who was brought up in a good family'. It was to be near that family and his own mother that made Henley opt to return to the vicinity of his roots.

He said: 'We decided to get the hell out of LA. We didn't want to be in any more earthquakes and we wanted to have children. We wanted them to grow up in Texas around people who still say please and thank you.' When Don and Sharon moved into their new house near Dallas, neighbours called by, cookies in hand, with the offer that if they ever needed help they only had to ask. As a brooding, intense young spirit, Henley had ached to flee an incestuous-type society where people got too involved in each other's lives. Older now, he appreciated such kind offers. He did not get too cosy, however. On 9 January 1995, the Hell Freezes Over tour resumed at the Dome in Tacoma, Washington, where they broke the house attendance record. Twelve days later, the Eagles played to over 65,000 people at the Rose Bowl in Pasadena, California.

Along the way, more singles spun off the album. In February, 'Love Will Keep Us Alive' made the US Top 40, but also hit number one in *Billboard*'s Adult Contemporary Singles chart, remaining on that survey for over seven months; during this time 'Learn To Be Still' entered the Adult Contemporary Top 20 chart. Having recuperated, Glenn Frey was asked for a band health check almost a year on from re-forming. 'What I see right now,' he replied, 'is some guys who are very happy and getting a tremendous amount of satisfaction out of the shows and enjoying each other's company.'

Glenn's solo album, *Solo Collection*, was released in March but didn't chart. Two months on, it was another chart no-show for Joe Walsh's solo work, *Look What I Did!* As Henley had said, the Eagles were a far stronger force together, as was proved when it was widely acknowledged that they had pulled off one of the most successful performance comebacks in rock history. In mid-May 1995, the tour ended for now, having grossed in excess of $135 million, and played to more than two million people. The Eagles scattered to be with their loved ones for the summer, with every reason to feel proud.

In Don Henley's case he happily left his drum kit and microphone behind to take another big step when he finally wed. Asked at the start of the decade whether he would ever get hitched, Henley had revealed: 'I just don't want to botch it.' He had been very wary of marriage, feeling that he had plenty of time. Now, five years later, almost 48 years old, he was ready, and on 20 May 1995, he and Sharon Summerhall married at his Vista Ranch, Malibu. Guests included the Eagles, as well as Jackson Browne, Bob Seger, John Fogerty, Sting, Bruce Springsteen, Billy Joel, David Crosby, Jimmy Buffett and Randy Newman. 'It was quite a show,' said Henley. 'We had a great wedding!' Within a few months, Sharon fell pregnant and over the next five years the couple had three children.

In November 1995, the Eagles regrouped to embark on the next leg of the Hell Freezes Over tour, which took them around the world. They played sold-out dates in Japan, New Zealand and Australia, racking up yet more impressive statistics – by the end of the year, the overall tour gross stood at over $165 million, and *Hell Freezes Over* was one of the Top Ten biggest selling albums of 1995.

That November Henley had a solo album release, *Actual Miles: Henley's Greatest Hits*, which just made it into the US Top 50. His attention, however, was centred on the Eagles' achievement. He let it out that the band privately joked that it was no mean feat to have come from the riotous 1970s and still be around, not having had any deaths in the band along the way. 'I take a sort of perverse pride from that,' said Don, adding, 'and I'm stubborn. I intend to outlive all my detractors!' On *Billboard*'s 1995 Top Album of the Year chart, *Hell Freezes Over* ranked fourth, and the Eagles were number five in the publication's list of Top Album Artists of the Year.

On 30 January 1996, at the American Music Awards, the Eagles walked off with three trophies: Favourite Pop/Rock

Group, Favourite Adult Contemporary Artiste, and Favourite Pop/Rock Album for *Hell Freezes Over*. Soon afterwards, when the Grammy Awards nominations were announced, the Eagles were listed in the running for three accolades: Best Pop Album (*Hell Freezes Over*); Best Pop Vocal Performance by a Duo or Group ('Love Will Keep Us Alive'); and Best Rock Vocal Performance by a Duo or Group ('Hotel California' (live)).

With the tour set to get underway again soon, though, some strain was starting to tell on the band, which was graphically exposed when Don Henley spoke out about life in the Eagles' eyrie. 'Deep down we all really respect each other,' he declared. 'Our personality quirks are annoying at times, but you can't go through what we've been through and not have an abiding love for one another. Some days I want to kill every fuckin' one of them, but I get over it.'

As the tour trundled through America and Canada during summer 1996, Glenn Frey showed up on the silver screen when he played the character of Dennis Wilburn in the Tom Cruise-Renee Zellweger movie, *Jerry Maguire*. The Eagles' roadshow next hit Europe, opening on 5 July at the RDS Concert Hall in Dublin, Ireland, and coming to an end on 4 August at Murrayfield Stadium in Edinburgh, Scotland. Glenn recalled: 'No one left the stage pissed off. There was no dark cloud hanging over the band. We hugged and congratulated each other.'

That was true of that final night, but it had been a two-year-long tour, and Henley remembered how there had sometimes been other, difficult, atmospheres. Inter-band relationships had frequently fluctuated, and the pendulum swing had been pronounced. He took four years to say so, but Don eventually revealed: 'There'd been moments of great joy and contentment. And there'd been moments of animosity, dissatisfaction and resentment. There's always tension, and a lot of it is self-created. There are still ghosts from the past that rear their ugly heads and can make things unpleasant.' It was as well then for future unity that their reunion tour had come to an end.

1997 was a quiet year, though the Eagles were not forgotten. In January, the Rock and Roll Hall of Fame produced its list of the 500 Songs That Shaped Rock and Roll and it included 'Take It Easy' and 'Hotel California'. On 21 February, Glenn Frey turned up on TV once more in an acting role, playing Inspector Phil Robbins in 'Rampage', an episode of the series *Nash Bridges*, starring Don Johnson.

In November, Joe Walsh released a solo album, *Little Did He Know*. Before that, on 29 September, in recognition of his role in the creation of the Thoreau Institute near Walden Pond, Don Henley was awarded the National Humanities Medal by President Bill Clinton at a White House formal ceremony.

Come 12 January 1998, the Eagles collectively were honoured when, in the very first year they were nominated for the distinction, they were inducted into the coveted Rock and Roll Hall of Fame during a dinner held at New York's Waldorf-Astoria Hotel. Irreverently, Don Henley said at the time: 'Old buildings, politicians and whores all become respectable if they stick around long enough!' Uniquely, however, all seven Eagles attended, and it was an historic night for the band and their fans when Glenn Frey, Don Henley, Don Felder, Joe Walsh, Timothy Schmit, Randy Meisner and Bernie Leadon all performed 'Take It Easy' and 'Hotel California'.

Although the Eagles had once more retreated from the live scene, their star continued to gleam brightly. On 1 January 1999, *Pollstar* issued its list of the all-time greatest money producing tours in rock history. The Rolling Stones came top, followed by Pink Floyd, then U2 and the Eagles. In March, the Eagles received the prestigious Diamond Award from the RIAA for sales (well) in excess of 10 million of both *Hotel California* and *Eagles: Their Greatest Hits 1971–1975*.

That summer, rumour had it that the band had spent

around six weeks in an LA recording studio. Don Henley was known to have commitments to a new solo album, but hopes rose of an all-new Eagles' studio album. The band's contract with Asylum Records had long since expired, and there was no word of Geffen Records, which had released *Hell Freezes Over*, being in the frame. But no one anticipated the Eagles encountering any problem in picking up a new lucrative contract – especially when, in November 1999, they reached a new rarefied pinnacle. The RIAA included the Eagles in its list of Artists of the Century, putting them in the select company of Elvis Presley, Barbra Streisand and the Beatles. But the RIAA also announced, with some fanfare, that *Eagles: Their Greatest Hits 1971–1975* had surpassed Michael Jackson's *Thriller*, and was now the biggest selling album in American recording history. RIAA president, Hilary Rosen, presented the Eagles with an official plaque to commemorate this crowning achievement.

In a different sense, certain Eagles had pulled off personal achievements this decade – most notably, Joe Walsh. The new millennium was fast approaching, and for many was an intensive time of taking stock. A noted wildman of rock and a zany character, Joe had kept well hidden the fears and demons he'd had to overcome to get himself sober and clean of drugs. Not a man prone to revealing private details in a serious vein, it was especially poignant when he did so in late December 1999. Talking publicly of how he had repeatedly tried to stop drinking and doing drugs and had previously been unable to, Joe admitted: 'It was terrifying. I was trying to stop but I had become so dependent, I couldn't. Anybody who is as scared as I was about substance abuse should do something about it. There is life after vodka and cocaine. And it's a good life.'

On a mini round of gigs in the dying days of December 1999, the Eagles played at the Mandalay Bay Events Center in Las Vegas, when their special guest was Jackson Browne. He and Linda Ronstadt were also on the bill when the Eagles played a millennium gig on New Year's Eve at the Staples Center in downtown Los Angeles. The Eagles took to the stage before an energised audience at 10.15 pm on that historic night, and the concert was recorded, to be included in an upcoming box set of retrospective work.

When *Amusement Business* produced details of the Top Ten Grossing Millennium Shows, Phish, who had played two nights at the Big Cypress Seminole Indian Reservation, came top. Number two were the Eagles, whose one-off show had raked in over $6.2 million, beating Billy Joel's Madison Square Garden, New York Y2K gig into third place. Having capped their successful comeback with these recent achievements, Glenn Frey remarked: 'With us, it's almost like the chapters keep ending, but the book isn't finished. There's more to do.'

There were certainly more milestones to pass; in February 2000, it was announced that Glenn Frey and Don Henley were to be inducted into the Songwriters Hall of Fame. Talk still swirled of a new Eagles studio album, and in spring Henley threw a little light on the subject when he confirmed that the band had cut a few tracks the previous summer, but nothing that had lit the touchpaper for them as yet. Henley also stated ominously: 'There's some disagreement about production values and song quality. There are things to be worked out before we can continue with that project.'

In the meantime, in May 2000, Henley released the solo album, *Inside Job*, which featured guest input from Frey and Felder. Sandwiching that, in March and September respectively, the albums *20th Century Masters: The Millennium Collection The Best of Joe Walsh* and *20th Century Masters: The Millennium Collection The Best of Glenn Frey* were released. In November a 4-CD box set, *The Eagles 1972–1999 Selected Works* followed, and went platinum.

It was not the past, however, that preoccupied Frey and Henley, but the political future, which they feared would switch into the hands of the Republican Party. Having served two terms, Bill Clinton was not permitted to stand for re-election. The Democrats then had to pin their hopes on Clinton's Vice President, Al Gore, who was up against former president's son, George W. Bush, in the 2000 presidential election. Bush had a worrying lead in the polls and as election day in November drew near, many music stars, such as the Eagles and Jon Bon Jovi, had been out on the stump trying to drum up support for Gore.

Dread at the prospect of George W. Bush reaching the White House in what would be a hugely controversial election, gripped the two politically active Eagles. Frey declared that he fervently hoped that people would wake up and see through 'the bumbling governor from Texas. He reminds me of a comedian on a 90-minute show with only 15 minutes worth of material. There's a lot at stake in this election'. Henley was just as scathing. He said he was 'horrified' at the prospect of a Bush win. 'I don't think the man's qualified in any way to be president. It's a joke. I wish the American people would snap out of it.'

George W. Bush squeaked into the White House, but the Eagles had problems closer to home to deal with – trouble they had kept a lid on. So it came as a complete shock in early February 2001, when it emerged that Don Felder had been newly fired from the band. Felder at once filed a lawsuit in the Los Angeles Superior Court against Glenn Frey and Don Henley, claiming that he had been wrongfully dismissed from the Eagles. He was reportedly also seeking the dissolution of Eagles Ltd., the band's corporation, and an accounting of record royalties, touring revenue and merchandising since 1974. Lawyers for either side refused to go into detail. Neither side would reveal why Don Felder had been ousted, and this tight-lipped attitude prevailed, despite the music press clamouring for the dirt.

The four remaining Eagles, equally unwilling to say a word on the subject, knuckled down to working on this elusive new studio album, while also preparing to hit the road again. The public's thirst for the Eagles remained undiminished, and in March 2001 they ranked as the third highest-selling band in America; the Beatles were top, followed by Led Zeppelin. The Eagles' new studio album was becoming a phantom thing. With no record label breathing down their necks, there was no deadline; Henley was even talking in terms of it possibly taking two years to complete. 'I don't think we'll go out in the desert, take peyote and puke like we did in the old days,' he declared, 'but to make this an authentic Eagles' project, Glenn and I are going to have to co-write at least four songs. I can't think of another band that hasn't made an album of new material for 22 years and then made a triumphant return. We believe we can.'

Work on the album was shelved, though, when the Eagles settled into an enormous hangar on an LA film studio backlot to rehearse for their upcoming tour, which would be a lower key affair than the Hell Freezes Over one. The linchpin figure at these rehearsals was Glenn, who became a wisecracking drill sergeant, determined to keep a gimlet eye on the troops. When they practised their vocal harmonies, Frey was ruthless. 'If it hurts and you're running out of air, *then* you're on the right note!' he declared.

Two weeks after Timothy Schmit released a solo album, *Feed the Fire*, the Eagles stirred their fans to turn out in their droves once more when, on 26 May 2001, the band launched themselves onto the road. They launched in Moscow, then hit Helsinki, Stockholm, Hanover and Cologne before arriving in Britain in early June. UK dates were played in Manchester, Sheffield and Birmingham, preceded by a four-night stint at London's Earls Court. They gigged throughout Europe, returning to Britain for more dates before staging one of their standout performances at the end of June in front of 18,000 people in the impressive grounds of Stormont, Northern Ireland's parliament building. The Eagles' only two US dates were on 28 July at the American Airlines Center in Dallas,

Texas, and on 11 August at the new Invesco Field at Mile High in Denver, Colorado.

Following a rest period, by early summer 2002, the band set out to tour America and Canada, ending mid-July. In August, Glenn Frey made another TV appearance, guesting in the 'It's All In The Game' episode of the series *Arli$$*. As if live gigging had got into their bloodstream, by November 2002, plans were announced for yet another tour in the new year. In April 2003, the Eagles announced that the new studio album, still in the works, would not be released on a major record label. Instead, they intended to bring it out on a label of their own, making it available via the internet. The first single was said to be called 'Hole In The World', and its release would coincide with the new tour, for which rehearsals got underway at Culver Studio in LA. The tour was to be dubbed Farewell Tour I, which was the Eagles' way of poking fun at those superstars who had been playing so-called farewell tours time and again for years, but the irony was missed by many.

With this tongue-in-cheek-title, the tour itself got seriously underway on 9 May 2003 at the Richmond Coliseum in Virginia, and ran through various states to land at the Boardwalk Hall, Atlantic City in New Jersey, on 25 July. Relations were generally stable, but not always completely smooth. 'We still have our differences,' Don Henley confessed. 'We certainly have our days when we don't see eye-to-eye, but we've learned to get through in a much calmer and more productive way.' Backstage life had been very different for a long time now, with everyone into fitness exercise and healthy eating. 'That's why we're not dead,' said Don succinctly. Joe Walsh concurred: 'We're all older now and we're a little more emotionally predictable. Plus, we don't have substances in our brains.' He added bluntly: 'We don't particularly love each other but the thought of playing with anybody else is worse.'

The fact that all age groups and both sexes flocked to see

them, surprised the outspoken guitarist. Walsh recalled being stunned when a very young lad wanted his autograph. When he enquired of the boy how he could possibly know who he was, the youngster baldly replied: 'Hey man, my grandfather turned me on to you.' To which piece of perceived impertinence Walsh later cursed: 'Little fuckin' brat!'

By the time this tour started, the Eagles had cut several potential tracks for their next album, and intended cutting more to give them a pool from which to select the best numbers. But instead of releasing an album, as promised, they brought out the single, 'Hole In The World'. It instantly received heavy radio airplay and was performed every night on tour. Don Henley had started this song off. 'I'm a news junkie', he explained. 'I was very affected by 9/11 and sat down one night at the piano and it just came out, or the first part of it anyway. Then Glenn finished it.' Don made it clear that he did not want 'Hole In The World' to be considered a controversial song. He pointed out that it could apply to situations other than that appalling terrorist atrocity. 'There's a lot of holes in the world metaphorically,' he maintained.

Speaking of missing pieces, there must have been Eagles fans who dearly wished Don Felder was still in the line-up. Felder's unfair dismissal court action was going through its various paces. It was sad that it had come to a legal wrangle, and that summer Felder needed to escape from the stress. He liked playing golf, and in September 2003 he wound up in Scotland at the famous Old Course in St Andrews, when the Pro-Am golf tournament was being staged. The event always attracts a plethora of celebrities, which that year included actors Hugh Grant and Samuel L Jackson, as well as Bon Jovi drummer Tico Torres. The evening entertainment, ironically enough for Felder, trying to get away from it all, was provided by a Scottish group of skilled musicians who stage an Eagles music show.

The group is run by bassist/vocalist Gus Boyd, and he recalls: 'I got a telephone call from Don Felder asking if he could join us for a few numbers on stage that night. I thought it was somebody winding me up and for a while I wouldn't take him seriously. But Don quietly insisted, "No, look, listen – it *is* me!" We were blown away. Don came to our hotel room and we rehearsed. His wife was with him and it was funny because at one point Felder was in full throttle and his wife yelled: "Hey honey? You're far too loud! You'll drown the guys out!" Don said: "Okay, dear," and he turned it down. But he was impressed with us. In his very American drawl he told us, "You guys have got it pretty much worked out, there!"'

According to Gus Boyd, Don Felder meticulously worked out which songs he would guest with them on, which Boyd took to be because of the court feud with the Eagles. Says Gus: 'Don didn't in any way talk about the court case, but it's my own personal impression that he was bitter about having been sacked.' The band's show, called 'The Eagles Story', went ahead that night, with a difference when Tico Torres came and drummed for a while, and Don Felder joined them for some numbers. As the band put it, simply having actually played on the same stage with Don Felder is something they will live on for a very long time.

Meanwhile, back in the States, the Eagles' tour rolled out across America as an extremely tight act. Said Timothy Schmit: 'We're not the Grateful Dead. We're very precise in everything we do. We pretty much know every note. It's what we are.' This three-month leg ended on 26 October 2003 at the Memorial Coliseum in Fort Wayne, Indiana. That month, the 33-track set, *The Very Best of The Eagles*, reached number three, and went double platinum by December. In February 2004, 'Hole In The World' received a Grammy nomination for Best Pop Vocal Performance By a Duo or Group. Then on 12 May, the Eagles' world tour resumed with a gig in Grand Rapids, Michigan.

On 15 October, they launched their very first Asian tour at the Impact Centre in Bangkok, Thailand. They trekked through Singapore, Hong Kong and Japan before heading to Australia in mid-November. There, the Eagles played such venues as the Subiaco Oval, Perth, the Rod Laver Arena, Melbourne, and the Sydney Superdome, as well as the Entertainment Centres in Brisbane and Adelaide. The record-breaking demand for tickets for all these shows meant they were sold out in under four hours, forcing extra dates to be added.

The blistering success of this Eagles' world tour left the band on a considerable high. In November 2004, Q magazine in Britain issued a poll of the 50 Biggest Bands of All Time, which was topped by Pink Floyd. Three US bands featured in the top 15 – Bon Jovi at 14, the Beach Boys at 12, with the Eagles placed 11th.

In January 2005, the band met up to discuss how the new studio album was shaping, and at the same time news leaked out that another television special was in the pipeline for transmission in summer. Before this, their tour resumed on 5 March at the Coliseum, North Charleston in South Carolina. Crisscrossing America, with a trip into Canada at the end of that month, the Eagles pitched up on 11 April at New York's Madison Square Garden. In May, *Eagles*, a 9-CD, 76-track box set was released, while the tour trundled on. Playing a string of sell-out dates in August and September, the Eagles then followed gigs in Anaheim, Oakland and San Jose with a blistering performance on 17 October 2005 at the Glendale Arena in Phoenix, Arizona. Towards the end of 2005, a 2-DVD set of the Eagles live in concert, filmed at the Rod Laver Arena in Melbourne, Australia, was released. It shot to number one in both the US and UK charts, providing the perfect springboard for the summer 2006 European leg of their tour. Speaking to BBC radio on the eve of their 23 June gig at Hampden Park Stadium in Glasgow, Scotland, Don Henley held out hope that the Eagles' new album would be released in spring 2007.

It had been a big task in 1994 to come back after a 14 year

gap and reclaim their position as one of the finest bands in music, but the Eagles did it. And in the ensuing decade and more, they further cemented their standing.

Their journey to become a top rock act has been a remarkable and volatile one and along the way it has produced a clutch of timeless classics. The Eagles have soared as startlingly high as they have, at times, been plunged drastically low, but they are undoubtedly a permanent part of music's brightest firmament. And with one of the most riotous, inspiring and sometimes poignant stories in rock, they have proved that they are natural born survivors.

Each Eagle is a vibrant, vivid character of lively, independent spirit. In a world crushingly obsessed with political correctness, Glenn Frey and Don Henley in particular are also refreshingly blunt in their inherent honesty, and engagingly funny with it. It is hardly surprising then, that when Don Henley was once asked why he wanted to outlive his rivals he replied drolly: 'I'd like to stick around for the Apocalypse – that's showbiz!'

INDEX